Privateering and Diplomacy, 1793–1807

Atle L. Wold

Privateering and Diplomacy, 1793–1807

Great Britain, Denmark-Norway and the Question of Neutral Ports

palgrave
macmillan

Atle L. Wold
Department of Literature, Area Studies & European Languages
University of Oslo
Oslo, Norway

ISBN 978-3-030-45185-1 ISBN 978-3-030-45186-8 (eBook)
https://doi.org/10.1007/978-3-030-45186-8

This Palgrave Macmillan imprint is published by the registered company Springer Nature Switzerland AG.
The registered company address is: Gewerbestrasse 11, 6330 Cham, Switzerland

Acknowledgements

The present book is the result of a research project I have been working on, on and off over a number of years. Although it began with the chance discovery of a primary source in the National Library of Scotland, it really only started to take form and find direction when I participated in the project 'The Transformation of International Law and Norwegian Sovereignty in 1814' at the Centre for Advanced Studies (CAS) at the University of Oslo in 2012–2013. I am very grateful to the organisers of the project, professors Ola Mestad and Dag Michalsen, for inviting me to partake, as well as to all the other participants for their feedback and comments and for the lively discussions we had on privateering and issues pertaining to international law. Researching the topic of privateers operating out of neutral ports led me to consult material held in several different archives and libraries, and I am grateful to the staff at the following institutions for their help and assistance: The National Records of Scotland, the National Library of Scotland, the Caird Library at the National Maritime Museum, the Kent Library and History Centre, the Danish National Archives, the National Archives of Norway, the Regional State Archives of Stavanger and the National Library of Norway. Last but not the least, however, I am grateful to the staff at the National Archives at Kew in London—where most of the research for this book was carried out—for their expertly assistance, particularly in navigating the Admiralty papers. The nature of this project meant that it was necessary to translate a number of primary documents, and high-quality translations were provided by—in chronological order—Torill Myreng, Nora Naguib Leerberg, Stéphanie Rodrigues de Miranda and Adam King (from French), and

Bjørg Tosterud (from Latin). All translations from Danish are my own. Over the years, a number of people have assisted me with various issues relating to the project, or presented ideas that have subsequently led to important discoveries, and I should like to register my appreciation for this. Frode Fyllingsnes in Stavanger alerted my attention to the documentation from the court hearings for the case against Captain Lawson conducted before the Magistrates' Court of Stavanger, and Dr. Arnvid Lillehammer at the University of Stavanger subsequently transcribed the court protocol from a very cumbersome Gothic handwriting. Professor Ulrik Langen at the University of Copenhagen assisted me with material on the French representatives at Copenhagen, and my colleague Svein Erling Lorås in French Area Studies at the University of Oslo helped me with a number of questions related to French history. Professor Éric Schnakenbourg at the University of Nantes very kindly took time to answer my queries concerning French policies on neutrality, as did Dr. Koen Stapelbroek at the Erasmus University of Rotterdam on Dutch privateers, and professor N. A. M. Rodger, and Drs. Marianne Czisnik, Tim Voelker and Roger Knight all shared their expertise on the Royal Navy. My thanks also go to cartographer Jon Karsten Ramsrud at the Norwegian firm *Karttjenester AS* for his professional production of the map showing the location of Consul John Mitchell's informants along the southern-Norwegian coastline. Finally, financial support from my own Department of Literature, Area Studies and European Languages at the University of Oslo was essential for my many visits to archives and libraries, and I am very pleased with the professional and efficient publication process conducted by Palgrave Macmillan, as well as for their belief in my book project.

Contents

About the Author

Atle L. Wold is Associate Professor of British Studies at the Department of Literature, Area Studies and European Languages, University of Oslo, Norway. He is the author of *Scotland and the French Revolutionary War, 1792–1802* (2015).

Abbreviations[1]

ADM	Admiralty
AMAE	Archives du Ministère des affaires étrangeres, Paris
CL	Caird Library (National Maritime Museum)
FO	Foreign Office
NA	National Archives (London)
NLN	National Library of Norway
NLS	National Library of Scotland
NRS	National Records of Scotland
RSAS	Regional State Archives of Stavanger

Note

1. Biographical details:
   All information about British individuals referred to in this book has been collected from the *Oxford Dictionary of National Biography* unless otherwise stated.

List of Figures

CHAPTER 1

Introduction

In the summer of 1799—or more specifically on 22 July—the editor of the Scottish newspaper the *Caledonian Mercury* found reason to raise an issue of considerable concern. Under the heading of 'DUNDEE—19th July', a worrying story was reported in the following manner:

> This morning brought intelligence of the capture of the Tay Greenlandman, a full ship, off Kennairdhead, 16 days ago, by a privateer of 16 guns, which carried her into Bergen. The crew were landed at Aberdeen yesterday from Norway. The ship and cargo are valued at upwards of 6000l. and will be a heavy blow to this place. It is to be hoped that Government will at last take some effectual measures to have this nest of pirates and robbers rooted out, which has so long been allowed to insult our country and injure our trade.

Discovered by the author when he was looking through the editions of the *Mercury* in the National Library of Scotland (NLS; this was before digitalisation) while researching a completely different topic, this brisk statement seemed to raise a number of questions. How could it be that a privateer—as a representative of a country at war—had brought a captured merchant ship into a neutral port since, at this point in time, the dual-monarchy of Denmark-Norway was neutral in the war that had raged in Europe since 1792? Was it compatible with neutrality for the government of a neutral country to permit this kind of activity to take place in its ports, and if not, why was it allowed to happen? The editorial certainly seemed to suggest that something was amiss, but did not say exactly what the problem was.

A. L. Wold, *Privateering and Diplomacy, 1793–1807*,
https://doi.org/10.1007/978-3-030-45186-8_1

Furthermore, was the Danish government, as well as the local officials and inhabitants in Bergen, not afraid of British reprisals, and why would, in any case, a small state such as Denmark-Norway risk provoking one of Europe's great powers? Perhaps the phenomenon of privateers operating out of Norwegian ports—and as we will see, Bergen was far from the only privateers' 'nest' in Norway—even played a role, first in the breakdown of British-Danish relations in 1801, and subsequently in the outbreak of war between the two countries in 1807? The privateer in question was French, and Denmark-Norway would, of course, become an ally of Napoleon in 1807.[1] Such, at any rate, were the early musings of this author after his discovery in the NLS' reading room.

While it can be stated straight away that the impact was arguably not *that* great, it gradually emerged from researching relevant source material that the question of French privateers and Norwegian ports was an ongoing issue in the diplomatic correspondence between the two countries throughout the 1790s, and a cause of almost constant tension. The British government tried to bring the practice to an end, while the Danish government insisted on keeping the ports open to privateers, and did so until a series of events forced it to call an official closure in July 1799. Why was that, and why was the British government not able to persuade its Danish counterpart to agree to a closure of its ports to privateers straight away, or at least before so many years had passed? These questions formed the main point of departure for the study underlying the present book, the central focus of which is the bilateral relationship between Great Britain and Denmark-Norway, and the attitudes the two countries held towards neutrality and privateering. This means that the approach adopted here differs from that of most works on Danish foreign policy, or British-Danish relations in the period in general. Existing research has focused primarily on the question of neutral *trade*, and the ways in which the Danish government tried to defend its right to trade with belligerent nations, particularly through the adoption of convoys for Danish merchant vessels.[2] Less work has been done on the Danish policy on privateering and the British response to that but, as it will be argued in the subsequent chapters, this was of greater importance than the lack of attention among historians so far would suggest. Moreover, just as the question of neutral trade raised issues concerning the relationship between neutrals and belligerents, and their relative 'rights' and 'duties' under international law, so the phenomenon of privateers operating out of neutral ports gave rise to equally thorny questions about what constituted 'proper' neutral behaviour. This legal element was central to the topic under discussion here, and while this is primarily a book on history, an attempt has been made to see the historical events and developments covered in the context of international laws and bilateral treaties. Alongside the more theoretical and legal questions pertaining to privateering and neutrality, however, there was also a more practical side—the experience of privateering as it unfolded—and both are investigated here.

Chapter 2, the first and longest of the regular chapters in this book, addresses the diplomatic debate that ensued between the British and Danish governments in the wake of first sightings of French privateers on the coast of Norway in the spring of 1793. Although the British side tried to argue that it was unacceptable for privateers to operate out of neutral ports, it proved difficult to establish quite why that should be the case. An agreement of sorts was reached in August 1793, whereby privateers were allowed to come into the ports of Norway (not Denmark) on certain conditions, but allegations of breaches of the agreement led to discussions lasting on-and-off until 1799. These debates form the mainstay of the chapter, but sections have also been devoted to the French point of view, and to the question of who had the better argument in the debates as seen from a legal perspective. The diplomatic debate was, as the term would suggested, carried out by the diplomatic representatives of the two countries, but a possibly even more important function was filled by the British consuls in Denmark and Norway, and Chap. 3 goes into detail on this. Emphasis has been placed on the many difficulties facing consuls who were asked to carry out war-related duties while based in a neutral country, as well as on the role played by the unusually industrious and resourceful British consul at the southern-Norwegian port town of Kristiansand, John Mitchell. This chapter covers the whole period from 1793 to 1807. Where Chap. 2 addresses the principled debate on privateering and neutral ports, Chap. 4 looks at what has been termed 'privateering in practice', the actual operations of French privateers from 1793 until 1799 (and from 1795, also Dutch privateers). This practical dimension concerned both general issues such as the use of 'false flags' by privateers, and individual cases of particular interest. It was often through controversial individual cases that the difficulties involved in applying the agreement of 1793, as well as other rules relating to the relationship between belligerents and neutrals really became clear. Among these individual cases, that of the British merchant vessel the *Bell & Ann* and Captain Robert Lawson stands out as more extraordinary than most, and has been examined in detail. Chapter 4 also looks at the sale of vessels brought into Norwegian ports through the example of auctions advertised in the newspaper the *Christiansand Weekly Gazette*.[3] These three chapters form the main bulk of the discussion contained in the book, but they are complemented by another two chapters that are somewhat shorter. Chapter 5 addresses the impact the French invasion of the Netherlands in 1795 had on the war in the North Sea. The Dutch Republic had been an ally of Britain from 1793 until the invasion, but was now forced to change sides in the war. One consequence of this was the introduction of Dutch privateers hunting for British merchant ships alongside those from France; another was the new threat posed by the Dutch Fleet, which had previously fought with the Royal Navy. Again, particular emphasis has been placed on one individual case of great interest, that of the Dutch 'Captain von Dirking'. Lastly, Chap. 6 picks up where Chaps. 2 and 4 left off, looking at the state of affairs in the Norwegian port towns after the official closure of these ports to privateers. For this period also, one particular case came to dominate, that of the French Captain Jean Jacques de St Faust in 1803–1804.

The primary sources consulted for this book consist mainly of correspondence, where the British Foreign Office Correspondence-series for Denmark forms the main source. It is the richness of this archive that has made it possible to investigate the topic at hand, and while the FO-series consists predominantly of British material, it includes 'non-British' documents such as official statements by the Danish government too. This series has then been supplemented by a number of other sources such as Admiralty papers, treatises, court transcripts and newspaper articles, as well as contemporary published works. Finding the relevant material has involved quite a lot of 'detective' work and, in that sense, this is a book based on a classic historian-in-the-archives-type study.

As is arguably the case for all historical investigations, there will be roads not taken, and issues of potential relevance and interest, which there was no room to include; so also with this book. The story of French and Dutch privateers operating out of Norwegian ports arguably has three to four main protagonists: Great Britain, Denmark-Norway, France and the Batavian Republic, if we are to see the latter as a protagonist and not simply a protégé of France. The focus of this book, however, is primarily on the first two, and particularly on Britain. Although the topic of privateering has an international ring to it, related as it was to the development of international law in this period, and the diplomatic debate between Britain and Denmark-Norway was a bilateral affair, this book has nonetheless been devised as primarily a work in British history. Its central focus is on the British government's approach to privateering out of neutral ports, and the ways in which it tried—through its diplomatic and consular corps—to address the problems this generated. This means that there are related and interesting issues, which have not been dealt with in depth here, as well as room for new detailed studies of the other three protagonists. Thus while the French response to the British-Danish agreement of August 1793 has been addressed, and the several changes to the French privateering policy thereafter have been included, this study does not go into detail on how the Republican governments in France devised their policies on privateering and neutrality, or what made them change tack from time to time. As of yet, no study of this exists. Similarly, the chapter on the Dutch change of sides does not go into detail on the policies devised by the Batavian governments on privateering, but focuses on the impact 1795 had on Britain's war in the North Sea. The policies of the Danish government have naturally been addressed in more depth, but the book is not a study of the internal workings of the government apparatus of the dual-monarchy. Finally, while the port towns along the southern-Norwegian coast feature prominently throughout the book, no attempt has been made here to carry out an extensive number-crunching exercise with respect to questions such as: exactly how many British vessels were carried into Norwegian ports and condemned there; what kind of goods did they carry; who purchased these goods and vessels; and what characterised attitudes to privateers in the various Norwegian port towns and outports affected by the activity more generally? Were people typically pro-French, pro-British or neither? The British representatives in the dual-monarchy certainly held views on this, but whether they were correct in their assumptions is another matter. While some work has been done on these types of questions in local-historical works on individual port towns, and estimates have been made as to the number of vessels brought into Norway, no comprehensive study of the 'Norwegian experience' has yet been carried out. The case of the auctions advertised in the *Christiansand Weekly Gazette* included in Chap. 4 arguably provides considerable information on the nature of the sale of captured vessels in the area covered by this newspaper—and this *may* very well have been representative of similar sales elsewhere—but more work could be done if the sources exist. The gauntlet has been dropped. As far as British policies on privateering and neutrality, and British diplomacy and consular work in the northern corner of Europe are concerned, however, it is the hope of this author that the present book may have an interesting contribution to make.

Notes

1. The nationality of the privateer was confirmed in the next issue of the *Caledonian Mercury*, 25 July 1799.
2. The leading authority on Danish foreign policy in the eighteenth century is the late Ole Feldbæk, who was professor of history at the University of Copenhagen.
3. The *Christiansand Weekly Gazette* was Consul John Mitchell's translation of the original Danish title: *Kristiansands Adresse Kontors Efterretninger*.

CHAPTER 2

The Debate on Privateering and Neutral Ports, 1793–1799

When the French Revolutionary War began on the European continent in 1792, the dual-monarchy of Denmark-Norway—a conglomerate state which also included the German Duchies of Schleswig and Holstein—had stayed successfully out of armed conflict ever since the end of the Great Nordic War in 1720. That war had ended in defeat for Denmark-Norway and its objective of regaining territories lost to Sweden in the wars of the seventeenth century, and 1720 came to mark a watershed in Danish foreign policies.[1] From now on, no further attempts would be made to regain lost territories and, instead, focus was on defending the territorial integrity of the state as it stood. The best way to achieve this was to stay out of the wars of other powers, and meant that, at the outbreak of war, Denmark-Norway would adopt the position of a neutral country. To make this possible, however, the Danish government had to conduct a careful peacetime policy aimed at avoiding 'political isolation'. Typically, an alliance would be formed with one or more of the great powers where Denmark would adopt a 'subordinate' position in return for guarantees of security, only to exchange this alliance with a new one as the need arose. As the main authority on Danish foreign policy in the eighteenth century, Ole Feldbæk has stated, this meant that the Danish government conducted 'a zig-zag course between the great powers' from time to time. Towards the end of the century, however, the main focus arguably came to be on securing the friendship and support of Russia as a counterweight to Sweden, and Swedish aspirations towards the kingdom of Norway.[2]

A. L. Wold, *Privateering and Diplomacy, 1793–1807*,
https://doi.org/10.1007/978-3-030-45186-8_2

Coupled with the policy of staying out of war was a strategy of utilising neutrality for commercial ends. This was partly a matter of exploiting the opportunities the outbreak of war gave to expand upon trade there and then—since there was typically an increase in the demand for neutral shipping during wartime—but it also formed part of a more long-term policy of generating economic development. As a third-rate power, Denmark-Norway had little chance of competing with the likes of Great Britain and France in the great eighteenth-century 'struggle for wealth and empire', let alone to get embroiled in commercial wars with any hope of success, but through a carefully conducted policy of neutrality, it was nevertheless deemed possible to obtain a smaller share of trade and commerce in the shadow of the great powers. And on this point, the Danish government was proved right.[3] A. P. Bernstorff, the Danish Foreign Secretary for most of the 1790s, summed up the Danish foreign policy in 1780 as 'Sicherheit und Wohlstand', or 'security and prosperity',[4] but it was nevertheless denounced by many outside observers—including many in Britain—as little more than an attempt at blatant wartime profiteering. Denmark only stayed neutral in order to make as much money out of the belligerents and the wartime situation as possible it was believed, and this perception of Danish motives led to a constant British suspicion of the Danish government. By the time war broke out in Europe in 1792, recent experience seemed to confirm such suspicions. As Éric Schnakenbourg has demonstrated, the Danes utilised their position and presence in the Caribbean to trade extensively with all the belligerents in that region during the American War. Not only did they conduct trade with both the British and the French Antilles, but they also traded with the rebellious colonies, the future USA, as well as with the Dutch once they had entered the war.[5] The period 1793–1807 was to prove no exception from this general rule, as we will see.

The Revolutionary and Napoleonic Wars period, however, with its frequent changes of alliances between the European great powers, and stop-start nature of warfare, placed the Danish foreign policy under increasing strain. For a long time, the Danish government was able to pursue its particular brand of commercial neutrality with a degree of success but, eventually, the policy failed. Crisis was first reached in April 1801, when the Danish government's decision to introduce convoys for neutral trade—as well as Denmark's entry into the League of Armed Neutrality together with Russia, Sweden and Prussia in August 1800—led to open conflict with Britain, and the well-known British attack on Copenhagen on 2 April 1801. Thereafter, the Danish government pursued a more toned-down policy of neutrality but, increasingly, even this was not enough to stay out of armed conflict. In 1807, the dual-monarchy was forced to enter the war on the side of France because of developments which were essentially outside of its control: Napoleon's demand that neutral countries enter the Continental System and Britain's pre-emptive strike on Copenhagen in August that year, which was aimed at preventing the Danish Fleet from falling into French hands.[6] Thus what has been termed the 'long peace' of 1720–1807 was followed by the 'short war' of 1807–1814.[7] It can be argued, therefore, that the main challenge facing the Danish government in terms of retaining neutrality was increasingly that of balancing the interests of Britain and France, the only two great powers which remained constantly at war with each other from 1793 until the final defeat of Napoleon in 1815 (apart from the brief interlude of the Peace of Amiens from 1802 to 1803). As the French side gradually gained control over an ever-greater part of continental Europe, culminating in Napoleon's French Empire of 1804, while a series of British naval victories consolidated Britain's dominance at sea, the Danish government found itself pushed from two sides. Yet, at the same time this development arguably provided the Danish government with a room of opportunity to exploit neutrality in the expectation that neither belligerent would wish to push the neutral power into the arms of the enemy.[8] For a long time this seemed to work quite well.

A central issue in the Danish balancing act was the question of how a neutral power such as Denmark-Norway should relate to the privateers of these two belligerent countries. While it may not have been of as crucial importance as the question of neutral trade—at least in the sense that it did not lead to outright armed conflict between Denmark and Britain—privateering and neutrality nevertheless formed the topic of a long-lasting debate in the diplomatic correspondence between the two countries in the period 1793–1799. The debate was extensive in terms of the numbers of letters exchanged, and arguably addressed a series of central questions relating to neutrality and what it really meant to stay neutral in a war. The issue at stake was very specific: was it compatible with neutrality—as the concept was understood and regulated by established international rules under the so-called Law of Nations and specific treaties—to permit privateers from the belligerent nations to use the ports of the neutral country as bases for their attacks on enemy trade? Quite what it would mean to use ports as 'bases' in this context was at the crux of the whole debate, and an issue we will return to throughout the book, but, first, more detail needs to be provided on the situation which arose when Britain entered the war against Revolutionary France in 1793.

Both Britain and France sent out privateers during the Revolutionary and Napoleonic wars, but the French did so in significantly larger numbers than the British. In the waters surrounding the dual-monarchy, the North Sea, the Skagerrak and the Kattegat in particular, but also the Norwegian Sea, the issue at hand was one of French privateers seeking to use Norwegian ports as bases for their attacks on the extensive and lucrative British Baltic Sea trade, and to some extent also, Archangel trades. All merchant vessels sailing to and from the Baltic Sea had to pass through the Sound, the narrow passage between Denmark and Sweden, and on the Danish side the British consul at Elsinore, Nicholas Fenwick kept a close watch on the number and nationality of the ships passing through and paying the required customs duties to Denmark. More than 10,000 ships were registered each year by the beginning of the 1790s and, for the year 1791, Fenwick's accounts revealed that out of a total of 10,452 ships passing through the Sound, 3720, or just over a third, were British. Only three other countries reached more than 1000 vessels, while the number of French ships stood at a mere 88.[9] The figures for 1792 showed a similar pattern with 4349 British vessels out of a total of 12,114, and just 25 French ships.[10] The situation was, in other words, a very uneven one. While there were numerous British merchant vessels French privateers could lay chase to, British privateers faced more meagre possibilities of a good catch. This was an important difference, and a main reason why British privateering in the North Sea was never much of an issue (though we will see that there were other reasons for the French predominance in privateering too).[11]

Shortly after Britain had entered the war against France in February 1793, the first report of the sighting of a French privateer landed on the desk of the British diplomatic representative to Denmark, Daniel Hailes in Copenhagen.[12] The vessel in question was a fairly large ship of 20 guns which had appeared off the town of Mandal on the southern coast of Norway.[13] The British government now moved to protest, arguing that allowing French privateers to operate from Norwegian waters was incompatible with neutrality, and the diplomatic debate which ensued took place on two levels: one was a more general and principled discussion about privateering and neutrality, and this rather special case of privateers using neutral ports; the other was the question of French privateering as it worked out in practice. While this may sound a bit odd—why would one discuss French privateering from Norwegian ports in practice, while at the same time discussing whether it should take place at all?—the reason is that the whole issue turned out to be more complicated than the British seem to have thought, or at least argued, at the outset. Moreover, while the discussions were taking place, French privateers kept operating out of Norwegian ports, and even when an agreement had been reached, the problem remained of applying the rules agreed upon in practice. As with all aspects of law, one might argue, one thing is the actual letter of the law or the rules adopted, another how to apply this in individual cases, and privateering tended to present a number of challenges in this respect. The current chapter addresses the more general, or principled discussion, while Chap. 4 explores the central individual cases which arose from time to time, and how these came to illustrate the many dilemmas privateering gave rise to (while Chap. 3 addresses the role of the British diplomatic and consular representatives in Denmark-Norway). Central to this was the problem of determining who was in the right and who was in the wrong in an individual case of dispute. Before we can move on to the debate, however, it is necessary to clarify what we mean by privateering, and what characterised French privateering in particular—why did French privateers seek to operate out of Norwegian ports in the first place?—as well as the understanding of neutrality at the end of the eighteenth century, and how neutral countries should relate to the privateers of the belligerents. The first two sections of this chapter address these issues.

Privateering

Privateering, as it had developed by the later eighteenth century, can perhaps best be described as a form of commercial warfare, organised and conducted by non-state, or 'private' operators—as, indeed the name 'privateer' would suggest—but sanctioned by the state. At the outbreak of war, the governments in the belligerent countries could issue so-called letters of marque or letters of reprisal whereby they authorised private entrepreneurs to hire a crew and equip one or more ships with the weapons needed to hunt for and seize the enemy's merchant vessels. Any enemy vessels caught would be brought back to the home port of the privateer ship in question, and a case would then be raised before a 'Prize Court' (provided, that is, the privateer was not caught by enemy warships before it could reach the safety of a port in the home country). The adjudication of the court would then determine whether the capture was in accordance with those rules and regulations that applied for privateering. If the court decided that the vessel was a 'fair' or 'good Prize', that is, that the capture was legal, both ship and cargo would become the property of the owner of the privateer, who could then proceed to sell both, usually at an auction. The owner of the privateer could not, however, pocket the entire profits earned from that sale, since the government that had issued the letter of marque might claim a part of this, and both the captain and crew members of the privateer were entitled to their shares as well. Exactly how large a share they were due varied considerably, and not all governments demanded a part. Moreover, if the capture involved neutral nations, be that either in the shape of an enemy vessel carrying neutral goods, or enemy goods on board a neutral vessel, the whole affair became more complicated.[14] We will return to the question of neutrality later, but for now it should suffice to conclude that the essence of privateering was one of utilising private resources in what one authority of French privateering, Patrick Crowhurst, has denoted a 'war on trade', carried out in order to undermine the war-effort of the enemy.[15] Since privateering involved an attempt to seize the (hopefully) valuable cargoes on board the merchant vessels of an enemy country, and was conducted as a private venture, privateering could be said to resemble piracy in some respects. Yet, while privateering is sometimes confused with piracy, it is important to draw up a clear distinction between the two. Whereas privateering had become a well-established and generally acknowledged and accepted institution by the later eighteenth century, piracy was seen by most states as a very serious form of criminal activity, and one for which severe punishments could be handed out. Immediate execution upon capture at sea was the commonly accepted punishment for pirates by the time war broke out between Britain and France in 1793.[16] But precisely because privateering and piracy resembled each other so closely in terms of the actual activity carried out, while they remained clearly distinct in a legal sense, it was crucial to keep them well apart (and not the least because of the punishment inflicted for piracy). Much, therefore, depended on whether the paperwork was in order, since the only certain way to distinguish a privateer from a pirate, when out at sea, was through the letter of marque that all legitimate privateers must carry.

Furthermore, because of its likeness to piracy, privateering could be said to constitute an open invitation to abuse, and in practice often led to controversy. One question was the status of the government which had produced the letter of marque. At a time of considerable upheaval in Europe such as the 1790s, privateers might be commissioned by new independent states which had not yet been recognised or, indeed, by the new government of an existing state—such as the republican government formed in France in 1792—before this had been acknowledged by the other governments of Europe.[17] Were letters of marque issued by such 'un-recognised' regimes to be accepted, or should they be seen as void, with the consequence that the privateers in question could be treated as pirates? It could clearly be in the self-interest of some belligerent countries to question the legitimacy of the privateers of their opponent in order to undermine the war effort of that opponent. Privateers, in turn, would sometimes operate in the very borderlands to piracy, tempted by the possibility of large gains made from the capture of merchant vessels which were not fully legitimate targets. One example of this was the tendency of French privateers in the 1790s to go after vessels flying the flag of a neutral nation in the hope that they could 'disprove' the neutrality of the vessel in question, and thereby, hopefully, seize a potentially valuable cargo as their prize. Although the general rule adopted by the French authorities was that 'just one valid piece among the ship's papers was enough to prove her neutrality', Éric Schnakenbourg has argued, French privateers would look for any kind of irregularity on the part of neutral vessels they had stopped at sea, however minor, in order to claim that they were, in fact, sailing in support of the enemy. In the case of the Danish vessel the *Norge*, caught by the privateer *Enterprise* in October 1797, the justification for bringing the vessels into port in France was that the captain's sea pass was invalid, and that the crew list lacked the signature of a Danish official. It was clearly not a British vessel, nor could it reasonably be argued that it was sailing in support of the British war effort, but it was nevertheless condemned by a Prize Court at Nantes on the basis of these technicalities.[18] In this case, one could argue that the French Prize Court in question had failed in its mission, since a main purpose of the Prize Court system was to prevent privateering from descending into piracy, and otherwise uphold the rules of privateering, but the problem was perhaps as much to do with a weakness in the (French) Prize Court system itself: the local organisation of the courts. One thing was that the judges at the court knew how important privateering was for the livelihood of many people in Nantes, and thus may have felt the 'pressures of their environment', another that they had invested in the privateering enterprises themselves, meaning that they had a self-interest in condemning prizes.[19]

With such borderline practices taking place, it was perhaps not surprising that privateers were sometimes accused of outright piracy, and the legally ambiguous nature of privateers operating from neutral waters arguably lent itself to suspicions on the British side that the French were prepared to bend any rule to their advantage. For merchants who had just lost considerable valuables in the shape of captured ships and cargoes, the possibility that the papers of the privateer was not fully in order, or that the capture could be deemed illegal in some other sense—if it had taken place in neutral waters for example—presented, of course, their chance of reclaiming their loss. Finally, the very particular case of privateers using neutral ports as bases opened up for a whole raft of additional problems and grey areas as we will see in the subsequent chapters. The history of privateering—both in general terms and with respect to French privateers in particular—is, however, central to how this kind of warfare unfolded in the 1790s and early 1800s, and we will address this first.

Privateering was, as we have seen, based on the issuing of letters of marque, and by the late eighteenth century, this practice already had a long history. Originating with the German word *Mark*, or similar French *marches*, in the meaning of a frontier, the implications of a letter of marque was 'the right to take action beyond the frontier of the issuing state'.[20] This arguably made it a special form of *reprisal*, and reprisals, in turn, had their origins in older Germanic law practice relating to family feuds. If—in a situation where revenge was sought for some or other wrongdoing—it proved impossible to obtain compensation from the person who had committed the deed, this could be sought from family members instead. Quite often, such conflicts would relate to stolen property, and the word reprisal itself was derived from the French word *reprendre*, meaning to recover or take back, and thus related to property.[21] If, however, the actual stolen goods could not be recovered from the person who had stolen them, similar goods, or goods of a similar value, could be seized from family members. The same kind of logic was then extended to cases where the injury had been caused by a foreigner. Again, if the person in question could not be apprehended or otherwise made to compensate, satisfaction could instead be obtained 'by seizing the property belonging to any fellow-national of the wrongdoer'.[22] Such action required the sanction of the government in the home country, and this was provided by a letter of reprisal. In its earliest practice, dating back to medieval times, such letters had related to the retaking of property within the territorial jurisdiction of the sovereign or government which had issued the letter, but with the extension beyond the borders of the state in a letter of marque, the possibility emerged of hunting for property on the high seas. In the 'special reprisals' of the medieval practice, such letters referred to individual cases, and the documentation was necessary to distinguish this legal and state-authorised quest for property from plain piracy. Privateering proper, however, first emerged in the early modern period with the issuing of 'general reprisals', which not only authorised *all* members of society to hunt for the property of a certain country upon the high seas, but also removed the requirement of an original injury to be redressed. Letters of marque were thus no longer aimed at a reprisal in the original sense of a specific recovery of property, and were now more clearly linked to the outbreak of war between two countries.[23] The letters themselves could still be very detailed, tailored to an individual privateer vessel, containing information on the size of the crew, the specific armament carried by the ship, tonnage and name of the vessel itself, and were often accompanied by a set of 'instructions' for the privateer, outlining the rules the privateer must abide by.[24] Moreover, letters of marque were almost invariably issued for one enemy country only, and if other countries entered the war on the opposing side, new letters would have to be issued to authorise the capture of merchant vessels from these countries. The importance of a legal framework to regulate privateering in order to uphold a clear demarcation against piracy was, in other words, no less crucial with the development towards general reprisals. The difference was that the letter of marque had moved from the sphere of the medieval feud, to that of the wars of the modern state system. In that sense, however, privateering also appeared a remnant of the past and anomaly in the modern warfare which emerged in the eighteenth century. As a kind of private war, it seemed to fit in poorly with the advent of a state monopoly on the legal exercise of physical force, and the professional armies and navies of the period. Perhaps a growing unease about privateering as an essentially outdated and uncivilised way of conducting war could be said to be emerging already by the 1790s. British responses, from the public as well as from the authorities, were certainly very fierce the moment information emerged which suggested that French privateers had overstepped the rules of privateering in some way or another. By the time privateering was abolished by the Declaration of Paris in 1856, British opinion seems to have swung decisively over on the side of seeing privateering as barbaric and barely any better than piracy. As the newspaper the *Daily News* stated in a pithy comment in 1854, a privateer was 'merely a pirate with a pardon in his pocket'.[25] Moreover, it took time to develop a set of commonly agreed international rules for privateering and, for a long time, governments might disagree on the status of a 'privateer' in individual cases. Thus where the famous Sir Francis Drake of the late sixteenth century was a privateer in the view of the English government, to the Spanish he was a simple pirate. It was only in the seventeenth century that clear legal regulations of privateering emerged in full force. This set of agreed rules on privateering was based partly on Prize Court rulings and the precedent they provided, and partly on numerous treatises entered into by two or more countries. By the mid-eighteenth century, this development had resulted in a body of international law on privateering which, in the view of Gary M. Anderson and Adam Gifford, provided for 'a complex and generally effective legal order'.[26] Coupled with the strenuous efforts made by many European states to eradicate piracy in the period—which necessitated the development of legal definitions of piracy as a crime, typically as high treason—privateering could finally emerge as a fully legitimate form of warfare.[27]

France was one of the main privateering nations of the seventeenth and eighteenth centuries, and French privateering in the later eighteenth century has been studied extensively by Patrick Crowhurst in particular. In his view, the perhaps most important feature of French privateering was that it constituted 'a substitute for trade when that collapsed'.[28] Clearly, privateering necessitated a state of war, but even when that existed, regular trade was usually preferred by those who might otherwise take part in privateering. There were specific reasons for this: the central figure in a privateering venture, Crowhurst stresses, was the *armateur* or 'managing owner', who was typically a merchant in one of the coastal towns which had a tradition for privateering, such as Dunkirk, St. Malo and Nantes. He was the person in charge of obtaining the licence from the government, providing a vessel and hiring a crew and a captain.[29] Knowledge of shipping was obviously an advantage for those who sought their luck in privateering, but it was also necessary to be able to raise the funds required to carry the cost of equipping a privateer, and the willingness and opportunity to risk this capital in what might very well turn out to be a loss-making venture. Wealthy merchants were, in other words, particularly well placed to become *armateurs*. If valuable prizes were captured, the profit earned could be formidable, but if the privateer vessel was caught by enemy warships, the whole investment was essentially lost. Thus privateering constituted a high-risk venture and, for most merchants, this was only seen as an attractive proposition when the opportunities for carrying out regular trade were poor. Consequently, French privateering fluctuated with the opportunities of trade, and this had a significant impact on *when* the French equipped privateers in significant numbers. When new opportunities for trade with the USA opened up in 1804, for example, French privateering activity went down markedly, only to pick up again when the US trade declined after 1806.[30] Combined with the changing policies on privateering adopted by the French governments of the period, and British counter-measures, the result was that the level of French privateering changed more or less from year to year. Initially, the new French republican government of 1792 even suggested that privateering should be banned altogether, but when it received little positive response to this initiative from Britain and others, it decided to encourage privateering the following year, in 1793.[31] After this first year of privateering, activity then decreased in 1794 as the French government placed 'an embargo on the movement of all French shipping' in preparation for an invasion of Britain. The invasion, however, never was, and from late 1795 onwards, privateers were again fitted out in increasing numbers. The peak came in 1797–1798, possibly spurred on by the new French government, the Directory's decree of 2 March 1797, which allowed French privateers to seize enemy goods carried by neutral vessels.[32] Thereafter, activity declined again, partly, it seems, because many privateers were caught by the Royal Navy, resulting in the imprisonment of many of the best French sailors, and partly because the British Convoy Act of 1798 made it more difficult to capture prizes.[33] Although the fear of French privateers was almost omnipresent in Britain in the 1790s, and the commonly held view was that the North Sea was 'infested' with privateers at all times, the reality was, in other words, a rather different one.[34] What is important in our context is that the fluctuations in French privateering seem to have had an impact on the British-Danish debate about Norwegian ports, as we will see later.

The nature of privateering as a high-risk *private* enterprise had important implications, both with respect to the organising of the activity and the strategy applied at sea. The *armateurs* would typically wish to minimise their cost in equipping and manning their vessels, and once at sea, the aim was to capture prizes as economically as possible. Three elements were central in this: the size of the crew, the armament carried by the ship and the type of vessel used. A privateer needed a fairly large crew. Not as big as that of a warship of a similar size, but significantly larger than what was the norm for merchant vessels. There were two reasons for this. Partly the privateer needed a crew large enough to successfully board and overcome the crew of a merchant vessel, if the merchantman refused to surrender upon a warning from the privateer; partly it had to be able to put a 'prize crew' on board captured vessels for the voyage home. In order to stop a merchant vessel the privateer had laid chase to, sufficient guns to overawe the ship in question were needed, but the number of guns was rarely on par with that of a similar-sized warship, and the cost of cannon was in any case a reason for restricting their numbers to what was strictly necessary only. Another reason for limiting the number of guns was the all-important element of speed. Privateer vessels clearly needed to be fast enough to catch up with merchant ships, but should also be sufficiently quick to outrun most naval vessels, and the weight of too many guns might slow down the ship. At the outbreak of war, a variety of vessels could be equipped and sent out as privateers depending on what was available, but the preference was clearly for faster-going ships and, soon, purpose-built high-speed vessels were launched specifically for privateering.[35] Thus the type of ship used, the armament carried and the size and training of the crew were specific for the privateering enterprise. Moreover, privateers normally sought to avoid actual combat as much as possible, and this applied to the merchantmen they were chasing as much as to the warships that were hunting for them. Typically, the privateer would try to impress upon the merchant ship it had caught up with to surrender without a fight. A shot across the bow and a display of guns—often including wooden dummy guns—as well as the presence of a large well-armed crew ready to board were aimed at convincing the captain of the merchantman that resistance was futile. Since the purpose of privateering was to seize both vessel and cargo, any damage done to the prospective prize, or to the privateer, would simply represent an unwanted loss. If the prize was seen as potentially valuable, however, privateers would not normally shy away from a fight they were well-placed to win. In such cases, the merchant vessel normally stood little chance of defending itself successfully, or of getting away, though exceptions to this did occur. In August 1797, for example, the 'armed Collier' *Exeter* of Newcastle put up such strong resistance against the attacking French privateer the *Courageux* that—after a battle lasting an hour-and-a-half—the privateer 'blew up' (probably a magazine explosion) with the loss of all but four of its 43-strong crew. The *Exeter* suffered no casualties.[36] Similarly, privateers very rarely picked a fight with regular warships, and usually only if they were defending particularly valuable prize vessels.[37] Neither the armament, nor the size or training of the crew was normally on par with that of naval vessels, and examples of French privateers who engaged successfully in combat with Royal Navy warships were few and far between.[38] One rare exception from this general rule was the exploits of Jean Jacques de St Faust, the commander of the privateer corvette *La Foi Batave*, who was able to fight off the Royal Navy frigate *Amethyst* in a clash off Bergen in March 1804.[39] Since privateers could not be legally caught in neutral waters, a common scenario in our period was therefore that of a French privateer racing towards the Norwegian coast, with a British warship in hot pursuit.

Although the British also sent out privateers in the 1790s and early 1800s, privateering was arguably never as important for the British side as it was for the French, and there was a particular reason for this.[40] In the situation which had developed by the later eighteenth century, where Britain had a superior navy to that of France as well as more extensive seagoing trade (particularly with respect to the Baltic Sea, as we have seen), privateering on a larger scale presented the perhaps best way in which the French might try to redress some of this imbalance. Not only could a significant number of privateers be launched in much shorter time than it would take to build up the navy, but it could be done at virtually no cost to the government. In order to facilitate privateering, the French government even decided to waive its share of the profit earned from the sale of prizes in February 1793.[41] Privateering also had the double benefit for the French government of potentially harming British trade, while at the same time ensuring that significant British naval resources were tied up in the protection of this trade. In essence, therefore, privateering could be said to constitute a kind of poor man's navy, and this became more apparent than ever when the European great powers decided to abolish privateering altogether in 1856. At that point, the main opponent of this move was the USA, which saw privateering as its only way to counter British naval superiority in a future war between the two countries.[42] Emphasising privateering over the build-up of the regular navy as a strategy for the war at sea was what the French themselves referred to as *la guerre de course*, or 'a war of chase', as opposed to a more regular naval war, or *la guerre de L'Escadre*, which they had largely abandoned by 1793.[43] French *armateurs* also found themselves in a more favourable position with respect to the task of recruiting men for their vessels, than did their British counterparts—or at least they did so until the number of skilled French seamen available for service was reduced by British captures. The poor state of the French navy—which had been run down before the war, as well as weakened by desertion and the persecution of officers by the Jacobin regime, and was generally held in poor regard—meant that there were more men available for privateer service.[44] In Britain, by contrast, privateers competed for men with both the Royal Navy and the merchant fleet, and the navy did not look favourably upon the privateers. There were even cases of impressment from privateers to navy vessels while both were out at sea.[45] Privateering thus constituted a central part of the French war effort at sea and, while it was never as extensive and successful in the French Revolutionary and Napoleonic Wars period as it had been in the heyday of the late seventeenth century, it was nevertheless a very real threat to British commerce.[46] Moreover, in terms of attacking the British Baltic Sea trade, the ability to operate out of Norwegian waters was a major advantage, partly because the long and cragged Norwegian coastline provided numerous opportunities for hiding away or escaping from British warships, but even more so because of its proximity to the main trade routes. As the British consul in the southern-Norwegian coastal town of Kristiansand, John Mitchell, explained to his superior in Copenhagen in 1796: for the British merchant vessels passing through the Skagerrak on their way home from the Baltic Sea, it was important to stay close to the Norwegian coast because the 'Jutland shores' were 'low and surrounded with dangerous Shoals', while the southern coast of Norway was 'bold, and safe, and full of good Harbours, and furnished with good Pilots'.[47] Much the same was the case for the British trade on Archangel, where Bergen on the western coast of Norway was ideally suited as a privateer base.[48] If French privateers could operate in and out of Norwegian ports, then that was clearly better than having to sail back and forth from France. The question was whether it was compatible with neutrality to allow them to do so, and this, in turn, depended on how neutrality was really to be understood.

Neutrality and Privateering

At the time of the outbreak of war between Britain and France in 1793, the concept of neutrality had not yet been fully developed in its modern form, and quite what it meant to be neutral in a war, as well as how neutral nations were supposed to relate to the belligerents, was a bone of some contention. Although a few states such as Denmark-Norway and the Dutch Republic had pursued a consistent policy of staying out of armed conflict for most of the eighteenth century, neutrality was still seen to relate primarily to situations of actual war. The notion of 'perpetual neutrality', that a country might declare itself neutral in peacetime also—as it applied to Sweden and Austria during the Cold War period of the twentieth century for example—would only emerge in full force after 1815.[49] Moreover, the understanding of neutrality emerged more out of state practice than from theoretical legal considerations, and the development of a law of neutrality was therefore more of a 'bottom up' than a 'top down' process. It emerged, Stephen C. Neff has argued, 'in a rather untidy piecemeal manner, to deal with the myriad practical problems that arose when some states were at war while others were at peace'.[50] There were particular reasons for this, and the implications were important.

The starting point was medieval European philosophy on warfare, which centred on the notion of a 'just war'. Ideally, Christians should not kill each other, or anyone else, due to the Sixth Commandment, but it was still possible to imagine a rightful exercise of violence in the shape of 'a war waged for the enforcement of right and the eradication of evil', and thus as a use of violence which was sanctioned by the Almighty.[51] Although it was usually very difficult, if not impossible, to establish such a clear right-and-wrong relationship in the actual wars which took place, the just war principle was nonetheless a very powerful one. It dominated European thinking on warfare until well into the seventeenth century, and was still influential by the later eighteenth century. From this perception of war as a conflict between right and wrong, it followed that neutrality, in the sense of remaining fully indifferent to, or detached from the conflict, was not really an option. All good Christians ought to side with the party who was fighting a just war and, although the just war doctrine did not necessary require everyone to enter the actual military conflict on the side of those who were fighting for justice, all countries ought at least to give their moral support to them. Neutrality was thus held 'in low esteem' by medieval European society.[52] A change to this dominance of the just war doctrine emerged only slowly with the rise of the early modern European state system in the sixteenth and seventeenth centuries. Gradually, war came to be seen more as a contest between two, or more, morally equal opponents, who were trying to resolve their differences on the battlefield. And when that was the case, it was increasingly not seen as necessary for other countries to pass any judgement on the conflict itself, or to decide which side to give their moral support. From this, it followed that it was also possible and legitimate for the non-belligerents to state the following: this is not a war that concerns us; we choose to stay aloof, or neutral. Acceptance of neutrality was further boosted by the frequent European wars of the early modern period, where most states found themselves in the position of being neutral relative to some or other conflict at some point. They might even be neutral with respect to one ongoing war, while at the same time a belligerent in another. Most states therefore realised that they had an interest in developing an international law of neutrality, or stated differently, that neutrality was an issue which should be dealt with in the man-made 'Law of Nations', the voluntary legal agreements states entered into and which would later be referred to as 'international law'.[53] This also applied to great powers such as Britain and France.[54] For a long time, this development was based on the forming of numerous bilateral treaties, and only in the second half of the eighteenth century was the topic addressed by legal scholars in a more systematic fashion. The debate then and later came to centre on the so-called rights and duties of neutrals, and on the extent to which they came into conflict with the corresponding rights and duties of the belligerents.

Neutrals were seen to have two main duties, *abstention* and *impartiality*, and the understanding of these two concepts was largely what defined neutrality as such. Abstention was arguably the more straightforward duty, and it related to what neutrals could not do, full stop. Most obviously, this meant that a neutral country had to stay out of the armed conflict itself; that neutrals could not engage actively in military operations in support of one of the belligerents. They could, however, act against a belligerent who violated the rights of the neutrals in some way or another—if one of the belligerents carried out a military attack in neutral waters for example—but in such cases the military actions of the neutral country was seen to be directed against the violation of its neutrality, rather than as an act in the ongoing war as such. This was a central point for both French privateers and British warships in our period. Neither could carry out legitimate captures or attacks of any sort in the waters of Denmark-Norway and, if they did, the Danish government could respond with military force without jeopardising its neutrality. The second duty of impartiality was also, on paper, simple enough. It related to what neutral countries could do, as long as it was done 'equally for each belligerent', that is, without giving undue preference to either of the two sides in the conflict.[55] In practice, however, this was not always so easily achieved, and quickly touched upon the question of rights.

The rights of neutrals had not been as clearly defined as their duties by the middle of the eighteenth century and to some extent consisted of what 'freedom of action' was 'left over' once the rights of belligerents had been defined (which could be seen as consistent with the unfavourable starting point for neutrality in the previously dominant just war philosophy).[56] Belligerents, on the other hand, were seen to possess a number of rights, such as the right to attack the military forces of their opponent, the right to occupy his territory, the right to blockade enemy ports and so on. In medieval times, these rights were based on the broader principle of 'necessity'—that a (just) belligerent had the right to take whichever action was necessary to subdue his (unjust) foe—but with the emergence of war as conflict between two morally equal opponents, belligerent rights were now simply seen to emanate from the state of war itself. Necessity still played a role, however, and while most belligerent rights related to the opponent in the war, some were also explicitly aimed at neutrals. In the words of Stephen C. Neff, they were: 'the right to capture enemy property at sea; the right to interfere with arms trading by neutrals; and the right to stop neutrals from trading with besieged areas'.[57] The underlying theme of belligerent rights *vis-à-vis* neutrals thus seemed to be that whenever the actions of neutrals had a direct impact on the conduct of the war, the principle of necessity gave the belligerents the right to interfere. How were the neutrals to respond to this? A main development in the second half of the eighteenth century was the formulation of arguments in favour of specific positive rights for neutrals. The main advocate of such rights was the Danish legal scholar Martin Hübner, who held that a state of war gave rise to a distinct set of rights and duties for both belligerents and neutrals, where the rights of one was the 'flip side' of the duties of the other. Thus where the belligerent had a duty not to carry out military attacks in neutral territorial waters, the sanctity of neutral territory constituted the right of the neutral. In Hübner's analysis, therefore, there was really no conflict of rights in war.[58] Not all legal scholars agreed that there was such a perfect balance between the rights and duties of belligerents and neutrals and, indeed, the second half of the eighteenth century was marked by a vigorous debate between different 'schools' on this question of rights and duties. The central point for us, however, is Hübner's attempt to lift neutrality to a level of parity with belligerency.[59] At a time of war, neutral countries had the same right to argue their case, as had belligerent countries, and belligerents ought to respect the rights of neutrals as much as the other way around.[60] More than anything, these discussions of neutrality in the later eighteenth century came to focus on seaborne trade—as indeed, the three belligerent rights relative to neutrals would suggest. To what extent could neutral countries trade with belligerents, and what rights did the belligerents have in terms of interfering with such trade?

Was it, for example, acceptable for neutral countries to 'take over' trade they were prevented from engaging in in peacetime, such as the colonial trade of one of the belligerents? The trade between the French colonies and the mother country was, for example, reserved to French merchant vessels in peacetime, and attempts to allow neutrals into this trade in wartime were opposed by the British as a violation of neutral duties.[61] More importantly, perhaps, to what extent could neutrals continue their own peacetime trade with one or more of the belligerents during the war and, if so, with what kind of goods? The duty of impartiality suggested that the pre-war trade could continue as long as no undue preference was given to one side in the conflict over the other, but what if a neutral country had had extensive trade with one of the belligerents, and not with the other before the outbreak of war? Should that be allowed to continue as before, based on the reasoning that neutrals had a right to carry on 'business as usual' as much as possible, and not be (too) adversely affected by a war they were not a party to, or should the belligerents have a right to interfere with trade which was clearly to their disadvantage, under the principle of necessity? In practice, the resolution to this conundrum came to focus on what constituted so-called contraband goods.

Although contraband was a concept originally linked to smuggling, in relation to warfare it had come to mean goods of direct use for combat, typically weapons and ammunition. Selling or shipping such goods to a belligerent could be seen as direct support for the war effort, and therefore as a violation of the duty of abstention on the part of a neutral country. For that reason, the general agreement was that neutrals could not trade with any of the belligerents in contraband goods. If trade in such goods had taken place before the outbreak of war between a country which was now one of the belligerents, and one that was neutral, it had to cease. For other goods, however, trade could continue as before, provided the neutrals did not try to enter blockaded ports. If they did, the belligerent mounting the blockade could seize both cargo and vessel.[62] The problem was that there was no general agreement on precisely which goods were to be classified as contraband. Specific lists of contraband goods were often drawn up in bilateral treaties, but that meant they only applied for the signatories in question. Moreover, there was a tendency over the course of the eighteenth century for such lists to grow longer, and to include so-called dual-use goods, that is, goods which could be used both for civilian and military purposes. To add to this, the understanding of contraband itself was rather elastic, and was stretched to include goods that were of use to the war effort in a wider sense, not merely of a direct military application.[63] This meant that the grey area between what was clearly contraband and what was clearly not contraband grew larger. Should timber—which could be used in the construction of warships (or privateer vessels for that matter)—be viewed as contraband, or would that be unreasonable because of its extensive civilian usage? Finally, precisely which kinds of goods were seen as vital to the war effort, and thus as contraband in the more extended meaning of the term, could change over time, sometimes in line with technological developments. With the advent of steamships in the nineteenth century, for example, the supply of coal by neutrals to the belligerents became an issue of contention. An abstention argument then held that neutrals should not supply coal to the belligerents, while an impartiality argument held that coal could be supplied, as long as it was done equally to both parties. Similarly, once warships were built of steel rather than wood, timber arguably lost its relevance as potential contraband. Contraband lists could therefore never be final, and were, as the great Swiss eighteenth-century legal scholar Emer de Vattel argued, in a 'permanent state of flux'.[64] Britain, as a country that was more often belligerent than neutral in the second half of the century, tended to promote comprehensive contraband lists. Two categories of goods proved to be particularly controversial in the later eighteenth century, and both caused friction between Britain and Denmark-Norway. They were 'provisions' and 'naval stores', where the first essentially meant food, while the second referred to ship-building materials, usually in a fairly broad sense. Most eighteenth-century treaties declared that provisions were non-contraband, while there was more variation for naval stores. For Britain and Denmark-Norway, the question of contraband was regulated by the Anglo-Danish Treaty of 1670, which stated that 'other necessaries of war'—that is, beyond weaponry—were to be seen as contraband, and the vagueness of this phrase led to repeated diplomatic disputes between the two countries over the course of the eighteenth century, focusing on foodstuffs in particular. Britain argued for a strict understanding where food was deemed contraband, while the Danish government held the opposite view. The issue was not fully resolved until 1780, when a compromise was reached and added in an explanatory article to the treaty. All naval stores were now seen as contraband, while all provisions were non-contraband.[65] Arguably, therefore, French privateers in Norwegian ports could not be supplied with naval stores, but Denmark-Norway could export food to France, as long as one did not try to ship it into blockaded ports. In the

1790s, however, the British once again tried to make food contraband, arguing that starving the enemy into submission was part of the British war strategy. A set of 'instructions' was issued on 8 June 1793 and sent to Copenhagen, forbidding neutral countries to export food to France. This unilateral decision was arguably in breach of the agreement of 1780, and was not accepted by the Danish side, which insisted on its right to supply the French with grain. On 18 August 1794, therefore, a new British proclamation rescinded the instructions of the year before. The question of grain exports to France remained a cause of controversy thereafter and led to a tug-of-war between the governments of the two countries. In May 1795, for example, Bernstorff was again pressured into suspending the corn trade with France, only for the order to capture neutral Danish grain-vessels *en route* to France to be recalled by Foreign Secretary Grenville about four months later on 15 September.[66] According to John Mitchell, the 'constant exportation of Corn from all Parts of the Danish Dominions to France' had by then 'rendered Grain of all Kinds so high priced & so scarce that the poorer Classes of the People in Holstein, Jutland, & Norway, are in a state of almost open Insurrection'.[67]

The particular case of the British-Danish debate on food as contraband, or not, can be seen as part of a more general development towards the end of the eighteenth century, where the rights of neutrals came under pressure from Britain in particular. As British sea power grew, Britain became the primary champion of belligerent countries' rights at sea, largely because that suited its interests as the dominant naval power.[68] In the second half of the 1790s, the pressure on neutral rights mounted even further as the two main opponents at sea, Britain and France, intensified their economic warfare.[69] The debate on privateering and neutral ports, which commenced in 1793, therefore took place between what was arguably the main proponent of belligerents' rights, Great Britain, and one of the main proponents of neutrals rights, Denmark-Norway.

First Round of Discussions

The initial British approach was to try to avoid the problem altogether by attempting to persuade the Danish government to give up its neutrality, and enter the war as an ally of Great Britain. In late March 1793, Lord Grenville instructed the British diplomatic representative at Copenhagen Daniel Hailes to work for this purpose.[70] Hailes was to 'propose to the Danish Ministers, that the Court of Copenhagen should accede to the

System of Measure now pursuing by so many Powers of Europe, for the Prosecution of a Vigorous War against France', and—in a statement which was typical of the British ruling elite's anti-revolutionary views at the time—'for Establishing an effectual Barrier against that System of Aggrandizement and Ambition openly avowed by France, and supported by the Propagation of the most atrocious and destructive Principles'. The Danish government should realise 'that all Civilized Nations have a common Interest in this Object', Grenville wrote. If, however, Denmark chose to stay out of the war, it

> should at least not afford, in consequence of this Neutrality, any Sort of Assistance or Protection direct or indirect to the Commerce, or to the Property of those who are the Common Enemies of all regular and Established Governments.[71]

The invitation to join the war on the side of Britain and her allies should, in other words, be accompanied by a clear warning from the British government. The focus on commerce in Grenville's statement was, of course, no coincidence. Denmark-Norway's 'profiteering' neutrality policy of the previous wars of the eighteenth century was well known, and Hailes had already provided Grenville with information that the Danish government was determined to pursue a similar policy in the current war. In late January, when an outbreak of war between Britain and France seemed 'inevitable', Hailes wrote, the Danish government was 'bent entirely upon the improvement of the finances and Trade of the Country', expecting 'great advantages from its neutrality, should the rest of Europe be embroiled in hostilities'.[72] His suspicions were confirmed once the war was a fact. It was now beyond doubt that 'the general disposition of this Country continues to be to take advantage of the War', so much so that 'there is little to be expected, in this quarter, from the effect of those sentiments of indignation and disgust which have been so justly excited against the French everywhere else'.[73] There was a ring of just-war thinking to this line of argument, based as it seemed to be on the notion that Britain had entered the war on the morally just side, fighting the reprehensible French republican regime. Viewing the French republicans and the revolution in a wider sense as an affront to humanity and as a breakdown of civilisation was commonplace among members of the British political establishment (and beyond) in the wake of the September massacres in France in 1792, and it would also resurface in the debate about privateers and neutral ports from time to time. While the focus of Hailes and Grenville was thus set on persuading the Danish government to give up its neutrality (a policy which, of course, failed), it was left to the British consul in Kristiansand in Norway, John Mitchell, to raise the issue of French privateers and Norwegian ports, and Mitchell was to play a central role in the subsequent debate.

It seems clear that Mitchell, who had been a British consul in Norway for nearly ten years by 1793, had anticipated the problem. Upon learning about the outbreak of war between Britain and France, he wrote in a letter to Grenville in late March that he had immediately 'requested of my Acquaintances at the Outposts to give me the earliest information of any French Vessels, Privateers &c that might be seen or heard of on the Coast'. His reason for doing so was the experience of the American War when 'anybody' who flew an American, French or Dutch flag had been allowed to seize vessels along the coasts of Norway and Sweden, bring them into port and have them 'Condemned & sold … with impunity'. Having just received information that 'two Cutters supposed by the description to be French Privateers' had been observed 'Cruising between the Dogger Bank and the Naze', he feared that the scenario of the last war was about to repeat itself now. He therefore asked for directions on how to act, and took the liberty to suggest two alternatives himself. Either, he said, Britain had to reach some agreement with both the Danish and Swedish authorities on 'some regular mode of proceeding with the Condemnation of Such Prizes in their Ports'. That is, if Britain were to accept the condemnation and sale of prizes caught by French privateers in the ports of Denmark-Norway or Sweden, an agreement would have to be reached on how this was to be done in practice. Alternatively, Mitchell wrote, Britain would have to 'prevail upon the Danish & Swedish Ministry to forbid entirely the Condemnation of British Property in their Dominions'. Based on the experience of the American War, Mitchell favoured the second alternative.[74] About a month later, on 27 April, Mitchell renewed his request for directions on how to act, and proceeded to outline his case further, now with a more principled argument:

> As the Court of Denmark have not yet Acknowledged the present Government of France, it appears to me, as if they cannot with consistence allow the Property of such Nations & States as are in Alliance and Friendship with Denmark, to be Condemned in the Danish Dominions by People who hold their Commissions from an Assembly of unknown individuals, such as

> I presume the Convention at Paris should be considered until their Authority is allowed to be legal.

Moreover, Mitchell argued, 'of all those Nations who Officially profess neutrality when Great Britain is at War, none require to be more circumspectly watched by Her, than the Danes'. Particularly the ports of Norway had tended to be 'open to all Adventurers in Privateering, and the legality of their Proceedings never Voluntarily examined by the Danish Magistrate'. There was, in other words, every reason to expect that the local authorities in Norway would be biased in favour of French privateers and against the owners of British vessels taken by these privateers, and that the Danish government would turn a blind eye to such breaches of neutrality. If British trade in the waters nearby Norway were to be secured, the British government would have to persuade the Danes to close all the ports of the dual-monarchy to all privateers.[75] The view presented by Mitchell in these two letters was subsequently adopted by the British government, and formed the basis for its argument in the diplomatic debate that ensued. These discussions took place primarily in Copenhagen, between the British envoy and the Danish foreign secretary Count Bernstorff, and took the shape of Hailes and his successors presenting a series of British arguments and demands for the closure of the Norwegian ports. The British side raised the debate, and kept it going. Initially, in the spring of 1793, the discussions went ahead in two main stages. First, Hailes met with Bernstorff at the Court in Copenhagen, and confronted him with the issue in what might be termed informal talks. Then, once the Foreign Office (FO) had received its reports from Hailes and had conducted some inquires of its own, an official exchange of arguments took place. This exchange clarified the relative positions of the British and Danish governments on the matter and, eventually, an unofficial agreement was reached.

Hailes first approached Bernstorff about a month after Mitchell sent his first letter to Grenville, and the occasion was that he believed he had caught the Danish government in acting inconsistently. From his subordinate, Consul Nicholas Fenwick at Elsinore, Hailes had received a copy of a circular order issued by the Danish government stating that it would be incompatible with Danish neutrality to allow the sale of prizes there. Since Hailes had already received reports from Mitchell that sales of prizes were taking place in Norway, he found this to be rather peculiar.[76] Armed with this piece of information he approached Bernstorff at court. First, he made sure that Bernstorff could confirm the circular order, and then he presented the following rhetorical question. Hailes 'beg'd to be informed', he wrote, 'whether the laws made for Denmark were not equally obligatory on Norway, and whether there was any difference in the Neutrality of the two Countries?' The question caused Bernstorff 'discernable' [*sic*] embarrassment, and he first responded that the order might not have reached Norway yet, before adding—'in a loose kind of way'—Hailes stated, 'that it was impossible to prevent the practices of which I complained in the numberless small ports and harbours of that coast so remote, and having so little communication with the seat of Government'. Essentially, Bernstorff's point seemed to be that the Danish government could not control the Norwegian coastline and whatever went on in the port towns there, at least as it was presented by Hailes in his letter to Grenville. Hailes found this to be a ludicrous argument. That a government should somehow 'have so little control over its subjects', he wrote, was that really to be believed? No, there had to be another explanation, and Hailes proceeded to present his own theory to Grenville. The Danish government had in fact adopted a deliberate policy of treating the ports in Norway differently from those in Denmark and the Duchies. These ports would be closed precisely so that the privateers would head for Norwegian ports instead, and it was done for a specific reason, Hailes argued:

> The extreme poverty of the Country, and the independent spirit of the inhabitants are the Causes, I believe, for the tenderness shewn by this Government towards Norway, and your Lordship remembers, no doubt, the endless discussions we had with this Court, upon the same business, during the last War.[77]

Hailes knew by this point, however, that the policy of closing the ports in Denmark and the Duchies to privateers, while the Norwegian ports were kept open, had been determined by a Danish ordinance of 10 November 1779. This was still in force in 1793, and the Danish government had no plans of repealing it.[78]

Once these initial reports from Hailes and Mitchell had been received in London, investigations were set in train to clarify precisely what Danish policies on privateering and neutral ports had been over the period when Denmark-Norway had claimed neutrality, starting with the Nine Years' War of 1688–1697. These investigations resulted in a relatively short historical account dated June 1793, which appears to have been written by the experienced diplomat Robert Liston. It provided Hailes and Grenville with much needed information. 'On a review of the conduct of Denmark as a neutral nation during the last hundred years', it was stated initially, it was clear that one thing had been consistent over time: the Danes had always allowed privateers entry into their ports. But during the wars of Louis XIV in the late seventeenth and early eighteenth centuries access had only been granted as refuge from stormy weather. The privateers had not been allowed to sell their prizes, and they had been obliged to leave the port again as soon as it was possible. In 1742, however, the French and Danish governments had agreed upon a treaty whereby French privateers had been allowed to sell their prizes in Norwegian ports, seemingly without a Prize Court verdict. This had led to complete anarchy with the 'immediate dispersion of every captured cargo which was carried into the ports of Norway by French Cruisers', and in order to remedy the situation, an edict had been issued by the Danish government in 1746, stating that a Prize Court verdict had to be presented before the sale of prizes could take place. In order for such a verdict to be obtained, the French consul in the Norwegian port town in question had to send a report to the Court of Admiralty in France, which would then carry out a 'summary Trial' and return the sentence of condemnation to the consul. This was deemed sufficient basis for a legal sale in Norway. Although the Treaty 1742 had expired soon after, the Danish government had stuck to this 'modified system of neutrality' ever since. In other words, Danish policy was that prizes could be sold in Norway, as long as a Prize Court ruling from France could be obtained.

The problem was that the Norwegians did not respect this arrangement. Not only did they assist French privateers as best they could, but the sale of prizes without a Prize Court ruling continued, and there were even some cases where 'inferior Judicatures' in Norway acted as Prize Courts on their own initiative. This was not officially accepted by the government in Copenhagen, but despite repeated British complaints and Danish promises to sort out the problem, nothing much was done about it. No Norwegians were ever tried or convicted for this kind of unlawful activity. The British government then suggested that the King of Denmark should demonstrate his independence and neutrality by closing all the ports in his realms to all privateers, independently of their nationality, but Copenhagen refused, and that marked the end of the diplomatic discussions too. Faced with the 'inefficacy' of its diplomatic overtures, the British switched tack, and resorted to a strategy of trying to defeat the French privateers by means of deploying superior naval forces in the North Sea. This was done in both 'the wars of 1742 & 1756', Liston noted. In turn, however, this British naval policy resulted in clear breaches of neutral territory, as British warships 'chased the French Ships into the Creeks and Harbours of Norway, from whence they cut them out & carried them off'. At times, the British naval crews even pursued their enemies on shore and into the towns, 'to the great alarm of the inhabitants'. Although the British authorities did not condone these actions, they frequently turned a blind eye to them. The American War then added a new problem. Although the British government was able to persuade their Danish counterpart to bar American privateers from Norwegian ports,[79] some of them were able to circumvent this particular obstacle by getting hold of French letters of marque, and sail under the French flag instead. The Danish government appears to have accepted this.[80] In just a few pages, therefore, Liston had provided a telling account of how both the Danish and the British governments, as well as the British Royal Navy and the local officials and inhabitants in the various Norwegian port towns, had acted with respect to French privateers in the past. Provided Liston was truthful in his account—and since he was presenting information to the Foreign Office, there is every reason to believe that he was—Grenville and Hailes had now been well briefed. What is striking about the subsequent development is partly that the British adhered to much the same strategy or approach in the 1790s, as they had done for the previous wars of the eighteenth century—this combination of diplomatic pressure and naval operations—and partly that events, as they unfolded in Norway over the course of the decade, seem to have followed much the same pattern too. This time, however, the diplomatic approach gave somewhat better results.

Second Round of Discussions

The second stage of the initial discussions, the official exchange of arguments, began in early July 1793, when the Foreign Office issued a note in French to the Danish government. The case presented in this note revolved around one single argument, which, in its essence, was the same as that presented by Mitchell a few months earlier. The current war was fundamentally different from previous wars, it was held, because there was no acknowledged government in France. No one, be that either those countries which were involved in the war against revolutionary France, or those who claimed neutrality, had recognised the current government of France if, indeed, it could be classified as a government proper. When this was the case, it was impossible to claim neutrality in any conflict involving France, and the note proceeded to give an outline of why this must be so.

The 'privileges' enjoyed by a neutral power in wartime, it was stated, were based partly on the 'general law of the nations' and partly on the 'particular treaties' signed by the nations in question, and on the strict adherence to this legal framework. Moreover, genuine neutrality meant the upholding of strictly equal relations to both (or all) the belligerents, and how could Denmark-Norway possibly achieve this equilibrium in its policies towards Britain and France respectively, when the Danes had not yet recognised the current regime in France? Thus while the relationship between Denmark-Norway and Great Britain was an orderly one regulated by the Law of Nations and treaties, the same could hardly be said for the relationship between Denmark-Norway and France where Danish neutrality had 'already been violated, and continues to be violated on a daily basis'.[81] No actual examples of such violations were mentioned in the note, but by the time it was sent to Copenhagen, Mitchell had already submitted reports of transgressions on the part of French privateers. In April, for example, he wrote to Grenville that 'Several Norwegian Vessels have lately been boarded by French Privateers off the Coast'.[82] The fact that the Danish government had not recognised the new regime in France—it was further stated in the note—necessarily had to have implications for the policies the Danish government adopted with respect to French privateers. It would not be possible to apply the 'ordinary laws of impartial neutrality', it was argued, as long as there was:

> no recognised authority in France that can settle the behaviour of French ship owners and to which a neutral government can appeal to punish them in the case of a breach of law. In violation of law, these will no longer be ship owners, but pirates.

In other words, as long as there was no acknowledged and functioning political regime in France, adherence on the French side to the established rules of privateering could neither be expected nor enforced and, consequently, French letters of marque were essentially worthless. For the Danish government, therefore, the only logical conclusion to this matter was the closure of all Danish ports to French privateers. In return for a Danish acceptance of this view, the British government would see to it that Danish trade was not 'troubled, molested or worried' by the Royal Navy.[83] Although the claim of a new kind of ideological war—what Emma Vincent

Macleod has termed a 'war of ideas'—was commonplace in British political rhetoric in the 1790s, it could arguably be said to form a part of a more long-standing British tradition too.[84] As the Danish legal authority J. F. W. Schlegel would later argue in his answer to the English judge Sir William Scott's verdict in the famous *Maria*-case from 11 June 1799, claiming that the current war was different from previous wars had been a standard British approach throughout the eighteenth century.[85] It was an argument to suit British interests, and Bernstorff was not going to accept it.

The official note from the British government was handed over to Bernstorff by Hailes on 18 July, but not before Hailes had made some changes to it. The text had come in draft form to Hailes, and in the report of the meeting which he sent back to Grenville, he pointed out that 'In transcribing the Note I took the liberty of making a Slight alternation, by changing the words *les Ports Danois* (towards the End) to *les Ports sons la domination de la Majesté Danoise*' (so from the ports of Denmark to the ports in the dominions of His Danish Majesty). Hailes was concerned that the word 'Danish', or *Danois*, might be 'construed' as excluding the ports of Norway, and thought it would be wise to avoid such an open invitation to a wilful misunderstanding on the part of Bernstorff. His subsequent meeting with Bernstorff confirmed his suspicions that the Danish minister would be less than accommodating. Repeated attempts by Hailes to persuade the Danish minister of the merits of the British proposal came to nothing, and the end result of 'this desultory conference' was that 'it was utterly impossible to bring him to the concession of anything', apart from the minor point of accepting the British blockade of the French Mediterranean ports. Bernstorff insisted on accepting the current political regime in France, and 'nothing short of compulsory measures will ever induce this Minister to deviate from the Line of Conduct in which he has hitherto persevered', Hailes wrote.[86]

By the time Hailes had his meeting with Bernstorff, several reports had come from Norway of French privateers bringing prizes into ports there. John Wallace, the British consul in Bergen, reported to the Admiralty on 22 June 1793 that the Dunkirk privateer *Sansparielle* had brought two British prize vessels, the *Janet* of Leith and the *Grove* of Whitehaven , into Bergen.[87] The same information was passed on to Hailes in Copenhagen, who proceeded to inform Grenville that he had instructed Wallace to 'enter up his protest against the sale of the English ships and their Cargoes, in case any steps should be taken there towards the disposal of them'.[88] Similar reports were sent from Mitchell,[89] who could also bring news that rumours, hearsay and general confusion with respect to the Danish government's policies seemed to be prevalent among French privateers. His source of information was 'an Englishman Gentleman' who had just arrived at Christiania from Dunkirk, and who had told Mitchell that many owners of privateer vessels had recalled their ships from the coast of Norway because they were concerned that the Danish government would prohibit the condemnation of prizes in the Danish dominions. But then—as they had received confirmations from their own 'Private Agents' at Copenhagen, that the Danish government had no such plans and were in fact intending to allow the condemnation of prizes to go ahead in Norway—privateer vessels had 'immediately' been fitted out and sent into the North Sea. Indications were, however, that some of these privateers were planning to bring any ships they might capture into a Norwegian port first, equip them with Danish flags and then attempt to sail them home to France under a false flag in order to condemn and sell them there instead.[90] Hailes had come across similar rumours in Copenhagen, which suggested that 'prizes might be brought into, Condemned and Sold in Norway, without demur' on the part of the Danish government.[91] So what *was* the Danish government's policy on the question of French privateers and Norwegian ports?

The answer came in a 'note and answer' to the British government dated 28 July 1793, in which Bernstorff presented the official Danish position. First, he rejected the notion of a new kind of war, and consequently also that it should have any implications for the Law of Nations, or existing treaties. Bernstorff admitted that he did not see himself as a great friend of the French revolutionary regime, but he nevertheless insisted that 'the Nation exists', and that it did have a reasonably well-functioning government and legal system. Moreover, the current French regime did respect existing treaties between France and Denmark-Norway, Bernstorff insisted. The Danish intention was therefore one of upholding a genuine neutrality in the conflict between Britain and France, relating in the same way to both parties. If it happened to be so that the neutrality of Denmark-Norway was 'more useful to one of the belligerent parties'—as it could be argued that privateering was more useful to the French than the British—then that was of no consequence for the neutral power, as long as it gave equal access to the privateers of both belligerents.[92] The principle of impartiality took preference over the principle of abstention in the reasoning of Bernstorff, it seems, and an underlying argument here appears to have been that it is not for the neutral power to evaluate what is or is not in the military or strategic interest of any of the belligerents. Moreover, as long as Britain continued to treat French privateers as prisoners of war, they 'cannot be considered as pirates or buccaneers by neutral powers', Bernstorff held. Second, Bernstorff re-emphasised his argument that the Norwegian ports should be kept open, when the other ports of the dual-monarchy were closed. Partly, this decision rested on historical precedent: the admission of privateers in Norway 'has existed forever in all maritime wars that have afflicted Europe. By turns all nations have profited from it and have anticipated it.' More importantly though, the 'immense' coast-line of Norway, with its innumerable ports, would be impossible to police, and attempting to do so would be merely 'illusory' and even counterproductive. If the Danish authorities tried to close the Norwegian ports, French privateers would simply destroy their prizes rather than bring them into port, he claimed.[93] Did this mean that French privateers would also be permitted to *sell* their prizes in Norwegian ports in line with the practice of previous wars, and not merely use these ports as a temporary stop on the way back to France? On this point, the note was not explicit in the sense of referring to Norway (or Denmark) specifically, but in a slightly cryptic passage it was nevertheless stated that: *Elle ne permettra pas la vente des prises; faites par des vaisseaux François, dans' ses États*, suggesting that the sale of prizes brought into port by French privateers was not to be permitted in *any* of His Danish Majesty's realms, Norway included.[94]

Subsequent correspondence confirmed that the Danish government had ceded ground on this question, though possibly more due to French than British pressure. In a letter to Grenville dated 27 July, John Mitchell stated that he had received a copy of a letter from the Danish Chancery to the local officials in Kristiansand 'in answer to my Protest against the Condemnation & Sale of the British Ships now Prizes to the French in Norway'.[95] The letter stated that the rules set down in the Ordinance of 1779 still applied, and that 'the bringing in, Condemnation, or sale of … Prizes' was to be permitted 'in the Danish Dominions' on an equal basis for 'all Nations'. There was, however, 'one *single* exception' from this general rule, namely, 'that the *French* are not to sell in our Ports the Cargoes of such Vessels as they may Capture'. The reason for this was quite simply that the National Convention in France had ordered all owners of privateers to bring their prizes home to France.[96] Or in other words, French privateers were not permitted to sell their prizes in Norwegian ports, but they could bring them into port temporarily on their way to France, and this led Mitchell to surmise that Bernstorff had 'minutely consulted the present necessities of the French Government' before 'dictating' the letters.[97] For Mitchell, it confirmed his impression of pro-French sympathies on the part of the Danish government. Hailes had come to the same conclusion with respect to the sale of prizes. Initially, it had been difficult to 'renew the discussion' with Bernstorff on this question, Hailes complained, but on 6 August, he could report that when he had asked Bernstorff in a recent meeting 'if he had given order to prevent the Condemnation and Sale of British Ships carried into Norway', he had been 'assured that such orders had been sent', and that they were 'punctually observed'. The only exception was if the ships carried goods of a 'perishable nature', in which case a sale could take place to prevent damage to the cargo.[98] The Danish government later confirmed that 'Corn and Fish' were the only goods to be deemed perishable, and that the proceeds from the sale of such goods in Norwegian ports should be 'deposited in the Royal Treasury until the Peace'.[99] By the end of August 1793, therefore, the Danish government's position had been clarified, and later correspondence would suggest that—broadly speaking—an agreement had been reached. The British side accepted that French privateers could operate out of Norwegian ports, and also somewhat grudgingly that they could bring their prizes into those ports, as long as they were not permitted to sell them there. One important concession had thus been won from the Danish side compared to the practice of the most recent wars. On the question of perishable goods, however, the debate continued, and Bernstorff's claim that his orders were being 'punctually observed' in Norway was decidedly not true. We will look at perishable goods first.

The Perishable Goods Question

The exception from the general ban on the sale of prizes, which the Danish government insisted on granting to perishable goods, was not readily accepted by the British side, partly, it seems, because it could be seen as an open invitation to abuse. This was evident in a report sent by Consul John Wallace in Bergen in March 1794. The 'French obtain permission to sell the Cargoes under the Specious Pretext of their being able to be damaged, and spoilled [*sic*]', Wallace complained, and added that 'it is expected they will soon obtain a liberty to sell the Vessels on the same pretext and terms'. Condemning and selling prize *vessels* had clearly not been allowed by the Danish government, and if Wallace was right in suspecting that local officials were due to allow such sales under the 'pretext' of the perishable goods rule, then that was no doubt in breach of the orders sent out by Copenhagen. In terms of the *cargoes*, however, the crucial question was whether they consisted of grain or fish, and since Wallace did not specify this in his letter, it is difficult to say if the permission which had been granted to carry out sales was unwarranted or not. Moreover, since he stated that the proceeds from the sales were to be 'deposited in His Danish Majesty Coffers', indications were that at least this aspect of the proceedings for sales was being upheld. Wallace's choice of words—the 'Specious Pretext'—suggests, however, that he did not see the perishable goods rule as legitimate.[100] The same view prevailed in London. In late August, Hailes was given instructions to investigate the case of the British merchant vessel the *Hopewell* of Leith which had been captured by a 'French Cutter' and 'carried into Fleckefiorden in Norway'. The *Hopewell* had carried a cargo of wheat, and its owner, a Mr. Claude Scott of London, was hoping to prevent the sale of the cargo. Scott had also informed the British government that a number of British vessels carrying grain had been brought into 'the Ports of Denmark and Norway', and that their cargoes had been sold, while the vessels were being detained. Hailes' task was therefore to raise the specific case of Mr. Scott with Bernstorff directly, as well as to investigate the extent of the problem, 'in order that His Majesty may judge of the measures which he may think proper to adopt, with a view to Circumstances so Novel, and unprecedented on the part of that Government'.[101] In response, Hailes wrote that while he would 'lose no time in following your Lordship's instructions', he had little hope of achieving success. Not only had 'all the applications which I made at the end of last year to the Danish Minister' on the subject of British vessels brought into Norwegian ports been declined, but similar complaints put forward by the Prussians more recently had 'not been attended to', leaving Hailes to conclude that 'I cannot flatter myself that even the strongest representation on my part will produce any effect'. Moreover, in a passage revealing a degree of exasperation with his superiors, Hailes pointed out that cargoes could only be sold 'when they consist of perishable commodities … as I was assured by Count Bernstorff, and as your Lordship has been informed'. Hailes had, however, instructed the consuls in Norway to provide him with 'the most accurate accounts which they can procure of all the British Vessels brought this summer by the Enemy into the Norwegian Ports'.[102] A week later, he could report that a recent meeting with Bernstorff had resulted in a predictable outcome. Bernstorff had insisted on allowing the sale of perishable goods on the basis of the 'principles of Neutrality' established by the Danish government, stressing that the proceeds of such sales would be 'paid into the Royal Treasury' in order that they may be 'adjudged according to the agreement made between the Belligerent Powers at the peace'.[103] The Danish government thus saw itself merely as a caretaker, looking after the value of cargoes consisting of perishable goods, and leaving it to the belligerents to decide the question of ownership at the end of the war. The principle seems to have been adhered to thereafter. In October the same year, for example, Hailes reported that the sale of certain prizes had been permitted by the 'Grand Bailiff' in Bergen 'on pretence of the cargoes being of a perishable nature'. Consul Wallace had protested against the sales, but to no avail and, this time, it was clear that the cargo of at least one of the ships in question, the *Janet* of Leith captured in June the year before, was grain and the sale thus permissible under the Danish rule.[104] With Bernstorff unwilling to yield on the point of perishable goods, the British side seems to have given up on making any further attempts to persuade him otherwise. There were, however, more serious causes for concern, and these came to dominate the more irregular discussions that took place in the subsequent years.

Norwegian-French Collaboration

Mitchell, and to a lesser extent the other British consuls in Norway, kept sending reports of French privateering activity to both Hailes' successor in Copenhagen from October 1794, James Craufurd, and directly to Grenville in London. These reports revealed that not only were French privateers selling cargoes of all sorts from prize ships in Norwegian ports, but they also suggested that the privateers found a market of eager buyers for the captured vessels in the Norwegian merchants there. By late November 1795, Mitchell felt the need to convey his frustration to Grenville, describing the situation in the port town of Kristiansand, were he was stationed. Notwithstanding the assurances given by the Danish government in 1793 that:

> the Prizes brought into Norway by the Enemies of Great Britain should not be sold there but remain in Deposit till the Peace, the Governor of this Province is selling them Daily. I Protest, & embarrass him as much as I can, but he is so much inclined to favour our Enemies.[105]

Indications were that the perishable goods rule was ignored too. 'I have received, My Lord, frequent complaints from His Majesty's Consuls in Norway', Craufurd wrote in a letter to Grenville in March 1796, 'of the permission given by the Danish Government to the French and Dutch to sell British Captured Vessels and their Cargoes, even though they are not in a perishable state'. This was clearly 'in violation of the agreement which took place between the two Courts at the Commencement of the war', Craufurd stated, and he had therefore confronted Bernstorff with the reports he had received from Norway. The Danish minister insisted, however, that 'the Governors in Norway had orders not to allow the Sales till it should have been legally proved that the Cargoes were in a perishable state'. Although he 'could not account for any deviation which might have taken place', he reassured Craufurd that he 'would write again to repeat and enforce these orders'.[106] By then the patience of the British government was beginning to wear thin, however, and in a government dispatch to Craufurd, Grenville stated that, seen in light of the agreement reached in August 1793:

> I have been extremely surprized to learn from your dispatch No 7, and from other sources of information that the practice continues to be prosecuted if not with the connivance of the Court of Denmark, at least without any interference on its part to prevent it.

The 'mischiefs' this practice produced were further aggravated by the 'circumstances of Danish Subjects becoming the purchasers of British Vessels and cargoes'. Craufurd was therefore to warn Bernstorff in his next meeting with the Danish minister that unless prize vessels or cargoes purchased by Danish subjects had been condemned by '*a legal Tribunal established in the dominions of the capturing country*', that is, in France, Britain would view such purchases as 'null'. Any vessels condemned outside of France would be reclaimed by Britain at the first opportunity for 'the purpose of being restored to their original British owners'.[107] Just as his predecessor Daniel Hailes had done, Craufurd continued to raise the issue of breaches of the agreement in successive meetings with Bernstorff, and Craufurd's successor from May 1796, Robert Stephen Fitzgerald, did the same. When confronted with the most recent news from Norway, Bernstorff would sometimes claim ignorance, but always assure the British envoy that he would do whatever he could to prevent further transgressions. He would also, however, often stress the difficulties involved in policing the long

Norwegian coastline, indicating that there was only so much the Danish government could do about the problem.[108]

While these discussions were taking place in Copenhagen, Mitchell sent a lengthy report to Fitzgerald, in which he outlined the development he had observed since the summer of 1793, and provided information on a recent and even more disconcerting turn of events in Kristiansand. As he had stated in his early dispatches in 1793, the expectation that the Danish government would permit privateers to use Norwegian ports and let them dispose of their prizes there had led to the capture of many British vessels in the waters nearby Norway. The cargoes of these vessels had subsequently been 'put up to publick [*sic*] Sale, by authority of the Danish Governor' in the port towns. Once the agreement had been reached between the British and Danish governments that no captured British vessels were to be sold unless their cargoes '*were of a perishable nature, and proved by a Jury of Experts to be in a state of decay*', however, privateers were 'discouraged' from operating out of Norwegian ports, and for the second half of 1793 and all of 1794, 'very few Ships were brought into Norway'.[109] After a French attempt to send warships to convoy their prizes home to France in the autumn of 1794 had failed, with several frigates frozen up in port and disease taking its toll on the crews, the 'Agents for the French and Dutch' in concert with their friends among the 'Civil Magistracy, and Mercantile Inhabitants, set all their Invention at work to find out ways, and measures to overturn, or, at all events to evade the Intention of the Copenhagen Arrangements'. Several ships which the French naval squadron had 'left behind' in port were now 'nominally surveyed, and Documents formally drawn up' stating that the cargoes were in a state of decay, notwithstanding the fact that some of them consisted of coal or iron. When Mitchell had asked the Governor of Kristiansand, 'Levitzow' (Levetzow), in a formal note to see the 'Survey and Deeds which authorized the Sales', this had been declined without explanation, though Mitchell himself thought that the sales had 'in all likelihood been sanctioned by the Danish Ministry'. Levetzow had proceeded to inform the French and Dutch consuls that privateers were now free to '*bring in, condemn, and dispose of their Prizes of every Description, and of the Proceeds arising from the Sale of such Captured Property, without condition or demur*' in Norway, Mitchell claimed, and he had then published a proclamation in the *Christiansand Weekly Gazette* on 4 September 1795 'in the name of the Provincial Government', stating the same. Although this proclamation 'could not be considered as a Government Ordnance', Mitchell wrote, it was 'instantaneously transmitted to all Enemies Ports', resulting in renewed privateer activity both in France and the Netherlands. When Craufurd then proceeded to raise the issue with Bernstorff in Copenhagen, the response was a predictable one. The Danish minister 'pretended that there was some Error in the Proclamation itself', and claimed that the publication had taken place 'without his Knowledge'.[110] Mitchell's letter thus seemed to present two alternative explanations for this turn of events: either that the local officials in Norway were operating contrary to the official instructions they had received from Copenhagen, or that the Danish government was saying one thing to the British side, and another to its local representatives in the Norwegian port towns. A third possibility was, of course, that it was all a matter of a misunderstanding. Which was true? The answer to this question clearly depended on the exact wording of the proclamation as it had been published in the *Christiansand Weekly Gazette*, and how this related to the instructions sent out by Copenhagen. The proclamation arguably contained two main points, of which the first was somewhat vague: it was stated that from now onwards, no particular 'rule' would apply for prizes brought into Norwegian ports by French privateers, and that the funds raised through the sale of these prizes at auctions would 'no longer need to be deposited in the royal coffers, but could be left at the disposal of the French consul'.[111] The second point was clear enough, but did the first point mean that the perishable goods rule from 1793 had been abandoned? Mitchell seems to have thought that this was the correct reading of the proclamation, and he proceeded to address the issue in a response to the proclamation, published in the same newspaper on 13 November. The 'Advertisement' which had been published in No. 36 of the *Gazette*, he wrote, had claimed that 'all' prizes brought in could be sold, and that the proceeds thereof could be disposed of by the 'Agents' of the privateers in question. Neither of this was, however, in line with the official policies of the Danish government, Mitchell stated, as Bernstorff had since declared the proclamation to have been 'unauthorised' and 'entirely unknown' to the Danish Ministry in his conversations with Craufurd. Consequently, the proclamation was nothing but the result of a 'high-handed undertaking on the part of the authorities at this place', and should therefore be disregarded.[112] Levetzow, however, issued a reply to Mitchell in the next issue of the *Gazette* refuting the claims of a 'high-handed undertaking' on his part. Partly, the issuing of the proclamation had taken place without his knowledge (which appears to be true, as he was not one of the signatories), and partly it conveyed the Royal Danish

Chancery's Order of 15 August the same year, which 'truly existed'. The Order of 15 August had, however, been 'changed' and 'clarified' by a later Chancery Order of 24 October, but this revision had obviously not been included in the proclamation published in September.[113] Levetzow's point thus seemed to be that the Order of 15 August had contained some or other mistake or omission, and that a second order had been issued to rectify this. What was the error in the first order? As Mitchell's letter to Fitzgerald from 1797 revealed, James Craufurd had raised the issue with Bernstorff, and in a letter Craufurd wrote to Grenville on the same day as the second order was issued, he explained what had happened: 'I find that in consequence of a mistake in the manner of wording an order sent about two months ago from the Danish Chancery here to the Governors of the Norwegian Province', Craufurd wrote, 'the French have been permitted to dispose of several British Prizes, and to receive the produce of the sales, contrary to the agreement entered into with this Court at the commencement of the war'. How could this have happened? 'The case is as follows', Craufurd explained:

> After the alliance took place between the French and Dutch, the Danish Chancery was instructed to write to the Governors in Norway, informing them that they might allow the French to dispose of any *Dutch* Prizes, which they had brought into the Ports of Norway during the war between France & Holland. The Chancery in their letter to the Governors, omitted the word Dutch, so that they conceived that the order extended to all Prizes whatever and accordingly have permitted the disposal of several British vessels.

It remained, however, to determine if this was an accidental omission, or a wilful one. To clarify this, Craufurd had shown Bernstorff a 'copy of the order', sent to him by Mitchell, and the Danish minister had 'assured' him 'that he had never been more astonished at anything in his life'. In Craufurd's view, the reaction seemed genuine. Bernstorff had then said that 'it arose entirely from a misconception on the part of the Chancery; that the Subject of British Prizes had never come under discussion in any way whatever since the summer of 1793, nor had any order been issued respecting them.' He had then promised to issue the 'necessary orders, for the prevention of any such irregularities in future', due to be 'sent to Norway by today's Post'. The meeting between Craufurd and Bernstorff took place on Thursday 22 October and, as we have seen, the order was issued two days later. Craufurd was less sceptical of Bernstorff than

Mitchell, and held that he had 'not the smallest doubt of Count Bernstorff's sincerity upon this occasion', but that did not prevent the possibility that someone else might have had questionable motives. In Craufurd's view

> the error appears so extraordinary that I am almost inclined to suspect some improper intention on the part of the Danish Chancery; the more so, as M. Colbiornsen, the Attorney General, a great partizan [*sic*] of the French, is the leading member of that Department.[114]

Craufurd's investigations thus seemed to suggest the possibility of a fourth alternative explanation: that forces in the government apparatus in Copenhagen were working against the official line of policy. He was not, however, able to present any conclusive evidence of such an 'improper intention' on the part of Colbiornsen or others in the Chancery. Meanwhile, Levetzow had been so 'offended' by Mitchell's claims that he had demanded the British consul be recalled from his station in Norway, and in a letter to Grenville, Craufurd admitted that 'Some parts' of Mitchell's 'advertisement are perhaps not altogether free from indiscretion as I have observed to Mr. Mitchell'. Summing up the case he concluded that Mitchell 'may perhaps have gone a little too far in the present instance, but I must in justice to him say that he is active & intelligent, and that he appears to me extremely attentive to the duties of his office'. A recall was therefore out of the question.[115]

While the issuing of the second order on 24 October seemed to put Bernstorff in the clear, the same was not the case for the local officials in Norway. Mitchell was, for one thing, undoubtedly correct in claiming that the sale of both prize cargoes and vessels was taking place well before the proclamation was issued in September 1795. In late August 1793, for example, the wealthy Kristiansand merchant, Niels Moe, advertised the sale by auction of the cargo from the captured British vessel the *Hope* in Egersund and, just over a month later, the ship itself was also put up for sale. Since the cargo of the *Hope* consisted of barley, the sale of this was permissible under the perishable goods rule, but not that of the ship, and subsequent sales revealed that non-perishable goods were sold too. In August 1795, for example, Niels Moe advertised the sale by auction in Kristiansand of the 'prize brig' the *Peggy*, including her cargo of coal and grindstones. Furthermore, the sale of both prize vessels and cargoes consisting of non-perishable goods continued with the approval of the local government officials thereafter.[116]

The reports of breaches of the agreement of 1793 led to the issuing of renewed instructions from London, now to Fitzgerald. The 'practices' adopted in the Norwegian ports, 'which afford to the enemy every facility that he could enjoy in his own ports', were 'contrary to every principle of neutrality' it was stated, and Fitzgerald was therefore to 'make the most serious and forcible representation upon the subject' to Bernstorff. Should the Danish minister claim ignorance yet again, Fitzgerald was to 'direct Mr. Mitchell to furnish you with the necessary evidence' to back up his case.[117] Fitzgerald acquiesced, and submitted an official note in French to Bernstorff, demanding that the Danish government take action to ensure the upholding of the 'regulations adopted in 1793'.[118] By this point it was, in other words, clear that the British government viewed the—in Mitchell's phrase—'Copenhagen arrangements' of August 1793 as a settled agreement between the two countries, and that, for the time being at least, any hopes of persuading the Danish authorities to close the Norwegian ports to privateers had been relinquished. Over the course of 1797 the problem intensified even further. With an increasing number of privateers being fitted out in France and the Batavian Republic, 'Every Letter which I receive from Mr Mitchell', Fitzgerald wrote in April

> brings me Information of Prizes made by the French and Dutch Privateers which infest that Coast, where the Encouragement they find and the Facility with which they dispose of their Captures leave very little hopes of seeing the Evil removed.[119]

The possibility of applying further diplomatic pressure was also hampered by the deteriorating health of Bernstorff, which prevented Fitzgerald from raising the issue with the Danish minister for a period of time.[120] Although Bernstorff's son Christian soon took over as Danish foreign secretary temporarily while his father was ill, and then on a permanent basis when A. P. Bernstorff died on 21 June, it remained difficult to achieve any improvement in the situation. By the middle of June, Fitzgerald could report that 'As the Summer advances, the Complaints which I receive from all quarters of the successful cruizes of the enemies Privateers on the Coasts of Denmark & Norway, multiply'.[121] It was in this frustrating situation that an attempt was finally made in late 1797 to investigate existing treaties between Britain and Denmark, in order to see if there was anything there which could be used to apply pressure on the Danes.

Resorting to Bilateral Treaties

Little information survives on the circumstances of the investigations which were set in train then, but it seems likely that they were spurred on by reports of increased French privateering activity. At least this appears to have been the reason why Sir John Sinclair of the Board of Agriculture raised the issue in a letter written to Dudley Ryder, the vice president of the Board of Trade and member of the Privy Council in early November that year. In Sinclair's view, the sheer number of French privateers, and the extent of their use of Norwegian ports, called for a renewed British attempt to scrutinise existing treaties with Denmark-Norway:

> It has been frequently stated in the papers, that considerable numbers of British Merchantmen have been captured on the coast of Denmark, carried into the Ports of that Power, and sold there. I conceive any circumstance of that sort, to be directly contrary to the terms, or at least to the Spirit of the existing Treaties between the two powers, particularly those of the 11th July 1670, & 20th Jany 1701, clause 3. Though the latter is temporary, the former, I conceive, is still in force.[122]

Sinclair was himself, of course, imprecise in referring to the 'coast of Denmark' and the 'Ports of that Power', but the problem was, in his view, so serious that something had to be done:

> It is of the utmost consequence, that this matter should be speedily attended to, as the number of French privateers now fitting out, is beyond all belief (I understand above 500); and if the same indulgences on the Coast of Denmark they have hitherto engaged, are continued to them, our trade to the Baltick [*sic*] must suffer considerably.

Sinclair stated his intention to raise the issue in the House of Commons, but, as his reference to the 'Spirit' of existing British-Danish treaties might suggest, he was uncertain about the validity of his case, and therefore sought further advice before proceeding with a motion in Parliament. The answer he obtained stated unequivocally that the Treaty of 1670 contained 'no stipulation whatever' whereby ships of war or privateers belonging to the enemies of Great Britain might be excluded from 'admission to the ports of His Danish Majesty's dominions', while the Treaty of 1701 was—as Sinclair had thought—'no longer in force, its duration having been limited to ten years only'.[123] Whether the Treaty of 1701 actually contained any relevant provisions was not stated, but it was in any case the Treaty of 1670 that had been the central one in regulating British-Danish relations concerning seaward trade in the eighteenth century, and it seems clear that there was no relevant clause there. The only one which came close was paragraph 23, which stated that if a ship from either of the two signatories to the treaty was seized by a ship from a power with which either of them were at war, *while* at anchor in one of the ports of the two countries, then both should do their outmost to recapture the vessel. Thus, it was crucial that the actual capture of any ship by French (or British) privateers had to take place outside of Danish-Norwegian waters. The treaty also underlined some other generally acknowledged principles related to privateering, such as that no captured ship could be seen as a good prize before a verdict had been reached in a Prize Court (§ 23), and that the inhabitants of the two countries could not take on 'commissions' for other powers, that is, become crewmembers on a privateer belonging to the enemy of one of the two countries (§ 31).[124] But while the treaty clearly addressed various issues relating to privateering, it did not say anything about that special case of privateers using the ports of a neutral power *as bases* for their activities. At one level, this should perhaps not come as a surprise as the phenomenon itself did not emerge in earnest until some 20 years later during the Nine Year's War—thus it seems likely that no one had really thought about it in 1670—but the negotiations which led to the signing of the treaty were also primarily concerned with the customs duties English merchants had to pay on passing the Sound, and the whole issue of privateering may therefore have been of less importance.[125] Consequently, there was little that could be done about the problem as far as appealing to treaties was concerned, but at least the Danish government had proved itself to be consistently inconsistent, in accordance with the policy presented at the initial discussions in 1793. It had resisted pressure from France and others to 'open its *ports in the Elbe to French Privateers and their prizes*', while keeping the ports on 'the coasts of Norway and Jutland' open, precisely because the Danish government viewed it 'scarcely possible' to fully police a coastline of that length, which was 'so thinly peopled and so little fortified'.[126] The reference to Jutland is odd, but otherwise the point made is a familiar one. Well before this investigation had been completed, however, the French government had decided to step up its war on trade. It was done in two stages, and resulted in a completely changed situation, which, in turn, would lead to the official closure of the Norwegian ports to French privateers in July 1799.

Before we go on to address this final development leading up to the closure, though, it is worthwhile to pause for a moment, and look at the question of privateers and neutral ports from the perspective of legal theory.

Who Had the Better Argument?

There was something rather unresolved about the situation which had been reached by the end of 1797. Neither of the two sides had really been able to persuade the other with his argument, nor had it proved possible to decide the question on the basis of bilateral treaties or law. Admittedly, references had been made from time to time to the 'Law of Nations' in a general sense, but neither side had been able to point to more specific rules which could have settled the issue once and for all. The result was what could perhaps best be described as an uneasy compromise. The problem was, of course, that there seemed to be little legal theory to resort to, and the British government had even admitted as much in a letter to Craufurd in April 1796, where it was stated that the 'right of a Neutral power to permit the sales of the property of a Friend within its dominions' was 'a point upon which the opinions of the best writers on the Law of Nations are divided'.[127] While there was a considerable body of work addressing neutrality in a more general sense, and particularly with respect to the issue of neutral trade, the same was not the case for privateers and neutral ports. At the same time as the British-Danish debate was taking place, however, one of the most influential eighteenth-century legal scholars, Georg Friedrich von Martens, wrote an analysis of legal theory on privateering, and this contained relevant passages.

Although Martens' main concern was the question of 'recaptures' in the many shapes and forms it might take, he also included a short section on what he called '*Cases in which a Prize is conducted into a foreign Port*', and what he meant by a 'foreign' port was, precisely, a *neutral* port. The analysis was written in 1795, and did not—as one might expect—include any references to the ongoing British-Danish debate. Moreover, there is no reason to believe that it came to the attention of either the Danish or the British side then, or later, and by the time it had been translated from French to English and published in London in 1801, the debate was, of course, over.[128] Nevertheless, Martens addressed the issue referring to several treaties, the work of legal scholars and the Law of Nations in a more general sense, and his enquiry resulted in several interesting observations. His starting point was that while 'in strictness' all maritime states required their privateers to 'bring their prizes into the ports of the sovereign from whom they hold their commission', this was not a rule without exceptions. Adverse weather clearly permitted privateers to seek refuge with their prizes into 'foreign ports', but also in 'very distant maritime wars' had privateers been allowed 'more liberty with respect to the choice of the port to which to conduct their prizes'. There was, in other words, nothing unusual in a government permitting its privateers to go into neutral ports. Did this mean that privateers could have their prizes condemned and sold in neutral ports, however? Martens' view was that it was really up to the neutral power to decide this. 'The universal law of nations' he wrote, gave neutral countries a free choice as to whether they would grant a 'privateer entrance and residence with his prize' in their ports, or 'refuse' him the same (except in cases of 'necessity' when access had to be granted). The neutral power was 'not obliged to take cognizance of the justice or injustice of the prize', that is, whether it was a legal capture or not, nor was it 'obliged to force the privateer to restore the prize to the first proprietor'. For that reason, the neutral power 'may suffer the prize to be unladen and sold within it', by which Martens presumably meant that sales could take place in the neutral port. As far as the Law of Nations was concerned, therefore, 'there are perhaps few points with respect to which a [neutral] power can have a more open field to act, according to what it thinks proper' or, posed differently, neutral countries seemed to have great leeway in terms of how they related to privateers and their prizes. Because there was such an 'open field to act', however, 'both the conduct of powers, and their treaties' had been 'so extremely varied' that one and the same country often had different agreements with other countries. Apart from the rule of access due to necessity, and the right all neutral countries reserved to themselves to adjudicate in cases where the prize had been caught 'within their jurisdiction', or when the prize, wholly or in part, belonged to one of their subjects, Martens summarised, there was little in terms of a general set of rules. The state of affairs he had described could arguably be seen to support the Danish position, yet, in Martens' own opinion, the conduct 'most conformable to a perfect neutrality' was one where the neutral power only permitted privateers to go into its ports for reasons of necessity, and required of them that they 'put to sea again as soon as the danger is past' without permission to unload, adjudicate of or sell their prizes. Martens' own view was thus arguably closer to the British position. The wide variety of arrangements which existed, however, led Martens to conclude that as long as the practice adopted in any given case was 'the same towards both belligerent powers', it had to be seen as 'consistent with neutrality'. This also included the Danish-French arrangement from the 1740s of allowing the French consul in the port town to administer the condemnation and sale of the prizes in agreement with the local magistrate, as it was described by Robert Liston in his historical account.[129] Martens' analysis of 'foreign ports' was short, and perhaps not very thorough or even clear, but it does underline the more general impression which emerged from the British-Danish debate: that there was no definite rule on privateers and neutral ports.

The Conflict Intensifies

On 2 March 1797, the French government issued a decree which stated that neutral ships carrying British goods could be seized by French privateers (or warships), and that British merchandise would automatically be declared a 'good prize' and confiscated. The neutral vessels would then be released.[130] Even more dramatic, however, was another decree issued almost a year later on 18 January 1798, which presented a whole new principle for privateering. Now, it was deemed acceptable for French privateers to seize not only any ship carrying goods of a British origin and have the goods in question confiscated, but to condemn the ship as well. This was based on the newly developed principle that the nationality of the vessel was decided by the nationality of the cargo, or at least part of the cargo. Thus, a ship carrying goods from various countries could be declared to be 'British' as long as at least some of the goods were of British origin.[131] In practice, Olav Bergersen has pointed out, this meant that a Norwegian or Danish ship carrying British wares could be taken into a Norwegian port and condemned by the French consul there. This novelty arguably led to a breakdown of the whole system of privateering. French privateers seized the opportunity the policy presented them with and pursued not only British vessels, but also any ship which had once been British, including ships which had been sold as prizes to Norwegians in Norway. The British retaliated by seeking to recapture ships of British origin, and one consequence of this tug of war between the French and the British was that, suddenly, it became very risky for Norwegian ship-owners or merchants to purchase ships brought in by French privateers. After all, the ships were essentially worthless and unusable when both the two main belligerents claimed the right to capture them. It was this impossible situation that eventually forced the Danish government to act, Bergersen argued, though there are some indications that the Danish authorities had begun to consider a closure even *before* the French decree of 1798 had led to this hopeless state of affairs, and that Russian pressure played an important role in bringing about the change of policy.[132] Moreover, as Bergersen discovered, the closing of the ports in 1799 took place in two distinct phases, suggesting, perhaps, that the Danish government had hoped to avoid the complete closure it declared in early July that year.

The Closure of the Norwegian Ports in 1799

Rumours that the Danish government had changed its policy first emerged in March 1798, when Grenville received a letter from the Admiralty Office stating that the French had been 'prevented from carrying Prizes to any part of the Danish Dominions'. This information had been conveyed by one 'Captain Hanson' who had recently arrived from Norway, though it does not seem to have been corroborated by anyone else.[133] About one month later, however, Fitzgerald himself reported that something was in the making in Copenhagen, and in a telling passage he stated that:

> The Danish Government seems to continue in a silent circumspect manner to take the necessary Precautions for the Protection of the Trade of this Country, and by a late Resolution the Ports of Norway are to be closed to all French Captures made on Neutral Navigation in Consequence of the Law of the 4th January; in other respects they will continue open as usual to the belligerent Powers.[134]

4 January was before the second French declaration had been issued, suggesting that the Danish government had begun to consider what action it could take on the basis of the impact of the first declaration—if Fitzgerald's information was correct, that is. Sometime later the same year, Mitchell reported on a change of mood among the Danes, which he thought was affecting the Danish government. Having recently visited Denmark from his new base at Hamburg, Mitchell had found that

> the Public Opinion in that Country, particularly the opinion of the Commercial Part of the Nation, is entirely turned against the French. And the Danish Government, which is Remarkably weak & passive, studies to Regulate its Conduct by the Publick [*sic*] opinion, with a scrupulous Attention.[135]

It is difficult to say if Mitchell's impression was accurate, but in January the next year, Fitzgerald decided to reopen the debate on privateers and Norwegian ports, asking Christian Bernstorff if there was any chance that the Danish government might come to a 'Determination to shut those Ports to Privateers'? He adopted an impartiality-type argument to back up his case, stating that the 'Advantages' derived therefrom for the French were 'great', while the 'Benefits resulting from the same to His Majesty's Subjects' were 'trifling'. Bernstorff did not respond to this principled argument it seems—an argument similar to the kind his father had dismissed six years earlier—but he did reply in an accommodating fashion to the question of closing the ports. As far as the 'Probability' of a closure was concerned, Bernstorff 'foresaw none at present, tho' he most sincerely lamented that that measure had not been adopted at the Commencement of the War'.[136] Indications were, in other words, that the French privateering activity in Norwegian waters was becoming a serious problem for the Danish government and, in March the same year, Bernstorff finally made an attempt to address the issue. In a declaration issued to all the pilot masters in Norway on 16 March, instructions were given that no privateer was to be piloted into *outports* except in cases of emergency. They could still bring prizes into the main ports, but it was stated unequivocally that the purpose of this new rule was to prevent privateers from using outports as bases and observation points. Since it was usually necessary to be at the outport in order to obtain direct visual observation of the merchant ships which passed by close to the Norwegian coast, this prohibition undermined the ability of French privateers to 'lay in waiting', and thus potentially their effectiveness. The declaration was, however, ineffective as many pilots ignored the instructions they had been given.[137] In fact, the activity in the Norwegian ports seemed to continue, more or less as usual, despite the new French policy. In late March 1799, Fitzgerald could report that 'the Enemies Privateers are collecting in force' on the coast of Norway, and in the middle of May that the 'fortunate' capture of a large French privateer by 'His Majesty's Sloop Martin' was somewhat offset by information that 'there are 15 other French & Dutch Vessels of that Description, now on the Coast of Norway'. In a revealing passage he added that:

> It appears pretty evident that the French are relaxing somewhat from their wonted indiscriminate Violence towards neutral ships, in favor [*sic*] of this Country, whose Merchants they are also flattering, with the Hopes of Indemnification for Losses by the Depredations already committed.[138]

Even so, the Danish government still decided to declare the ports closed to privateers in July the same year, and the question which arises then is: what caused this final change of policy, and exactly what the closure entailed? Intelligence suggesting a development in Copenhagen had emerged by June. 'It has come round to me, in the circuitous manner', Fitzgerald wrote to Grenville on 4 June, that the Danish government,

> anxious to accommodate the Differences subsisting between Great Britain and Denmark, is disposed to give a Proof of its Sincerity in that Respect, by ordering the Ports of Norway to be, henceforward, shut to all Privateers.

Fitzgerald thought the British government ought to seize this opportunity and apply pressure on its Danish counterpart to speed up the process as this was 'an Affair of great Magnitude to the interests of the British Trade', but had to admit that he was uncertain about the 'real Existence of such a Plan', since he did not quite trust his source of information.[139] By the end of the month he could confirm 'that the Plan of shutting the Ports of Norway to Privateers, is not a mere Conjecture ... but a real Project, on the Point of being carried into Execution'. Only the 'Assent of the Prince Royal' remained before the decision could be carried into execution, and once again, Fitzgerald stressed the 'Advantages which must result to the Trade of Great Britain from the Adoption of this measure'.[140] On 2 July, he could confirm that the Royal Assent had been given.[141] Further correspondence from Fitzgerald's successor Anthony Merry, sent after the declaration had been issued, however, indicated that the Russian government had applied pressure on the Danes to close the Norwegian ports to privateers, and that the reason for this was that they had taken 'Notice of His Majesty's Complaints against the Danish Government, particularly on the Subject of the Admission of French Privateers into the Ports of Norway'.[142] However this may have been it seems clear that it was, in the end, Russian pressure which persuaded the Danish government to close the ports. Ole Feldbæk, who studied the Danish-Russian diplomatic correspondence in connection with the forming of the Coalition of Armed Neutrality in 1800 closely, confirmed that it was Russian demands that forced the Danish government to close the ports.[143] On 6 July, Fitzgerald sent Grenville a copy of a Royal Danish declaration, which was styled to 'England, France and Holland'.[144]

In the opening passage the Danish king (meaning the Danish government[145]) absolved himself of any responsibility for the problems which had ensued from the policy of allowing privateers into the ports of Norway, and the declaration also carefully avoided any reference to the Norwegians:

> His Danish Majesty has long but vainly prided himself that the welcome afforded in the Ports of Norway to privateers from all Nations, and the rigorous Impartiality, the neutrality of which imposes this duty towards all these foreign Shipowners, would guarantee him on the part of the belligerent Powers the care and the consideration due to the friendliest intentions and to the most impeccable conduct.

Such hopes had, however, been 'disappointed' by the 'blind greed' of these very same shipowners, as well as the conduct of 'the Enemy Vessels of War and the excesses committed by the Crews of Privateers in the Ports of Norway'. For that reason, the Danish king saw himself with no other alternative than to declare that 'Permission to enter upon the Shores and into the Ports of Norway, or to dispatch their Seizures from there, will no longer be accorded to Privateers of any Nation'. Privateers seeking refuge from adverse weather were, in line with common practice, exempted from this prohibition, but so were also privateers who were being pursued by enemy warships. They were allowed to 'seek momentary refuge', but were 'obliged to turn back to the Sea once the Danger is passed, without being permitted to unload, to evaluate and to sell their Seizures or Cargo thereof'.[146] *One* aspect of the use French privateers had made of Norwegian ports as bases—the possibility of escaping from enemy warships into neutral waters—thus remained in place, but *sales* were no longer permitted under *any* circumstances. While it seems unlikely that the British side would have subscribed to the version of events presented in the declaration, they no doubt welcomed the decision finally to close the ports. The question now was whether the closure would be honoured by all parties involved. London was not convinced that it would, and this was made clear in a set of instructions issued to Anthony Merry, Fitzgerald's forthcoming replacement in Copenhagen, on 9 July. At that particular point in time, the final confirmation about the closure of the ports had not yet reached London, but it was made clear that once the ports were closed, Merry was to:

> instruct His Majesty's Consuls and Vice Consuls to be upon their Guard against the Possibility of these Privateers attempting to elude the Determination of the Danish Government by entering it's [*sic*] Ports under

> the Pretence of being driven in by stress of Weather or under some other subterfuge of a similar Nature.[147]

As it turned out, the declaration of 1799 did not mean the end to French privateers operating out of Norwegian ports, but it did mean that the principled discussion on privateering and neutrality came to an end. No attempt was made on the part of the Danish government to reopen the ports to privateers from any of the belligerent countries thereafter and, for that reason, there was no need to renew the debate on the principles of neutrality and privateering on the part of Britain either. The question now was whether the closure could be effectively maintained and, as could have been expected, that was easier said than done. The conclusion to the diplomatic debate was therefore a somewhat inconclusive one. The closure of the ports had not come about because the Danish government had, at last, been persuaded by the original British argument—the argument which held that it was incompatible with neutrality to allow the privateers of the belligerents to operate out of neutral ports—but because certain developments in the war had made it unfavourable for Denmark-Norway to continue this practice (and, finally, Russian pressure). It was more of a pragmatic answer to practical problems, than a resolution of a disagreement over principles relating to international affairs and the Law of Nations. Or posed differently: the British-Danish debate of 1793–1799 provided little in terms of clear precedence one could resort to, should a similar case emerge in the future. A few questions, however, present themselves at the tail end of this British-Danish diplomatic debate, of which the two more central ones are: what did the French authorities think about the question of privateering and neutral ports, and why did the British not press harder for an effective policing of the Norwegian coastline on the part on the Danish authorities, and particularly with respect to the (unauthorised) sale of prizes in Norwegian ports? We will address the question of the French perspective view first.

The French Point of View

For a debate that concerned the operations of French privateers, the lack of references made to either the French policy on privateering, on neutral ports or on neutrality more generally is rather conspicuous. Although the British side insisted that the French point of view could not be heard as long as Denmark-Norway had not recognised the new republican regime in France, it is still a bit odd that there seemed to be so little interest in French policies. The French were obviously a party to the issue at hand, but they were not seen as a party to the debate, it would seem. This did not mean that the French were not paying attention however. While the British-Danish debate took place in 1793, the French representatives in Copenhagen reported back to Paris, and were given instructions in return. This exchange of letters reveals a sympathetic attitude towards neutrals, and arguably also towards the particular situation Denmark-Norway found herself in. For this, there was a historical precedent too because, where Britain had increasingly become the defender of belligerent rights towards the end of the eighteenth century, France had arguably adopted a different position, partly in opposition to Britain. Although France was, of course, also a great power, and one often involved in wars against, precisely, Britain in the eighteenth century, the French foreign policy had been one of defending that freedom of trade which neutral third-rate powers such as Denmark-Norway cherished. The French monarchy even sought to enlist the support of neutral countries in its own struggle to resist British 'tyranny'—the supposed attempt made by the British to gain supremacy over the oceans and world trade—from time to time, and portrayed Britain and British policies as the greatest threat to the rules and conventions established through treatises and the Law of Nations.[148] While it was not immediately obvious that the new republican governments of the 1790s would wish to carry on the policies of the French *ancien régime*—as, indeed, the initial attempt to abolish privateering would suggest—indications are they *did* retain the traditional pro-neutral French stance, at least until the intensification of the war on trade in 1797–1798.

The issue of 'the admission of our armed vessels en route and of their seizures ... in the ports of their dominions' was raised by the French chargé d'affaires in Copenhagen, P. Framery, in a meeting with Bernstorff sometime after the outbreak of war between Britain and France on 1 February 1793. At this point, Framery reported back to Paris, and Bernstorff had replied that:

> You will still find me firm and steadfast in the principles for which you know me, there is a treaty between us and France, as long as it is not formally breached, and on our part it certainly will not be, we will fulfil our obligations in good faith. Thus our ports will continue to be open to you as they will to other warring powers.

Bernstorff also confirmed that 'we will not abandon the strict neutrality that we have always observed', and pointed out that Sweden intended to follow the same line of policy as Denmark. In Framery's view, there was every reason to believe that the Danish government would adhere to this salutary policy.[149] A similar position was adopted by the French Minister for Foreign Affairs, François Louis Michel Chemin Deforgues, in a letter to the President of the French National Convention from early July 1793. The French government ought to adopt an accommodating approach towards Denmark (and Sweden), he argued, because these two 'old allies of France' were 'constantly goaded by our enemies' who were hoping that they would 'renounce their system of neutrality' and 'make common cause' with the coalition against the French Republic.[150] By then, however, the French government had already decided to demand that all prize vessels caught by French privateers be brought home to France—possibly due to uncertainty about what line of policy the Danish government would adopt—and this left Framery a bit puzzled.[151] He had obtained information from the French Consul Cheraulx at Bergen, of a decree issued by the National Convention stating 'that privateers should transport seizures made by them against enemies to French ports', he wrote in a letter to the French Foreign Minister Le Brun on 9 July. In Framery's view 'some changes must be made in this regard' as the North Sea was 'too distant from our ports for it be possible to make the crossing'. In order to see what could be done he had approached Bernstorff and asked if the Danish Court would not '*permit the sale of our seizures in the same manner as that which was practised during the previous war*'? To this, however, Bernstorff had replied that it could not—'for the moment'—allow such sales to go ahead 'without compromising itself to the highest degree; that England was already too angered by the Danish government's consent to the admission of our privateers and their seizures into the ports of Norway'. This 'resentment' felt on the part of the British meant that the situation could easily develop into an open conflict if the Danish government did not tread carefully, Bernstorff prophesised. For that reason, the Danish government had resorted to a temporary solution whereby French captures would be entered into 'storage' by 'our bailiffs and commanders in Norway', and only cargoes containing perishable goods would be sold. At the same time, the officials in Norway had been 'advised' to 'accord every facility for the sale under the pretext of your consul'. This was all that the Danish government was able to do in the current situation, Bernstorff explained, but he also assured Framery that the value of the property 'so deposited' in Norwegian ports would be guaranteed by the Danish authorities. 'In this way', he concluded, 'your privateers can continue to bring their seizures to Norway, where they will receive every assistance and the protection assured them by our friendly attitude towards the French nation', even if they would not be able to sell these prizes in port.[152] Provided Framery's account was truthful, indications were, in other words, that Bernstorff was prepared to open up for a return to old practices at some point in the future. Paris seemed to be content with the Danish explanation, and prepared to accept the Danish policy for the time being. As it was stated in a set of instructions sent out in mid-August:

> We have no right to complain about this course of action because Article 37 of our former trade treaty limits itself to stipulating that judgments regarding seizures made at sea will be rendered according to the law, but it does not determine anything about the sale of these seizures. By insisting on this latter point, we expose the Danish government to accusations of partiality and to all manner of violence on the part of the English. But we do have a right to demand that the free departure of our seizures from the ports of Norway is permitted when the captains believe it possible to send them to our own ports in safety.[153]

Although the 'reluctance of the Court of Denmark to permit the sale of our seizures in its ports is very awkward for the French privateers', it was stated in a subsequent letter, 'we have no right to demand condescension'.[154] By June the next year, however, the decree on the return of prizes to France appears to have been rescinded. In a couple of letters to Lord Grenville, Mitchell suggested that something was in the making, and stated that the 'French Plenipotentiary at Copenhagen has obtained permission of that Court to Sell by Publick Sale the Prize Ships now in Norway, on condition that the Produce be deposited in the Danish Treasury'.[155] Half a year later, in 1795, sales commissioned by the French consuls in Norway began in earnest.[156] In addition to this correspondence, copies of the official notes that were exchanged between London and Copenhagen were also passed on to Paris, and the overall impression that emerges from the year 1793 is that the French paid close attention to the British-Danish debate, and adjusted to the developments that took place.

Conclusion

A striking feature of the British-Danish debate is how often the British representatives in Copenhagen, as well as consul Mitchell in Kristiansand, approached the Bernstorffs with complaints about the state of affairs in Norway, and received confirmation that the issue would be looked into and dealt with, only to observe that nothing much changed. Although there are clear indications that particularly A. P. Bernstorff retained the confidence of the British representatives and was seen as an honest and well-meaning man, it is odd that the British government simply accepted his reassurances, and let this state of affairs pass year after year. While a definite answer to this question is hard to establish, a few reasons for this reticence on the part of the British government may be suggested nonetheless.

The French Revolutionary War from 1793 to 1802 was in many ways a desperate struggle for Britain. The threat of a French invasion was almost omnipresent, resulting in frequent 'invasion scares' and general concern, and an actual invasion was probably only averted by a series of crucial naval victories against the French.[157] In this situation, the British government could not afford to lose too many friends, and the perception on the British side seems to have been that Denmark-Norway was, on balance, a 'friendly neutral', its profiteering attitude notwithstanding. The question was therefore whether the privateer issue was important and serious enough to risk disrupting this friendly relationship, possibly causing an armed conflict and, in the worst-case scenario, pushing the Danish government over on the French side in the war. Increasing French control over the northern parts of mainland Europe from 1795 onwards made it obvious to anyone that mainland Denmark was very exposed to a French invasion. A neutral Denmark-Norway was better than one allied to France, and the British government was well aware that Copenhagen was under pressure from both sides. The activities of the French 'agents' in various parts of the dual-monarchy, including the Republic's unofficial representative in Copenhagen from 1793 to 1796 (official from 1796 to 1800), Philippe-Antoine Grouvelle, were reported by the British representatives from time to time, and there seems to be little doubt that they applied pressure on the Danish government to keep the Norwegian ports open to privateers. Daniel Hailes, for one, was particularly concerned about Grouvelle's close contact with, and possible influence on, A. P. Bernstorff.[158] As Fitzgerald reported in June 1798, 'the undisguised Fear of giving offence to the French' was prevalent among 'all descriptions of People here, in and out of office', and it seems likely that this concern was the main reason why it took so long from the first indications emerged of Danish plans to close the ports, until a full closure was actually implemented.[159] If Britain and Denmark-Norway were to retain their friendly relationship, it was important to apply the diplomatic pressure in measured terms. That the problem of French privateers using Norwegian ports was serious when seen from the point of view of the British government is, however, beyond doubt, and can also be deduced from the sheer amount of correspondence relating to it. About half the letters contained in the Foreign Office Correspondence-series for Denmark for this period concern privateering, compared to a roughly similar number for Danish neutral shipping and British captures of Danish vessels suspected of carrying goods to France. Despite this concern about French privateering, however, the actual number of British vessels brought into Norwegian ports was arguably not very high. Olav Bergersen found that, by the end of 1798, a total of 190 ships had been condemned in Bergen and Kristiansand, with 119 and 71 ships as the individual figures.[160] Of the possibly as many as 11,000 British merchant vessels captured for the whole period 1793–1815, this was obviously not a very significant share, but no one could *know* that this would be the outcome at the time of the most intense French (and Dutch) privateering activity such as in 1797, and both the Baltic and Archangel trades *were*, no doubt, very valuable and important for Britain.[161] Nevertheless, it was precisely neutral Danish shipping, and the introduction of convoys for such shipping in the summer of 1798, which led to a British military response in the shape of the attack on the Danish Fleet at Copenhagen on 2 April 1801.[162] Neutral convoys meant that Britain could not exercise its traditional belligerent right of *visitation*—that is, the opportunity to check that neutral ships were not carrying contraband goods to the enemy—and this was seen as unacceptable. In the end, therefore, one could say the need to *prevent* supplies from coming through to France was seen as more important than the need to *protect* the importation of supplies to Britain—even when the supplies in question came through the crucial Baltic Sea trade which, in the view of one historian, was Britain's 'principal source of naval stores'.[163] Yet, this contrast can be misleading since Britain could, and did, devise its own means of protecting the Baltic Sea trade from the depredations of privateers in the shape of convoys and a naval presence off the coast of Norway. This may have made it less pressing to force through a closure of the Norwegian ports, than to prevent the adoption of a system of neutral convoys.[164]

British reticence may, however, also have been caused by sensitivity towards other challenges one knew the Danish authorities were facing, most notably the difficulties involved in policing the long Norwegian coastline (partly due to insufficient naval resources), and in controlling the Norwegians themselves. Although Hailes had thought it 'ludicrous' that the Danish government could not control its own subjects at the time of the initial discussions in 1793, he had also made the very perceptive observation that Copenhagen needed to tread carefully because of the 'independent spirit of the inhabitants' in Norway.[165] The later eighteenth century was a period of growing national awareness in Norway, a development that would culminate in the claim for independence in 1814, and it may well be the case that the British government appreciated this state of affairs. Apart from Hailes' comments there is, however, little direct evidence to confirm this.

Finally, one might also ask why the Danish government did not do more to satisfy British demands. The answer, it seems, is partly linked to the aforementioned point. As it has been alluded to in this chapter, and as will be explored further in Chap. 4 in particular, there were many people in Norway who profited from cooperating with French privateers, to obtain both prize cargoes and prize vessels. It was, however, arguably also in the interest of the Danish government to allow, or at least turn a blind eye to, the condemnation of prize *vessels* in Norway. Since the domestic capacity for ship construction did not even come near to satisfying the need for tonnage caused by the Danish government's policy of 'commercial neutrality', Olav Bergersen has argued, the condemnation of merchant ships from the belligerents presented the only realistic way of acquiring the necessary number of ships, quickly enough.[166] Daniel Hailes appears to have suspected as much already in February 1794, when he wrote to Grenville that 'the Trade of this Country is so flourishing as to cause a demand for Shipping'. The country in question was Norway.[167] The wish to keep the ports open to *all* privateers and to allow them to condemn their prize vessels there should be seen in the light of this policy. In this, the Danish government and Norwegian merchants arguably had a common interest—until the French decree of 1798 turned the situation upside down that is.

Notes

1. While the term 'Denmark-Norway' is used here to refer to the whole of the dual-monarchy, the term 'Danish' has been adopted for the government or state, in line with what has been the common practice.
2. Ole Feldbæk, *Denmark and the Armed Neutrality 1800–1801: Small Power Policy in a World War* (Akademisk forlag, Copenhagen, 1980), pp. 15–16, 202–204. See also: Ole Feldbæk, 'The Anglo-Danish Convoy Conflict of 1800: A study of small power policy and neutrality', *Scandinavian Journal of History*, 2 (1977), pp. 3–21; and Lars Bangert Struwe, 'Allieret eller neutral? Dansk sikkerhedspolitikk 1740–1807', in Eric Lerdrup Bourgois and Niels Høffing (eds.), *Danmark og Napoleon* (Højberg, Hovedland, 2007), pp. 17–31.
3. See two articles by Ole Feldbæk: 'Eighteenth-Century Danish Neutrality: Its Diplomacy, Economics and Law', *Scandinavian Journal of History*, 8 (1983), pp. 10–11; and 'Privateers, Piracy and Prosperity: Danish Shipping in War and Peace, 1750–1807', in David J. Starkey, E. S. van Eyck van Heslinga, J. A. de Moor (eds.), *Pirates and Privateers: New Perspectives on the War on Trade in the Eighteenth and Nineteenth Centuries* (University of Exeter Press, Exeter, 1997), pp. 227–229.
4. Feldbæk, 'Anglo-Danish Convoy Conflict', p. 161; and: Feldbæk, *Armed Neutrality*, p. 18.
5. Éric Schnakenbourg, *Entre la Guerre et la paix: Neutralité et relations internationales XVIIe–XVIIIe siècles* (Presses Universitaires de Rennes, Rennes, 2013), pp. 283–330. See also: Finn-Einar Eliassen, 'Kameleon, stråmann eller trojansk hest? Danmark-Norges nøytralitet og indiahandel under den amerikanske frihetskrig, in Finn-Einar Eliassen, Bård Frydenlund, Erik Opsahl and Kai Østberg (eds.), *Den rianske vending: Festskrift i anledning professor Øystein Rians 70-årsdag 23. februar 2015* (Novus Forlag, Oslo, 2015), pp. 49–63.
6. See, for example: Feldbæk, 'Danish Neutrality', pp. 20–21, and N. A. M. Rodger, *Command of the Ocean: A Naval History of Britain, 1649–1815* (Penguin, London, 2006), pp. 549–552.
7. Ole Feldbæk, *Danmark-Norge 1380–1814*, iv, *Nærhed og adskillelse 1720–1814* (4. volumes, Universitetsforlaget, Oslo, 1998), p. 12 [translated from Danish].
8. Feldbæk, 'Convoy Conflict', p. 164.
9. The three other nationalities at over 1000 vessels were the Swedes at 1860, Dutch at 1736 and Danes at 1394. National Archives [NA], FO 22/15, Foreign Correspondence, Denmark, f. 32, N. Fenwick to Lord Grenville, Elsinore 21 January 1792 [Fenwick always wrote 'Elsingoer', but for clarity and consistency, Elsinore has been used here].

10. NA, FO 22/16, fo. 30, N. Fenwick to Lord Grenville, Elsinore 19 January 1793. By comparison, the figures for 1788, the first year in which British ship had made up more than one-third of the total, were 3279 British, 64 French and 9216 in total. NA, FO 22/11, fos. 21–22, N. Fenwick to the Marquis of Carmarthen, Elsinore 20 January 1789.
11. As David J. Starkey has pointed out with respect to British privateers: 'privateering was a demand led activity, in the sense that the perceived abundance and vulnerability of the prey conditioned the extent and the character of the predatory response'. David J. Starkey, 'A Restless Spirit: British Privateering Enterprise, 1739–1815', in David J. Starkey, E. S. van Eyck van Heslinga, J. A. de Moor (eds.), *Pirates and Privateers: New Perspectives on the War on Trade in the Eighteenth and Nineteenth Centuries* (University of Exeter Press, Exeter, 1997), p. 128.
12. At this point, the British diplomatic representative to Denmark-Norway normally held the title of 'envoy extraordinary', one step short of full ambassadorship. See: D. B. Horn, *The British Diplomatic Service, 1689–1789* (The Clarendon Press, Oxford, 1961), pp. 29–30, 42–45.
13. NA, FO 22/16, ff. 43–44, D. Hailes to Lord Grenville, Copenhagen 26 February 1793.
14. For a good discussion of the practice of privateering and Prize Courts, see: Gary M. Anderson and Adam Gifford Jr., 'Privateering and the Private Production of Naval Power', *Cato Journal*, Vol. 11, No. 1 (1991), pp. 99–122.
15. Patrick Crowhurst, *The French War on Trade 1793–1815* (Scholar Press, Aldershot, 1989).
16. See, for example: Anderson and Gifford, 'Privateering', p. 110.
17. This problem emerged very clearly when the American 'rebel' government issued letters of marque during the American War of Independence. See: Robert C. Ritchie, 'Government Measures against Piracy and Privateering in the Atlantic Area, 1750–1850', in David J. Starkey, E. S. van Eyck van Heslinga, J. A. de Moor (eds.), *Pirates and Privateers: New Perspectives on the War on Trade in the Eighteenth and Nineteenth Centuries* (University of Exeter Press, Exeter, 1997), p. 22.
18. Éric Schnakenbourg, 'Chasing the enemy under neutral cover: French seizures of Danish ships in Nantes during the Directory period', in *The International Journal of Maritime History* (2016), Vol. 28 (1), p. 142.
19. Schnakenbourg, 'Chasing the enemy', p. 140. On the role of the prize courts, see: Carl J. Kulsrud, *Maritime Neutrality to 1780: A History of the Main Principles Governing Neutrality and Belligerency to 1780* (Little, Brown, and Company, Boston, 1936), pp. 17–37.

20. Stephen C. Neff, *War and the Law of Nations: A General History* (Cambridge University Press, Cambridge, 2005), p. 81 [quote], and Theodore M. Cooperstein, 'Letters of Marque and Reprisal: The Constitutional Law and Practice of Privateering', *Journal of Maritime Law & Commerce*, Vo. 40, No. 2 (2009), p. 222.
21. The word 'prize' was in turn derived from 'reprisal'.
22. Neff, *War*, p. 77.
23. *Ibid.*, p. 108. On the development of reprisals, see also: Stephen C. Neff, 'Britain and the Neutrals in the French Revolutionary Wars: The Debate over Reprisals and Third Parties', in Koen Stapelbroek (ed.), *Trade and War: The Neutrality of Commerce in the Inter-State System* (COLLeGIUM Vol. 10., the Helsinki Collegium for Advanced Studies, Helsinki, 2011), pp. 236–239.
24. Good examples of both letters of marque and the accompanying instructions, in this case issued by the American government in 1776, can be found in a brief, but useful booklet written by Angus Konstam: *Privateers & Pirates, 1730–1830* (Osprey publishing, Oxford, 2001), pp. 16–18.
25. *Daily News*, 10 March 1854, cited in: Jan Martin Lemnitzer, *Power, Law and the End of Privateering* (Palgrave Macmillan, London, 2014), p. 39.
26. Anderson and Gifford, 'Privateering', 107. See also *ibid.*, footnote 12, p. 109.
27. Ritchie, 'Government Measures', pp. 10–17; and Ola Teige, 'Priser, profit og nøytralitet: Kaperfarten i Norge under den store nordiske krig 1709–1720', in *Sjøfartshistorisk årbok* (2012), pp. 8–10.
28. Crowhurst, *French War on Trade*, p. 1. Privateering as a substitute for trade was not unique for the French experience, however. See: Anderson and Gifford, 'Privateering', p. 114.
29. Crowhurst, *French War on Trade*, pp. 84–85, and R. P. Crowhurst, 'Profitability in French Privateering, 1793–1815', in *Business History*, 3 (1982), p. 48.
30. Crowhurst, *French War on Trade*, p. 51.
31. Ritchie, 'Government Measures, 21; Stephen C. Neff, *Justice among Nations: A History of International Law* (Harvard University Press, Cambridge, Massachusetts, 2014), p. 207; Joh. H. Tønnessen, *Kaperfart og Skipsfart 1807–1814* (J. W. Cappelens Forlag, Oslo, 1955), pp. 17–18; and Olav Bergersen, *Nøytralitet og Krig: Fra Nordens væpnede nøytralitets sage, en sjømilitær studie* (2 vols., Tveitan, Oslo, 1966), i, p. 191.
32. For a further discussion of the French decree of 2 March 1797, see below, p. 50.
33. Crowhurst, *French War on Trade*, pp. 31, 43, 50–51, 91, 199; and Ritchie, 'Government Measures', pp. 21–22. Approximately 130 French privateers were caught in 1797 alone, Crowhurst, *French War on Trade*,

p. 50. See also Chap. 6 in Crowhurst on 'French Prisoners of War in Britain'. We will return to the British Convoy Acts and other countermeasures in Chap. 4.

34. Crowhurst, *French War on Trade*, p. 46. The British Envoy in Copenhagen, James Craufurd, used the term himself in a letter to the foreign office in October 1795, when he argued that privateers 'infest the North Sea'. NA, FO 211/5, Foreign Office and predecessor, Embassy, Consulate and Legation, Denmark: General Correspondence—Secret Communications, No. 52 to My Lord, Copenhagen, 17 October 1795. Concern about privateers was perhaps particularly marked in Scotland where the common perception was that Scotland lacked the necessary naval defences. See: Atle L. Wold, 'Scottish Attitudes to Military Mobilisation and War in the 1790s', in Bob Harris (ed.) *Scotland in the Age of the French Revolution* (John Donald, Edinburgh, 2005), pp. 140–163.
35. Crowhurst, *French War on Trade*, pp. 101, 202.
36. NA, FO 22/29, fos. 3–4, Robt Steph Fitzgerald to Lord Grenville, Copenhagen 19 August 1797.
37. The crew on board the French privateer which had captured the *Tay Greenlandman* (referred to in Chap. 1, p. 1) had, for example, been 'terribly afraid when they first saw the Greenlandman, taking her for a British man of war', but as they discovered that the ship had no guns, 'they recovered their courage, and took possession of her'. *Caledonian Mercury*, 25 July 1799.
38. See: Patrick Crowhurst, 'Experience; Skill and Luck: French Privateering Expeditions, 1792–1815', in David J. Starkey, E. S. van Eyck van Heslinga and J. A. de Moor (eds.), *Pirates and Privateers: New Perspectives on the War on Trade in the Eighteenth and Nineteenth Centuries* (University of Exeter Press, Exeter, 1997), pp. 165–167; Crowhurst, *French War on Trade*, Chap. 3, 'Privateering: the reality. 1793–1815' in particular. The features of French privateering outlined here applied more generally too, and a good account of 'privateering in practice' can be found in the article by Anderson and Gifford: 'Privateering'.
39. R. P. Fereday, *Saint-Faust in the North 1803–4: Orkney and Shetland in Danger, An Abortive Raid and its Consequences* (Tempvs Reparatvm Monographs, Oxford, 1995), Chap. 11, 'Campbell versus Saint-Faust'.
40. The main authority on British privateering is David J. Starkey. See, for example: 'A Restless Spirit: British Privateering Enterprise, 1739–1815', in David J. Starkey, E. S. van Eyck van Heslinga and J. A. de Moor (eds.), *Pirates and Privateers: New Perspectives on the War on Trade in the Eighteenth and Nineteenth Centuries* (University of Exeter Press, Exeter, 1997), pp. 10–28.
41. Crowhurst, *French War on Trade*, p. 88.

42. Lemnitzer, *Power*, pp. 80, 100.
43. *La guerre de course* can also be understood as a strategy, which gives priority to commerce raiding over more conventional naval operations, even if the raiding itself is carried out by regular warships rather than, or in addition to, privateers. We will return to this issue in Chap. 4, pp. 143–146.
44. Crowhurst, *French War on Trade*, p. 47; Paul Kennedy, *The Rise and Fall of British Naval Mastery* (Penguin, London, 2004), pp. 130–131; Rodger, *Command of the Ocean*, p. 437; and Robert Gardiner (ed.), *Fleet Battle and Blockade: The French Revolutionary War 1793–1797* (Chatham Publishing, London, 1996), pp. 9–11, 61. On the origins of the French privateering policy, see also: J. S. Bromley, *Corsairs and Navies 1660–1760* (Hambledon Press, London, 1987), Chap. 11, 'The French Privateering War, 1702–13'.
45. Anderson and Gifford, 'Privateering', p. 118, footnote 31.
46. Crowhurst, 'Profitability', p. 59.
47. NA, FO, 22/27, fos. 96–100, John Mitchell to Lord Robert Fitzgerald, Christiansand, 18 November 1796 [quote, fo. 98v].
48. Bergersen, *Nøytralitet*, i, p. 275.
49. Stephen C. Neff, *The rights and duties of neutrals: A general history* (Manchester University Press, Manchester, 2000), p. 101.
50. Neff, *The rights and duties*, pp. 7–8.
51. Neff, *War*, p. 49.
52. Neff, *The rights and duties*, p. 7. For a detailed discussion of the just war doctrine, see: Neff, *War*, Part 1, pp. 7–82.
53. Neff, *The rights and duties*, p. 50. The 'voluntary' Law of Nations was seen as distinct from *natural law*, 'the idea that the entire world was under the rule of a single universal, transcultural set of moral principles'. Neff, *War*, p. 10.
54. Neff, *The rights and duties*, pp. 27–29; Anderson and Gifford, 'Privateering', pp. 106–107.
55. Neff, *The rights and duties*, p. 13.
56. *Ibid.*, p. 14.
57. *Ibid.*, p. 18.
58. *Ibid.*, p. 49.
59. Stephen C. Neff has described these schools as 'The conflict-of-rights (or necessity) theory'; 'the code-of-conduct school'; and 'the community interest school', where Hübner belonged to the second. See: *ibid.*, pp. 45–53.
60. For a recent and comprehensive analysis of Hübner's work, see: Nora Naguib Leerberg, *The Legal Politics of Neutrality in the Age of Privateering: Martin Hübner's Law of Neutrality and Prize* (Dreyersforlag A/S, Oslo, 2015).

61. Neff, 'Britain and the Neutrals', p. 233. This was also known as the 'Rule of 1756', see: Neff, *The rights and duties*, pp. 65–66. The increasing naval character of the wars fought in the second half of the eighteenth century arguably played a role in spurring on the debate about neutral rights, since, invariably, the trade of neutrals was adversely affected by wars at sea. See: Finn-Einar Eliassen, 'Kameleon, stråmann eller trojansk hest', p. 53.
62. See for example: Neff, 'Britain and the Neutrals', pp. 232–235. For a comprehensive discussion of the origins and development of contraband, see: Kulsrud, *Maritime Neutrality to 1780*, chapter VI 'The Definition of Contraband of War', pp. 244–294.
63. Neff, *The rights and duties*, pp. 19–23; and Leerberg, *Legal Politics of Neutrality*, Chap. 6, 'The Issue of Cargo: Free Ship, Free Goods and the Contraband Exception', pp. 104–128.
64. Neff, *The rights and duties*, p. 54. Coal issue: *ibid.*, p. 107; and Lemnitzer, *Power*, pp. 98, 112–113, 159.
65. Kulsrud, *Maritime Neutrality*, pp. 278–285.
66. Jørgen Hornemann, *Danmarks statsmand: A.P. Bernstorff og hans samtid* (Borgen, Copenhagen, 2001), pp. 516–550; and Neff, *The rights and duties*, p. 64.
67. NA, FO 22/23, fos. 117–118, John Mitchell to Lord Grenville, Christiansand 30 June 1795.
68. Writing in support of the British position in 1801, the English lawyer Robert Ward argued for a very comprehensive understanding of contraband. In his view, it was 'the activity and labour shewn in the service of an enemy, and not the production or trade in the particular articles, which, and which alone, form in reality the essence of Contraband'. *Any* goods were potential contraband, if it could be demonstrated that the supply of them aided the war effort of the recipient belligerent nation. Robert Ward, *An Essay on Contraband: being a continuation of the Relative Rights and Duties of Belligerent and Neutral Nations, in Maritime Affairs* (J. Wright and J. Butterworth, London, 1801), p. 185.
69. Neff, *The rights and duties*, pp. 41–42, 85.
70. Hailes held the title of 'Envoy Extraordinary'. We will return to the question of the British diplomatic representation in Denmark-Norway in Chap. 3.
71. NA, FO 211/4, Foreign Office and predecessor, Embassy, Consulate and Legation, Denmark: General Correspondence. Lord Grenville to Daniel Hailes Esq, Whitehall, 29 March 1793.
72. NA, FO 22/16, fos. 31–32, D. Hailes to Lord Grenville, Copenhagen, 28 January 1793 [quote fos. 31–31v].

73. *Ibid.*, fos. 62–63, D. Hailes to Lord Grenville, Copenhagen, 14 March 1793 [quote, fo. 62].
74. *Ibid.*, fos. 68–69, John Mitchell to Lord Grenville, Christiania, 23 March 1793 [Copy sent to the Admiralty].
75. *Ibid.*, fos. 121–122, John Mitchell to Lord Grenville, Christiania, 27 April 1793 [quote fos. 121–121v]. Mitchell re-emphasised the need to 'forbid the French the use of the Danish or Norway ports' in a letter to Grenville in late June. *Ibid.*, fos. 174–175, John Mitchell to Lord Grenville, Christiania, 24 June 1793 [quote fo. 175v].
76. *Ibid.*, fos. 136–137, D. Hailes to Lord Grenville, Copenhagen, 18 May 1793.
77. *Ibid.*, fos. 141–142, D. Hailes to Lord Grenville, Copenhagen, 21 May 1793. Jørgen Hornemann has argued that Bernstorff anticipated demands for the closure of the Danish ports; meaning he cannot have been entirely unprepared. Hornemann, *Danmarks statsmand*, p. 513.
78. See: Bergersen, *Nøytralitet*, i, pp. 211–214. Hailes had been informed about the ordinance by Mitchell, and stated so in a letter to Grenville. See: NA, FO 22/16, 136–137. Mitchell had also informed Grenville directly: NA, FO 22/16, fos. 138–139, John Mitchell to Lord Grenville, Christiania, 18 May 1793.
79. The reason for this seems to have been that Denmark-Norway had not yet recognised the new American republic. Liston did not mention this in his account, but it is referred to in other correspondence from the period, for example: NA, FO 22/27, fos. 219–221, Robert Fitzgerald to Lord Grenville, Copenhagen 22 April 1797 [see: fo. 220].
80. NA, FO 97/117, Letters and Papers Supplementary to the Denmark Correspondence in the Years 1793–98, fos. 80–85, 'Statement of the Conduct of Denmark as a Neutral Power, in former Wars, R. 3d July, by Mr. Liston'.
81. NA, FO 22/17, fos. 9–16, 3 July 1793 [translated from French]. The document does not have a title or signature, but it was enclosed with a government order sent to Hailes, see: *Ibid.*, fos. 3–8, No. 9 to Mr. Hailes, Whitehall 3 July 1793.
82. NA, FO 22/16, fo. 107. John Mitchell to Lord Grenville, Christiania, 13 April 1793.
83. NA, FO 22/17, fos. 9–16. The Danish government did not officially recognise the French Republic until February 1796. See: Feldbæk, *Armed Neutrality*, p. 17.
84. Emma Vincent Macleod, *A War of Ideas: British Attitudes to the Wars Against Revolutionary France 1792–1802* (Aldershot, Ashgate, 1998).
85. Ola Mestad, 'Schlegel mot Sir William Scott i 1800—Schlegels internasjonale priserettsstudie', in Ola Mestad (ed.), *Frihetens forskole: Professor*

Schlegel og Eidsvollsmennenes læretid i København (Pax Forlag A/S, Oslo, 2013), p. 306.

86. NA, FO 22/17, fos. 33–38, D. Hailes to Lord Grenville, Copenhagen, 22 July 1793.
87. NA, ADM 1/3841, Admiralty, Letters from British Consuls, J. Wallace to Philip Stephens, Esq., Secretary of the Admiralty, Bergen, 22 June 1793. See also Nicholas Fenwick's report on the same: *ibid.*, N. Fenwick to Philip Stephens, Elsinore 25 June 1793.
88. NA, FO 22/17, fos. 19–20, D. Hailes to Lord Grenville, Copenhagen, 6 July 1793 [quote fo. 19].
89. *Ibid.*, fos. 23–24, John Mitchell to Lord Grenville, Christiania, 6 July 1793; and *ibid.*, fos. 31–32, John Mitchell to Lord Grenville, Christiania, 13 July 1793.
90. *Ibid.*, fos. 21–22, John Mitchell to Lord Grenville, Christiania, 6 July 1793 [Mitchell sent two separate letters to Grenville that day].
91. *Ibid.*, fos. 27–28. D. Hailes to Lord Grenville, Copenhagen, 9 July 1793 [quote fo. 28].
92. *Ibid.*, fos. 63–69, Note, the Department of Foreign Affairs, Copenhagen, 28 July 1793 [translated from French; quote fo. 65].
93. *Ibid.*, fos. 63–69 [translated from French; quotes: fos. 68–69].
94. In a more direct translation, this passage would read 'He will not permit the sale of prizes made by French vessels, in his states'. *Ibid.*, fo. 64.
95. *Ibid.*, fos. 57–59, John Mitchell to Lord Grenville, 27 July 1793 [quote, 57v].
96. *Ibid.*, fos. 59–60, 'Copy of a Letter from the Danish Chancery to the Government of the Province of Christiansand respecting French Prizes brought into Norway', signed by [Christian] Colbiornsen, Copenhagen, 22 June 1793 [original emphasis; the letter appears to have been translated by Mitchell himself.]. We will return to the question of French policies on the sale of prizes in Norwegian ports later.
97. *Ibid.*, fo. 57.
98. *Ibid.*, fos. 73–74, D. Hailes to Lord Grenville, Copenhagen, 3 August 1793 [first quote fo. 73]; and *ibid.*, fos. 77–78, D. Hailes to Lord Grenville, Copenhagen, 6 August 1793.
99. NA, FO, 22/25, fos. 122–124, 'To Mr Craufurd, Downing Street, 3 April 1796' [quote fo. 122v]; see also: NA, FO 22/17, fos. 106–107, D. Hailes to Lord Grenville, Copenhagen, 31 August 1793; and NA, FO 211/5, No. 53 'to My Lord', Copenhagen, 17 October 1795.
100. NA, FO 22/18, fo. 79, J. Wallace to Lord Grenville, Bergen, 8 March 1794.
101. NA, FO 22/20, fos. 206–207, 'To Mr. Hailes', Downing Street, 26 August 1794 [quote fos. 206v–207].
102. *Ibid.*, fos. 214–216, D. Hailes to Lord Grenville, Copenhagen, 6 September 1794 [quotes fos. 214v–215].

103. *Ibid.*, fos. 222–224, D. Hailes to Lord Grenville, Copenhagen, 12 September 1794 quotes. fos. 222–222v].
104. *Ibid.*, fos. 263–265, D. Hailes to Lord Grenville, Copenhagen, 4 October 1794 [quote fo. 263v]; and NA, FO 22/17, fos. 106–107, D. Hailes to Lord Grenville, Copenhagen 31 August 1793 [on the cargo of the *Janet* of Leith].
105. NA, FO 22/24, fos. 185–186, John Mitchell to Lord Grenville, Christiania, 23 November 1795 [quote fo. 186].
106. NA, FO 22/25, fos. 90–91, James Craufurd to Lord Grenville, Copenhagen 5 March 1796 [quote fos. 90v–91].
107. *Ibid.*, fos. 122–124. 'To Mr. Craufurd, Downing Street, 3 April 1796' [quotes, fos. 122v–123v; original emphasis].
108. See: NA, FO 22/17, fo. 161, D. Hailes to Lord Grenville, Copenhagen 30 November 1793; FO 22/25, fos. 194–195, James Craufurd to Lord Grenville, Copenhagen, 21 May 1796; *ibid.*, fos. 249–250, James Craufurd to Lord Grenville, Copenhagen, 28 June 1796; *ibid.*, fos. 251–256, James Craufurd to Lord Grenville, Copenhagen 2 July 1795; NA, FO 22/26, fos. 204–205, 'To Lord Robert Fitzgerald', Downing Street, November 1796; *ibid.*, fos. 244–245, Robert Fitzgerald to Lord Grenville, Copenhagen, 26 November 1796; and FO 211, No. 27 to 'My Lord', Copenhagen, 2 July 1796.
109. NA, FO 22/27, fos. 73–76, John Mitchell to Lord Robert Fitzgerald, Christiansand, 19 November 1796 [quotes fos. 73–73v; original emphasis. This letter has been misplaced in a volume of letters dating from January to April 1797]. Fenwick confirmed this impression in May 1794, when he wrote to the Admiralty that there were 'no late Accounts of any Privateers in the North Sea'. NA, ADM 1/3841, N. Fenwick to Philip Stephens, Elsinore, 13 May 1794.
110. NA, FO 22/27, fos. 73–76, John Mitchell to Lord Robert Fitzgerald, Christiansand, 19 November 1796 [quotes fos. 73v–74; original emphasis]. On the Dutch privateers which emerged in 1795, see: Chap. 5. The governor's full name was Hans Christopher Diedrich Victor von Levetzow. See: Terje Bratberg (2016, 4. februar). Levetzow, in *Store norske leksikon*. Accessed 14. februar 2020 from https://snl.no/Levetzow.
111. National Library of Norway [NLN], *Christiansand Weekly Gazette*, No. 36, 4 September 1795 [the original title of this newspaper was *Kristiansands Adresse Kontors Efterretninger* and *Christiansand Weekly Gazette* appears to have been Mitchell's own translation of this. We have used Mitchell's English version here].
112. *Ibid.*, No. 46, 13 November 1795 [translated from Danish].
113. *Ibid.*, No. 47, 20 November 1795 [translated from Danish].
114. NA, FO 22/24, fos. 141–142, James Craufurd to Lord Grenville, Copenhagen 24 October 1795 [original emphasis].

115. *Ibid.*, fos. 220–222, James Craufurd to Lord Grenville, Copenhagen 8 December 1795 [quote 221b]; and NA, FO 211/5, No. 59 to 'My Lord', Copenhagen 8 December 1795.
116. NLN, *Christiansand Weekly Gazette*, No. 35, 30 August 1793; No. 40, 3 October 1794; and No. 36, 4 September 1795. We will return to the sale of prize vessels and cargoes in Chap. 4.
117. NA, FO 22/27, fos. 131–132, To 'Lord Robert Fitzgerald', Downing Street, 2 March 1797.
118. *Ibid.*, fos. 175–176, 'Nôte', Robt Steph Fitzgerald to le Comte de Bernstorff, Copenhagen, 23 March 1797 [translated from French].
119. NA, FO 22/28, fos. 3–4, Robt Steph Fitzgerald to Lord Grenville, Copenhagen, 29 April 1797 [quote fo. 3v].
120. See: *ibid.*, fos. 41–43, R. S. Fitzgerald to Wm Höyer Esq, Copenhagen, 20 May 1797.
121. *Ibid.*, fos. 69–70, Robt Steph Fitzgerald to Lord Grenville, Copenhagen, 13 June 1797 [quote fo. 69].
122. NA, FO 97/117, fo. 458, John Sinclair to Dudley Ryder, Whitehall 6 November 1797. Sir John Sinclair was a Scottish aristocrat who, while he sat on the Board of Agriculture, led the work of setting up the *Statistical Account of Scotland* from 1790, but it is not clear why he took a particular interest in the problem of French privateering.
123. NA, FO 97/117, fos. 460–461, signed: 'G. H.' [probably an attachment to the above letter]. The G. H. here may have been George Hammond, who was under-secretary at the Foreign Office from October 1795 to February 1806, and whose responsibility was dispatches relating to what had been the 'Northern Department' before the merger with the 'Southern Department' into the Foreign Office in 1782.
124. Jacob Henric Schou, *Chronologisk Register over de Kongelige Forordninger og Aabne Breve, samt andre trykte Anordninger, som fra Aar 1670 af ere udkomne, tilligemed et nøiaktigt Udtog av de endnu gieldende, for saavidt samme i Umindelighed angaae Undersaatterne i Danmark og Norge, et alphabetisk Register. 1 Deel*, i (Copenhagen, 1795). Forbund imellem K. Christian V og Carl II af Stor-Britanien, 11 Juli 1670.
125. On the negotiations leading to the treaty, see: L. Laursen, *Danmark-Norges Traktater 1523–1750, ii: 1665–1675* (6 vols., Copenhagen, 1923), pp. 305–333. The original treaty is held by the National Archives: NA, SP 108/35, Secretaries of State: State Papers Foreign, Treaties, part 1 and 2, Anglo-Danish Treaty of 1670 [in Latin].
126. NA, FO 97/117, fos. 460–461 [original emphasis].
127. NA, FO 22/25, fos. 122–124, 'To Mr Craufurd', Downing Street, 3 April 1796 [quote fos. 123–123v].

128. M. de Martens, *An Essay on Privateers, Captures, and particularly on Recaptures, according the laws, treaties, and usages of the maritime powers of Europe. To which is subjoined a Discourse, in which the rights and duties of neutral powers are briefly stated. Translated from the French, with notes, by Thomas Hartwell Horne* (London, E. and R. Brooke, and J. Rider, Bell Yaro, Temple Bar; J. Sewell, Cornhill; and J. Hatchard, London, 1801), p. 98 [original emphasis]. The title for the original in French was: Mr. de Martens, *Essai concernant les Armateurs les Prises et sur tout les Reprises. D'après les loix, les traitès, et les usages des Puissances maritimes de l'Europe* (Gottingue, 1795).
129. Martens, *Essay on Privateers*, pp. 98–102. For Liston's account, see above, pp. 30–32.
130. 'Decree of the Executive Directory concerning the navigation of neutral vessels, loaded with merchandise belonging to the enemies of the republic, and the judgments on the trials relative to the validity of maritime prizes. 12th Ventose, 5th year, (2nd March, 1797.)': (*The Napoleon series*-website, published March 2003). Accessed 23.04.2018: http://www.napoleon-series.org/research/government/france/decrees/c_decrees8.html. See also: Feldbæk, *Armed Neutrality*, p. 28. Although the official decree was issued on 2 March, Mitchell claimed that orders to the same extent had been sent out to French privateers already by late January. See: NA, ADM 1/3842, Letters to British Consuls, John Mitchell to Evan Nepean Esq., Christiansand, 24 January 1797.
131. 'Law which determines the character of vessels from their cargo, especially those loaded with English merchandise. 29th Nivose, 6th year, (18th January, 1798.)': (*The Napoleon series*—website, published March 2003). Accessed 23.04.2018: https://www.napoleon-series.org/research/government/france/decrees/c_decrees9.html, see also: Bergersen, *Nøytralitet*, i, pp. 402, 486.
132. Bergersen, *Nøytralitet*, i, pp. 619–620.
133. NA, FO 22/30, fo. 154, Spencer and Stephens to Lord Grenville, Admiralty Office, 29 March 1798; and *ibid.*, fo. 156, 'Copy', 24 March 1798 [enclosed with the Admiralty-letter].
134. *Ibid.*, fo. 206, Robt Steph Fitzgerald to Lord Grenville, Copenhagen, 24 April 1798.
135. NA, FO 22/33, fos. 102–103, John Mitchell to Lord Grenville, Hamburg 16 November 1798 [quote fo. 102]. We will return to Mitchell's move to Hamburg in Chap. 3.
136. NA, FO 22/34, fos. 35–36, Robt Steph Fitzgerald to Lord Grenville, Copenhagen, 29 January 1799 [quote fo. 36].
137. Bergersen, *Nøytralitet*, i, pp. 606–609.

138. NA, FO 22/34, fos. 229–230, Robt Steph Fitzgerald to Lord Grenville, Copenhagen, 23 March 1799 [quote fo. 229]; and *ibid.*, fos. 416–417, Robt Steph Fitzgerald to Lord Grenville, Copenhagen, 14 May 1799 [quotes fos. 416–416v]. See also: *ibid.*, fo. 459, Evan Nepean to George Hammond Esq., Admiralty Office, 24 May 1799; and *ibid.*, fos. 452–456, Robt Steph Fitzgerald to Lord Grenville, Copenhagen, 25 May 1799.
139. NA, FO 22/35, fos. 4–6, Rob Steph Fitzgerald to Lord Grenville, Copenhagen, 4 June 1799 [quote fos. 4–5]. Fitzgerald described his source as 'a Colleague with whom I have not the best reasons for being well satisfied', thus probably another diplomat. *ibid.*, fo. 5.
140. *Ibid.*, fos. 38–40, Robt. Steph. Fitzgerald to Lord Grenville, Copenhagen 22 June 1799 [quote fos. 38–38v].
141. *Ibid.*, fos. 58–62, Robt. Steph. Fitzgerald to Lord Grenville, Copenhagen 2 July 1799.
142. *Ibid.*, fos. 172–174, Ant. Merry to Lord Grenville, Copenhagen, 3 August 1799 [quote fo. 173].
143. Feldbæk, *Armed Neutrality*, p. 17.
144. NA, FO 22/35, fos. 71–72, Robt Steph Fitzgerald to Lord Grenville, Copenhagen, 6 July 1799. Fitzgerald wrote that he had obtained this copy from the 'Russian Minister', which presumably meant the Russian envoy to Copenhagen. The formal handover of the declaration from Bernstorff to Fitzgerald as the British representative only took place several weeks later, see: *ibid.*, fos. 139–140, Robt Steph Fitzgerald to Lord Grenville, Copenhagen, 23 July 1799.
145. Although Denmark-Norway was officially an absolutist state, the mental illness of Christian VII meant that the king took no active part in the government of his realms.
146. NA, FO, 22/35, fos. 73–75, 'Declaration a l'Angleterre la France, et la Hollande' [undated; translated from French].
147. *Ibid.*, fos. 91–100, To 'Mr. Merry', Downing Street, 9 July 1799 [quote: fos. 98v–99].
148. See: Schnakenbourg, *Entre la guerre et la paix*, chapter IV, pp. 181–233.
149. Archives du Ministère des affaires étrangeres, Paris [AMAE], Correspondance politique, Danemark, vol. 169 [CP, Danemark, vol. 169], fos. 41–46, Framery to Citoyen Ministre, Copenhagen, 5 March 1793 [translated from French]. A microfilm copy of this correspondence series was kindly lent to me by Professor Ulrik Langen at the University of Copenhagen.
150. AMAE, CP, Danemark, vol. 169, fos. 149–150, Deforgues to Citizen President, Paris 5 July 1793 [translated from French].

151. This was confirmed in the Danish Chancery letter from 22 June, of which Mitchell had obtained a copy around the same time. See: NA, FO 22/17, fos. 59–60.
152. AMAE, CP, Danemark, vol. 169, fos. 155–164, Framery to Le Citoyen Le Brun Ministere des affairs etrangeres, Copenhagen 9 July 1793 [translated from French; original emphasis].
153. *Ibid.*, fos. 219–220, to Grouvelle, Paris 18 August 1793 [translated from French].
154. *Ibid.*, fos. 226–227, to Framery, Paris 26 August 1793 [translated from French].
155. NA, FO 22/19, fos. 241–242. John Mitchell to Lord Grenville, Christiania 14 June 1794 [quote fo. 241v]; and *ibid.*, fos. 226–227, John Mitchell to Lord Grenville, Christiania 8 June 1794.
156. We will return to the issue of the sale of prizes with official French approval in Chap. 4.
157. There is a comprehensive literature on this topic, but for the invasion scares and the forces for 'internal defence' which were set up in Britain to deal with a French invasion, should one come about, see, for example: Atle L. Wold, *Scotland and the French Revolutionary War, 1792–1802* (Edinburgh University Press), Chap. 3 'Military Recruitment'.
158. For a detailed account of Grouvelle's activities in Copenhagen, and Hailes' protests against his presence there as the representative of a regime not yet officially recognised by the Danish government, see: Ulrik Langen, *Revolutionens skygger: Franske emigranter og andre folk i København 1789–1814* (Lindhardt og Ringhof, Copenhagen, 2005), especially pp. 42–47, and 216–219.
159. NA, FO, 22/31, fos. 80–82, Robt Steph Fitzgerald to Lord Grenville, Copenhagen, 19 June 1798 [quote fo. 81v].
160. Bergersen, *Nøytralitet*, i, p. 621. D. S. Reid looked at Lloyds Lists for the period 1793–1799, and found that 160 vessels were categorised as having been sent into Norway, though he though it likely that the actual number exceed 200. D. H. Reid, 'Danish Neutrality and the Royal Navy 1795–7', in *Mariner's Mirror*, Vol. 76, Issue 2 (1990), p. 179.
161. On the total number of ships captured, see: Kennedy, *Rise and Fall*, p. 131.
162. See for example: Feldbæk, *Armed Neutrality*, pp. 29, 34–39, and 139–165.
163. A. N. Ryan, 'The Defence of British Trade with the Baltic, 1808–1813', in *The English Historical Review*, vol. 74, No. 292 (July, 1959), p. 444.

164. We will return to the issue of the British defence strategy in Chap. 4.
165. NA, FO 22/16, fos. 141–142.
166. Bergersen, *Nøytralitet*, i, pp. 375–376.
167. FO 22/18, fos. 38–39, D. Hailes to Lord Grenville, Copenhagen 22 February 1794 [quote fo. 38v].

CHAPTER 3

The Consular Service and the Role of John Mitchell

The official contact between Great Britain and Denmark-Norway on a government level was conducted by the respective diplomatic representatives in Copenhagen and London. The general pattern in this contact was that the British representative presented British policies to the Danish government, while the Danish representative in London raised Danish concerns with the British authorities. On the British side, this was in line with what had become the established procedure by the later eighteenth century. The government preferred to use its agents abroad to communicate with foreign powers, in favour of the alternative: to raise its concerns with the diplomatic agents of these powers in London. Although this exposed the correspondence to 'the danger of interception and deciphering by the foreign government with a consequent strengthening of its negotiating power', D. B. Horn argued in his central work on British diplomacy, it also meant that the government could be certain that its 'point of view was accurately and vigorously impressed' upon that foreign government.[1] The Danish government seems to have adopted the same general approach, and in practice this meant that, while it was the British envoy in Denmark who led the debate on privateering, a similar role was filled by the Danish ambassador to London on the question of British captures of Danish vessels, and the debate on neutral shipping. It is, however, striking that the British representative seems to have been more involved in cases relating to Danish complaints, than the other way around. Only very rarely did the Danish ambassador address issues pertaining to

A. L. Wold, *Privateering and Diplomacy, 1793–1807*,
https://doi.org/10.1007/978-3-030-45186-8_3

privateering, and this may serve to underline the impression of a passive approach adopted by the Danish government on this issue. It seldom acted to enforce due adherence on the part of the local authorities in Norway to the agreement of 1793, unless when pressed by the British side, as we discussed in Chap. 2. But whereas the British representative in Copenhagen was in charge of the more general and principled debate on privateering and neutral ports, the British consuls to Denmark-Norway played the central role in terms of privateering in practice. They were the ones who were on-site and could observe the activity as it unfolded, and both London and the envoy at Copenhagen relied on their intelligence. In our period there were several consuls in Norway, as well as one in Denmark at Elsinore, and among them, John Mitchell in Kristiansand came to adopt a particularly important function. This chapter focuses on the consuls, on the system of intelligence gathering which Mitchell built up along the southern coast of Norway and on the various challenges the consuls experienced, operating in a neutral country at a time of war. First, however, we need to look at the nature of the British diplomatic and consular representation in Denmark-Norway since this arrangement was crucial for the practical operations of the consular service in particular.

The British Diplomatic and Consular Representation in Denmark-Norway

Although Denmark-Norway, and Denmark before that, had one of the longest-standing British diplomatic missions, the representative did not have the full status of ambassador, but was normally an 'envoy' or, more specifically, an 'envoy extraordinary', the second highest ranking representative after ambassador. The reason for this intermediate level of representation was the strategic position Denmark held relative to the Baltic Sea trade. The passing of so many British merchant vessels through the Sound necessitated a continuous British presence at Copenhagen, but otherwise the country was not important enough to warrant a full ambassador, and there were, in any case, few British ambassadors in the eighteenth century.[2] Another striking feature of the British diplomatic service in this period was the quick turnover of personnel. Individual diplomats were rarely on one station for very long, but kept moving to new posts every other year. None of the representatives at Copenhagen from 1793 to 1807 stayed in the post for more than three years, and this was far from unusual for the service as a whole. In total, no fewer than 13 individual diplomats were stationed at Copenhagen as envoy extraordinary, chargé d'affaires or minister plenipotentiary on an extraordinary or special mission. For a short time in early 1801, Nicholas Vansittart and William Drummond even held 'joint full powers' as plenipotentiary on a special mission and chargé d'affaires respectively.[3] Consuls, by contrast, could remain on the same station for decades, and this was the case for the British consuls to Denmark-Norway too. Thus, Mitchell had the advantage of first-hand knowledge of the development of French privateering in the North Sea from the start to the end. The diplomats in Copenhagen did not, and sometimes this meant that they were not fully on top of their brief. The argument Robert Fitzgerald presented to Christian Bernstorff in 1799 on the relative usefulness of privateering for France and Britain had, for example, been dismissed by Bernstorff senior six years earlier, and it seems likely that Fitzgerald was unaware of this.[4]

Alongside the advantage of a permanent diplomatic mission to Copenhagen, the British service in Denmark-Norway benefitted from the stationing of relatively many consuls, particularly in Norway. In addition to the consul at Elsinore in Denmark, and at Kristiansand in Norway, there were consuls at Bergen and Trondheim, and a varying number of vice consuls were appointed at the smaller port towns from time to time. Mitchell was also responsible for Christiania (present-day Oslo), and when he was there, a temporary appointment was made for a vice consul at Kristiansand, and vice versa.[5] By comparison, there were just three British consuls for the whole of the United States.[6] In relation to privateering, therefore, this arrangement of consular posts along the Norwegian coast meant that the consuls could perform an important role as the eyes of the diplomatic service. Yet, consuls were not strictly speaking a part of the diplomatic corps, so what exactly was the relationship between the British diplomatic and consular services? In theory, a relatively clear distinction could be drawn up between the two.

A diplomat was a politically appointed, official representative of the government, sent out to reside in the capital of the country where he was stationed. By the later eighteenth century, he earned a regular fixed salary drawn from the civil list and enjoyed high social prestige. The duties he was expected to carry out were also normally well-defined, and set out in the shape of the instructions he received upon his appointment to a new post. Typically, a diplomat was required to adopt a dual role, presenting British policies to the government in the country where he was stationed in official contexts, while at the same time collecting intelligence about the country and its government to be sent back to the Foreign Office in secret. For this latter task, ciphers were provided by 'Deciphering Branch' in London to ensure full secrecy, and the intelligence part of the job tended to make up the most detailed part of the instructions.[7] When Daniel Hailes was appointed envoy extraordinary to Copenhagen in 1792, for example, his instructions were set out in no fewer than 13 individual points, which required him to procure information on issues such as the 'Disposition and Character, as well of the King of Denmark, as of those employed by Him, in the Management of his Affairs', on the state of the Danish defences and on the expenses and revenues of the Danish government. Hailes was further to provide 'an Account of the Population of the King of Denmark's Dominions; and the Extent and Nature of the Commerce and Manufactures carried on in the different Parts of them', and it was his responsibility to 'protect and countenance Our Subjects, trading to, or residing in, any of the Danish Dominions'.[8] Clearly defined, yet extensive in scope, it is difficult to see how Hailes could have carried out these many tasks from his station at Copenhagen, without the support of government men stationed locally. As a diplomat he arguably therefore relied on the assistance on the consuls.

A consul, by contrast, was clearly not the official representative of one country to another in the same way as a diplomat, but was normally appointed to look after the interests of the merchants of the country he represented in the port town where he was stationed. Unlike the diplomatic representative who covered the country as a whole, a consul was usually responsible for a more restricted area only. The main task of the British consuls in Denmark-Norway was therefore to promote and defend the interests of those British merchants who had business to do in the port town of their station, or who for other reasons needed the support of their government—such as if a vessel of theirs had been captured by privateers. The institution of the consul predated the international system of diplomacy as it emerged in the early modern period—the concept of 'consul' itself being of Latin, and hence of Roman origin—and the first English consuls to be appointed had been merchants, elected by their fellow traders in a foreign port to represent their interests relative to the authorities in the host country. At this early stage (in the fifteenth century), recognition by the local sovereign was more important than royal authorisation from home and, consequently, D. C. M. Platt has argued; 'Consuls before the middle of the seventeenth century were not state officials.'[9] This situation began to change, however, with the first government-appointed English consuls in 1649, and thereafter the English—and later British—governments sought to gain full control over the appointment of consuls representing English/British merchants. Although consuls now became public servants, they never achieved the kind of social prestige associated with the diplomatic service, and were generally looked down upon by both diplomats and their superiors in the Foreign Office.[10] Few funds were allocated to the service and new consuls were often of questionable quality. Appointed more often on the basis of patronage than competence and experience, many of them lacked the knowledge of trade needed to perform consular tasks well. Yet, for Denmark-Norway, at least, the appointment of merchants as consuls appears to have continued as the main rule. John Mitchell, the consul at Kristiansand in Norway was, for example, a potato importer.[11] Another main difference between service as a diplomat and as a consul was that consuls were normally unpaid, in the sense that they did not receive a regular salary (though there were exceptions from this general rule).[12] Instead, they relied mostly on 'consulage', the duties merchants paid a consul for his services. While this could be lucrative in some stations—to the extent that it even surpassed the salary of a diplomat—it was clearly an unpredictable form of income. Moreover, since consuls were required to perform a variety tasks—some of which paid no consulage—and the Foreign Office was generally reluctant to cover their expenses, appointment as a consul involved the risk of facing an outlay that could not be easily redeemed.[13] This was a problem for all the British consuls in Norway in the 1790s, as we will see. The consular service also lacked a clear career 'ladder' of the kind which existed for the diplomatic service. Consuls, as was stated earlier, usually stayed in the same post for much longer than did diplomats and, apart from the possibility of rising to a post as Consul General, the service offered little opportunity for betterment. The long duration of consular service could also be a mixed blessing. While John Wallace in Bergen seems to have carried out his duties in a sterling manner right up until his death in March 1797, to the point of even naming his own successor, there are clear indications that Nicholas Fenwick at Elsinore was beginning to struggle towards the end. In May 1797, the British envoy at Copenhagen, Robert Fitzgerald, complained to Foreign Secretary Lord Grenville that Fenwick was well past his prime. To fill the role of consul at Elsinore, Fitzgerald stated, 'a Man of Intelligence is absolutely necessary', but as matters now stood, the office was held by one 'who has the misfortune to have become in his old days, the Ridicule and Scorn of the Place in which he resides'.[14] Fenwick was not removed from his post, however, and by early September Fitzgerald could inform Grenville that the consul, 'who is far advanced in Years, has at length fallen into a State of second Infancy or complete Dotage', and that it was unlikely he would survive the winter.[15] He did not, and was succeeded by his son Charles before the end of the year.[16] By contrast, when Daniel Hailes' temper and frequent outbursts against the Danish government—caused largely by the presence and activities of the French republican representative Philippe-Antoine Grouvelle in Copenhagen, and the Danish authorities' compliance with this—made him an embarrassment to the British government in 1794, he could quickly be sent on leave, and replaced on a temporary basis by James Craufurd as chargé d'affaires.[17] It was not until July 1796 that Hailes was actually recalled officially and replaced as envoy by Robert Fitzgerald. He was then appointed as the new British envoy to Sweden from January 1797.[18] Presumably, it was thought that he could handle that station better. Less of a well-organised service than diplomacy—if indeed, it could be called a 'service' proper—the British consular arrangements of the later eighteenth century arguably lacked the institutional framework necessary for such swift movements of personnel, and it was consequently not always that easy to replace consuls.[19] Consulates also differed from diplomatic missions in that they were usually set up on the basis of bilateral treatises—the Treaty of 1661 in the case of England/Britain and Denmark-Norway—and consuls were normally expected to master the native language of their station.[20] Indeed, this was seen as absolutely crucial by some. As Alexander Grieg stressed when he had resigned from the consulship in Bergen in 1798: if he was to be replaced by a person who was 'unacquainted with the Language & Laws of this Country', or if the foreign secretary appointed 'a Native here who is ignorant of the English Language, His Majesty may as well have no Consul here'.[21] For diplomats who moved to new stations far more frequently, this could clearly not be expected, and the language of diplomacy in this period was, at any rate, French. Finally, the actual appointment of consuls was also different from that of diplomats and—in the case of Denmark-Norway—the various appointments which were made in the second half of the eighteenth century shed light on the organisation of the consular service there.

Where a newly appointed British envoy to Copenhagen was given a set of specific instructions for the job, styled to him alone and written in English—as we saw in the case of Hailes—the appointment of British consuls from around 1760 onwards took the shape of a royal letter or commission, stating to 'anyone' it might concern that the person in question had been authorised by the British monarch to take up the post of consul at a specific, named place. These letters were written in a formal and highbrow Latin, starting with the name and many titles of the reigning British monarch, and were much more general in their wording than the instructions given to diplomats. The first appointments made by such royal commissions were those of Alexander Wallace at Bergen and Nicholas Fenwick at Elsinore, both of whom were instituted as consuls by letters signed 20 February 1761.[22] These two and subsequent letters adhered to much the same broad set-up and formula, and they were therefore, in most parts, quite similar, but there were nonetheless a couple of important differences with respect to the actual appointments. The letter to Wallace stated that His Majesty had seen fit to appoint a consul at Bergen on the grounds that this would be of use to those of his subjects who traded on Norway, and who often used the port of Bergen. As a man of great 'skill, loyalty, honesty and experience', Wallace was held to be well-suited to the task and—importantly—was to exercise his authority as consul in all the ports of Norway, although he would have his 'seat and residence' (*Sedem et Residentiam*) in Bergen. Although the term 'consul general for Norway' was not used in the letter, the appointment seemed to point in that direction. The letter proceeded to outline Wallace's responsibilities, which were all to do with a consul's traditional tasks relative to trade. Wallace was to assist, protect and give advice to British tradesmen in Norway (based on those treatises which existed between Great Britain and Denmark-Norway), and was to act as an intermediary between such traders and the local authorities in Norway, both magistrates and judges. This would be partly a matter of 'defending' the vessels, goods and property of these British subjects against claims made by local officials, and partly required the new consul to investigate, decide and, if possible, settle differences in opinion or issues of direct conflict between the two. The primary responsibility of Wallace as consul was therefore to 'defend' and 'look after' the interests of British subjects trading on Bergen, but he was also expected to promote the friendship of the two countries and work to increase the trade between them. The final part of the letter asked the Danish monarch to recognise the appointment, and to award Wallace all those 'rights, honours, privileges, freedoms and advantages' which British consuls normally enjoy 'everywhere', and enjoined all others to respect the appointment, British subjects in particular.[23] Compared to the instructions issued to diplomats this was a short text, and it did not address two—in our context—crucial issues. There was no mention of war, or how a consul was to operate if he found himself to be in a neutral country at a time Britain was at war, nor was there any mention of funding, through either consulage, other kinds of fees or, indeed, a salary. Essentially, therefore, the royal commission given to consuls was a combination of proof of appointment and a set of very general instructions for the job. The letter issued to Fenwick was almost identical to the one Wallace had received, and stated that Fenwick was to exercise his authority as consul in all the ports of Denmark and the Sound, but that his station was to be at Elsinore.[24] Another three consuls were appointed by royal commission before the 1790s. In 1773, Alexander Brown was set up as the consul of the *province* of Trondheim in Norway, with the *town* of Trondheim as his station. His authority was, in other words, limited to one part of the country. Two years later, John Wallace succeeded his father as the consul at Bergen, but notwithstanding the fact that there was now another consul in Norway, he was appointed on the same conditions as his father, meaning that he could exercise his authority in all the ports of the country.[25] Finally, in 1784, John Mitchell was appointed consul for the provinces of Kristiansand and Akershus, with his residence set to Kristiansand. It is worth noting that the word 'Akershus' (*Aggershouse*) had clearly been added to the text after it was first written, as it appears in-between the lines, but since it is written in the same hand as used elsewhere in the letter, and the ink has the same shade, it seems likely that it is an immediate addition, and not something which was done later. It also explains why Mitchell was sometimes referred to as the consul at Christiania.[26] Another two appointments were made before 1807. Upon the death of John Wallace in 1797, Alexander Grieg was appointed the new consul at Bergen, and Charles Fenwick, as we have seen, succeeded his father at Elsinore in 1802. No changes were made to the commissioning letters, and both were granted consular authority for the whole of Norway and Denmark respectively.[27] On paper, therefore, the consular arrangement for Norway per 1793 seemed to be one of two consuls with territorially limited authority and responsibility, and one whose remit in theory was the whole country, but whose primary responsibility was also a certain region.

In practice, however, the distinction between diplomats and consuls was not always as clear as these many differences between the two services would suggest. One thing was the inconsistent use of terminology. When Robert Fitzgerald went home on leave in 1799—while officially still the

British envoy to Denmark-Norway—his temporary replacement, Anthony Merry, was appointed as chargé d'affaires *and* Consul General, and this was by means an isolated example.[28] More importantly, though, the actual work diplomats and consuls were expected to do often overlapped. Diplomats could be required to carry out typical consular tasks—such as Hailes who was expected to assist British tradesmen—and consuls could be involved in work, which was strictly speaking a part of diplomacy. Mitchell's direct contact with Bernstorff on matters relating to the *principled* and *legal* aspects of privateering and neutrality certainly stretched the traditional role of the consul.[29] To an extent, this tendency towards overlapping tasks had a pragmatic explanation. Consuls and diplomats were rarely in the same place, and 'when there was no diplomatist on the spot', D. B. Horn has argued, 'the secretaries of state had no hesitation about employing the consuls for exactly the same kind of work'.[30] This was not unique for the British services and, as Jan Melissen has argued, 'the consular function has always been enmeshed with diplomacy'.[31] In the case of the British consuls in Denmark-Norway, however, it can be held that they adopted an unusually independent role relative to the diplomatic service, and this was particularly the case with John Mitchell in Kristiansand.

As we saw in Chap. 2, Mitchell often corresponded directly with Lord Grenville at the Foreign Office, not going via the British envoy at Copenhagen, but what is more is that all the British consuls in Denmark-Norway conducted a correspondence with the Admiralty which bypassed the more regular diplomatic channel and the Foreign Office altogether. Much of this correspondence was concerned with details of French privateers on the Norwegian coast and the number and names of British vessels brought into the ports there and, in this sense, the consuls made up an almost separate service in the British defence of trade, a topic we will address further in Chap. 4.[32] Mitchell, in particular, also corresponded directly with the Commander-in-Chief of the North Sea Fleet Admiral Adam Duncan and, more generally speaking, demonstrated an eagerness in service which went well beyond that of most consuls. This made him a great asset to the British government at times, but also meant that he sometimes overstepped the line of his authority. Central to Mitchell's work as a consul was the system of intelligence gathering which he organised on the southern coast of Norway.

System of Intelligence gathering

John Mitchell was a Scotsman from Edinburgh, whose nearly ten years' tenure in office by the outbreak of war in 1793 meant that he knew his station well. Moreover, the fact that he had worked both in Kristiansand and in Christiania, travelling back and forth between the two towns, no doubt added to his knowledge of the southern coast of Norway. He also mastered the native language, if not quite to the standard he might have wished for himself.[33] What Mitchell lacked, on the other hand, was experience in working as a consul at a time of war, but he approached that task with great energy and with clear ideas as to what his responsibilities were. An early example of this came in January 1794, when Mitchell reported on a specific mission he had set out to complete in the autumn of the preceding year:

> Since September last I have been employed for the Benefit of His Majesty's Service in examining every Port, Harbour, & Creek on this Coast from the Frontiers of Sweden, to the Confines of Bergen in all 21 Sea Ports, and an immense number of Harbours & Creeks. In these Ports, Harbours, and Creeks, are at this moment upwards of 200 Sail of so called neutral Vessels, loaded with Corn, Ammunition, Stores &c. from the Baltick, Copenhagen, & Gottenburgh, bound to France.[34]

Mitchell would later confirm that what he meant by the 'Frontiers of Sweden' was the city of Gothenburg, and that he had, in fact, 'visited every Port and Creek' from there to Bergen himself.[35] This tour of the coast had revealed that, while the 'Publick Papers' these vessels carried stated that they were 'all cleared out for Spain, Portugal, & Italy', information Mitchell had obtained from 'unquestionable authority (although private)' said otherwise. Not only were these ships 'bound to French Ports', but 'the greatest Part of their Cargoes is actually the Property of the French Government, having been purchased, and paid by their Commissaire Residing at Copenhagen'. At the moment, Mitchell wrote, these vessels were 'put into Norway' due to adverse weather, but that 'as soon as wind & weather will permit they will proceed on their Voyage'.[36] Although it was not fully clear from Mitchell's reports if the 'Publick Papers' in question had been issued by the Danish authorities—which would have constituted a breach of neutrality on their part—the whole case was seen as serious enough that no lesser a figure than Henry Dundas, the Home Secretary and Prime Minister William Pitt's right-hand man, moved in to deal with it. In a letter to the Admiralty, he stated that since 'a great number of Ships laden with Corn or Naval and Military Stores may speedily be expected to sail from the Ports of Denmark and Norway, with colourable Papers but really destined for the Ports of France', the Lords Commissioners were to 'instruct the Commanders of any of His Majesty's Squadrons or Vessels who may be likely to meet with such Vessels to be particularly vigilant in order to bring in and detain all such Ships'.[37] Mitchell's tour had clearly provided the British government with very valuable intelligence, yet in terms of Mitchell's consulship, it was the opening passage of the first letter which was the more telling. He had been 'employed for the Benefit of His Majesty's Service' he stated, but there is no evidence to suggest that he was ever instructed by either the British government or the envoy in Copenhagen to conduct this investigation. Rather, it seems to have been his own initiative, which in turn was based on what Mitchell himself *perceived to be* his appropriate role as a consul. This approach to consulship on Mitchell's part would become even clearer with the intelligence system he devised along the southern-Norwegian coast.

An early indication of Mitchell's plans came in one of his first letters to Lord Grenville, the one he sent on 23 March 1793. Here, Mitchell stated that upon hearing about the outbreak of war between Britain and France, he had requested information on French privateers from 'my Acquaintances at the Outposts'.[38] This was the beginning of what would soon become an elaborate system of informants and supporters, pitted along the coast from Stavanger to the border of Sweden, and involving all the 21 'seaports', as well as a number of outports, creeks and bays within what Mitchell denoted as the 'British Consulate Office Christiansand'. Mitchell's own reasoning behind this initiative was outlined in detail in an account of his system which he presented to the British government in April 1804. In the wake of the French privateering onslaught in the spring of 1793—when 'British vessels were daily taken, and brought up' in Norwegian ports, only to be 'condemned by the French consular tribunals and put up for sale' without a proper investigation into the legality of the capture—Mitchell explained, his 'first step' had been to protest against these sales, and otherwise to try to prevent the public auctions of prize vessels and cargoes from going ahead. These actions had been 'highly approved by the [British] King's ministers at the court of Denmark', Mitchell claimed, and he was of the decided opinion that he had been encouraged to continue in a similar vein:

> I considered the approbation of His Majesty's mission at Copenhagen, of what I had done, as not only an authorization but as imposing upon me a duty to persist and do all that existing circumstances put in my power to provide for the safety of the trade and property of His Majesty's subjects during the war.[39]

The question was how this was to be done, and it was at this point that Mitchell could draw upon his detailed knowledge of the port towns on his station, the structure of local government there and the disposition of the inhabitants relative to French privateers. Mitchell had already observed the joint interest the 'neutral merchants' and 'municipal magistrats [*sic*]' had in allowing the sale of prize goods and vessels. Although the local officials received a set salary from the Danish government, he explained, 'their appointments are so scanty that they are in some degree dependent upon the mercantile class of the community' and, therefore, the 'official emoluments' they derive from 'the condemnation and sale of captured property' came in as a valued supplement. Consequently, Mitchell stated, 'here exists a chain of connivance which from the tide-waiter up to the provinceal [*sic*] Governor is strengthened by mutual interests and is not easily contra-acted'. There were, however, people in the ports towns of Norway whose interests lay elsewhere, namely the many pilots who were stationed there, and the navy officers they answered to:

> In Norway, at every sea port and creek a certain number of branch and extra pilots, with a senior or as he is called in this country an Elderman at their head, are placed under the inspection of a naval officer of rank ... such a naval officer resides in every province and draws his appointments from a certain proportion of the pilotage paid by the vessels that come in and go out of the several ports and creeks of his Department.

Since privateering reduced the number of British merchant vessels coming into Norwegian ports—partly because of the British convoy policy, and partly because the presence of French privateers acted as a deterrent for individual British merchantmen—the amount of work for pilots, and therefore their income, fell markedly from its peacetime level.[40] As this also affected the income of the navy officers in question, there was 'little mutual attachment between them and the merchants and civil magistrats [*sic*]'. It was 'amongst these men' that Mitchell had,

> found in every province many who wished the neutrality of their country to be maintained upon principles of honor [*sic*] and justice and who were therefore well disposed to afford me every assistance which, consistent with their respective situations, was in their power to oppose the illegal operations of the enemies privateers as well as to defeat the connivances and clandestine practices of other avaricious speculators.

This conflict of interest among the Norwegians themselves provided Mitchell with an opportunity to enlist men for British service and, 'Warranted by the approbation of His Majesty's ministers in pursuance of what I considered my duty to the service', he had proceeded to recruit some of the 'most respectable Eldermen, superintendent branch pilots officers and others' to provide intelligence on French privateering activity. Mitchell organised these informants in a system of correspondence where the 'ordinary pilots' would provide intelligence on what they observed on the coast; the 'Elderman or superintendent of the Pilots' would report on the vessels going in and out of his district, and on 'their force and destination'; while the navy officers, who 'has the King's authority to visit every ship, man of war, or others that come within the reach of his boats', could use this power to 'embarrass and detain privateers' when possible. Finally, the 'brokers, Customhouse and other civil officers, where they can be trusted know the nature of the mercantile transactions carried on under their inspections', and could therefore determine whether, for example, French property was being shipped under neutral colours. The intelligence thus provided would then be passed on, either directly to Mitchell's office in Kristiansand, to his 'agents in their respective districts' or in some cases even to Royal Navy ships on the coast.[41] For this latter purpose, Mitchell had employed 'a faithfull [*sic*] intelligent Englishman who speaks the Norway language', Adam Walker, and hired a boat he could use to 'convey information' to the British warships.[42] The system was then organised into 'districts' of varying size, starting with the 'District of Laurwick' which covered the Oslofjord region, and included the ports of Frederichshall (present-day Halden) on the border to Sweden, via Frederickstadt (Fredrikstad), Moss, Droback (Drøbak), Christiania (Oslo), Dram (Drammen), Holmstrand (Holmestrand), Tonsberg (Tønsberg) and Laurwick (Larvik). The 'District of Longsund' followed, comprising the ports of Longsund (Langesund), Porsgrund, Skeen (Skien) and Kraggeröe (Kragerø), while the 'District of East risoer (Risør)' did not really include any actual ports, but was crucial because the coast of this district was ideally suited to privateering activity. Distant from the government officials at Christiania and Kristiansand, and without 'military works' or garrison, but with a thirty-five mile continuous 'chain of creeks wherein all discriptions [*sic*] of vessels may anchor in safety', it was the 'daily resort of the enemies Cruisers'. The 'District of Arandal' included the 'well known' roadsteads of Oxfiord (probably Oksefjorden by Tvedestrand), Tromöe (Tromøy), Mardoe (probably Merdø, the outport of Arendal), Grimstadt (Grimstad) and Brekkestedt (Brekkestø), as well as 'fifty others of less note'. Mitchell claimed that 'On the sea coast of this district are upwards of 400 branch and extra pilots regularly appointed and daily on the outlooks'. Mitchell's own station 'Christiansand and District' included the outport of Fleckkeroe Island (Flekkerøy), the 'principal pilot-station on the coast of Norway', and Kristiansand itself was crucial as the 'capital and seat of the provincial Government', as well as the 'residence of the British, French, Dutch and Prussian Consuls'. It was at Kristiansand that 'the Dutch and French Tribunals' carried out their condemnation of prize vessels and cargoes brought in by their privateers. On the southern tip of the coast was the 'District of the Naze' which comprised the ports of Helligsund (probably Ny Hellesund), Mandal, the Clove (possibly Klovholmen), Swinoe (Svinør), old and new Salo (possibly Austre Seli and Vestre Seli), Corshaven (Korshamn) 'and an infinite number of creeks'. Importantly for the Naze (Lindesnes) was its function as a point of rendezvous for ships bound for the Baltic, and—Mitchell claimed—'There is no point of sea coast in Europe nor in the world where so much British property is daily exposed as there'. Finally, as the last port of call, came the 'Bay of Fahrsund', a place which had presented Mitchell with some challenges of its own. Since the 'people who reside here neither respect Magistrats [*sic*], Government nor laws', Mitchell complained, Farsund could 'hardly be said to belong to any district'. As the 'haunt and safe resort of all sorts of illicit dealers, privateers smugglers and others of worse discriptions [*sic*] still', it had not proved possible to recruit anyone for British service 'from this nest of thieves' and, as a consequence, Mitchell had to employ the Elderman at Mandal to send a boat to 'Egvoy' (Eikvåg), the outport of Farsund, two times a week to 'see what is going on there'.[43] In addition to his own area of direct responsibility, Mitchell also tried to organise a system of intelligence gathering for the south-western and western coasts up to the town of Trondheim, but in this he was only partially successful. For the south-western coast, Mitchell instructed the 'acting' vice consul at Stavanger, Gabriel Schanche Kielland, to be in charge of a stretch of the coast covering a distance of 200 miles from 'Liesterland' (Lista) to Bergen. This included the port of Flekkefjord, and the 'creeks of Hitteroe (Hidra, formerly Hitterø), Sogendahl (probably the outport of Sogndalstrand), Eggersund (Egersund), Sirevaag (Sirevåg), Maldo (probably Madla by Stavanger), Skuttesness (Skudeneshavn), Karmmoesund (Karmsund) and Udifier 'the westernmost Island' (Utsira), as well as the port of Stavanger itself. Kielland appears to have carried out this task in a satisfying manner.[44] For the western coast from Bergen to Trondheim, however, Mitchell had approached 'the Messrs Griegs of Bergen', but as they had 'declined to enter into what they call political correspondence or to give any information beyond the limits of their trade' to British officials, he had instead directed Kielland to 'extend the chain of correspondence through all the ports and pilot stations from Stavanger by Bergen and Drontheim [Trondheim] as far as the stattenland' (Stadt/Stadlandet). It is not clear why Mitchell approached the Grieg family on this matter, rather than consul Wallace at Bergen, nor is it clear if the chain of informants on the coast from Bergen to Trondheim was ever as well established as it was for his own and Kielland's stations. At least, Mitchell never provided any similar kind of detailed account for this. But where the southern coasts were important for the British Baltic Sea trade, the western coast of Norway filled a similar role as the point of rendezvous for the 'homeward bound ships from Archangel', as well as for the 'Greenland and Hudson bay ships', Mitchell claimed. With French privateers sending prizes into Bergen, it was important to keep an eye on this part of the coast too; thus, ideally, a similar chain of informants should have been established there.[45] The location of the many ports and outports covered by Mitchell's arrangement can be seen in Fig. 3.1, 'Mitchell's System'.[46]

In 1797, Mitchell left his station in Norway for Hamburg, and appointed the long-standing vice consul at Kristiansand, Christian Höyer, as acting British consul. About the same time, the defeat of the Dutch Fleet at Camperdown on 11 October 1797 had a favourable effect on the situation in Norway, as seen from the British side. It 'not only diminished the number and force of the enemies in these seas', Mitchell wrote, but also 'lessened the consequences and influence of their agents and adherents in Norway', rendering it easier for the 'British Consul to procure the necessary information'. For that reason, Höyer was left to administer a

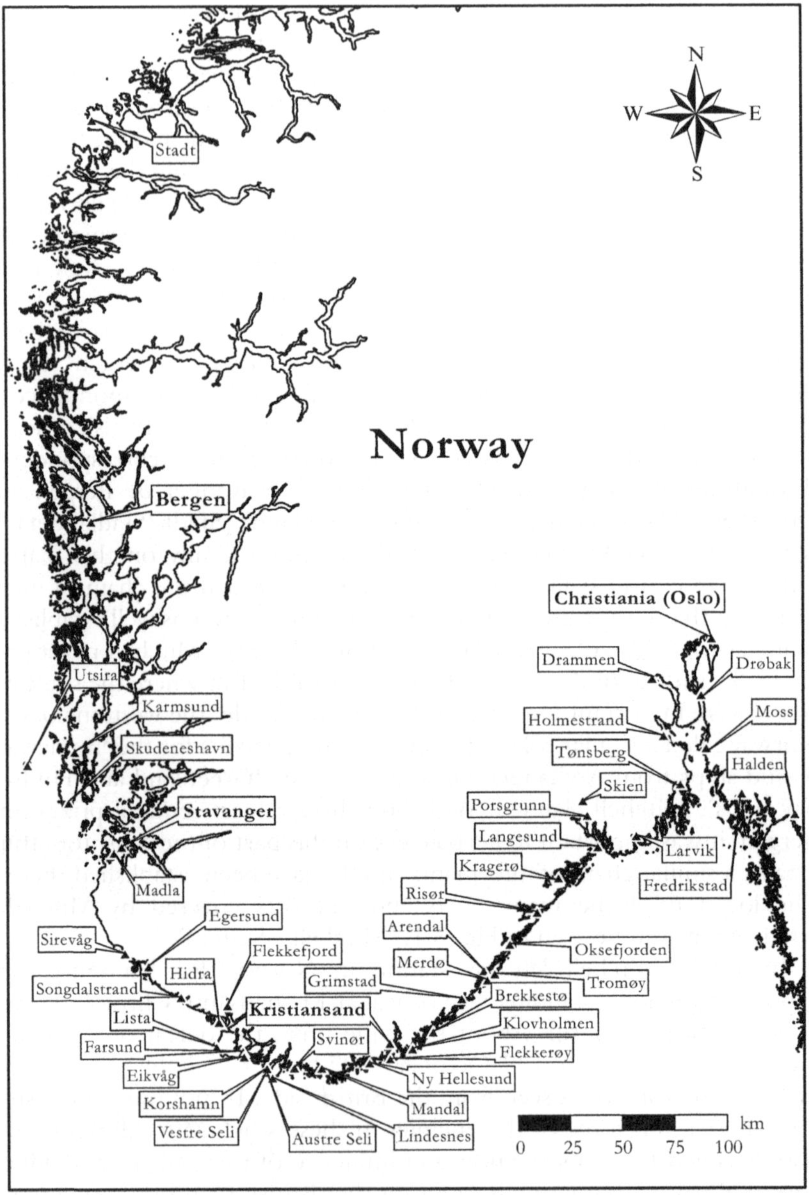

Fig. 3.1 Mitchell's System

somewhat scaled-down version of the system Mitchell had built up in 1793, until the whole arrangement was wound down in the year 1800, following the official closure of the ports to privateers.[47] This decision on the part of Mitchell appears a bit odd. For one thing, it is not clear exactly what he meant by 'enemies in these seas'. Was that a reference to warships only, or did he mean to say that the pressure from French and Dutch *privateers* had also lessened in the wake of Camperdown?

A statement he had made in a letter to Grenville in April 1800 seemed to point in that direction, but without being conclusive. Here Mitchell stated that: 'Since the Enemies Squadron were entirely driven out of the North Sea and only Privateers now and then on the Coast of Norway', he had left his 'Consular Service' in the hands of Höyer.[48] If Mitchell meant that there were fewer privateers, that does not seem to agree with the more general impression of intense privateering activity over the course of 1797–1798, which he also reported on. And even if the number of privateers went down for a time after Camperdown, it would appear somewhat premature to build down the system he had so carefully constructed on the basis of what might turn out to be a short-lived development only. After all, privateering activity had fluctuated considerably before 1797 too. Whatever assessments Mitchell made about the actual situation, however, his decision to scale down may have been prompted as much by his move to Hamburg as by any actual developments in privateering and, as we will see later, his reasons for going to Hamburg were not related to privateering.

Apart from the sheer energy and industry on Mitchell's part, which the organising of this elaborate system of intelligence procurement must have required, the success he had in recruiting so many men from different walks of life arguably speaks to his social skills. Presumably, it would take a personable character to persuade so many different people to work in the interest of Great Britain, and one would expect the British government to have appreciated the effort Mitchell had put in. There were, however, a couple of snags. One thing was the hiring of Norwegian nationals and even navy officers for British service. To what extent was this compatible with neutrality? While it was not uncommon for natives to be appointed as vice consul—Kielland and Höyer were just two examples of the kind—it was arguably a different matter to enlist military personnel.[49] As the prominent Kristiansand businessmen Ole Clausen Mørch and Johannes Nyrop stated when they testified to Mitchell's accounts in December 1796:

> The ordinary pilot cannot in all cases be told by His commander that the information required is for the use of the English Consul: such a disclosure might compromise the Commodore and be detrimental to the service.[50]

There are no indications, however, that the Danish government ever objected to this, if they even knew about it, and Norwegians were, in any case, hired by the belligerent powers for a variety of tasks. Not only did the French and Dutch (after 1795) consuls in Norway hire pilots and informants to assist them and their privateers in an analogous way to what Mitchell did, but they also appointed Norwegian merchants as commissioners to carry out the sale of prize goods and vessels. There were Norwegians working for either side in the conflict all the time.[51] Another and more serious problem for Mitchell was the issue of expenses. The hiring of so many people for British service, as well as the organising of the system in a general sense, obviously came at a cost. As he admitted himself in an understated kind of way: 'To carry this service into effect it was indispensibly [*sic*] necessary to allow a pecuniary encouragement' to those men he enlisted for service.[52] Indeed, his reason for submitting the detailed accounts of the system he had organised—about which little information emerges from the running correspondence of the 1790s—was his claim for a reimbursement of the 'money disbursed by me here on His Majesty's service as Consul in Norway'. This amounted to the sums of £1600 for Mitchell's station for the four years he was in charge, 1793 to 1796 inclusive; £1000 for the four years Höyer was in charge, 1797 to 1800 inclusive; and £430 for Kielland's station for the entire period, or a total of £3030.[53] Reclaiming this outlay was not, however, a straightforward matter, and points to the next issue we will address in this chapter—the financing of consular activities.

The Problem of Consular Fees

None of the British consuls in Denmark-Norway received a government salary, yet some of the tasks they were meant to perform paid no consulage, nor was it clear how the expenses could be covered in any other way. Part of the problem was that finances or funding, as we have seen, was not an issue which was addressed in the royal commissions to the consuls in Denmark-Norway, but at the same time, they were expected to carry out a range of more or less well-defined tasks,[54] the variety of which arguably made the consul a 'maid of all work'.[55] This was characteristic of the consular institution elsewhere also, and gathering information was one of these many traditional consular tasks. Although such collecting of intelligence was typically linked to the ongoing commerce in the port where the consul was stationed, it is possible to see Mitchell's intelligence system as a natural extension of this (peacetime) consular function at a time of war. As we have seen, Mitchell believed that the encouragement he had been given in 1793 had authorised him to go ahead with his plan, and he stressed this point further by enclosing a letter from James Craufurd with his accounts. In this letter dated 24 October 1795, Craufurd had, among other things, written that: 'I return you many thanks for the regular intelligence which you have been so good as to send me of what pases [*sic*] in your quarter, and I beg you will continue doing so'. Mitchell had added his own 'Remark' at the end of the letter, stating that on 16 January 1795, Lord Grenville had asked him to 'continue and maintain a regular communication of whatever occurred on any part of the Coast', and that the letter from Craufurd demonstrated 'that His Lordship's orders were not neglected'. Moreover, Mitchell claimed to have received confirmation on the point of expenses too, and in a passage which demonstrates his thinking on the matter, he stated that:

> To see with indifference British property condemned when there was the most distant prospect of rescuing it, was to me as an individual impossible; but after I had stated the annual expense of interrupting both the capture and condemnation of such property at £400, and had received such orders to carry through every such measure as appeared to me as beneficial to the service, I considered myself not only authorized but as in duty bound to pursue the line of conduct I had at first adopted, and consequently to confirm the arrangement I had made with the out Ports and Pilot-Creeks at the aforesaid expense.[56]

That Mitchell's own conscience and sense of duty as a consul compelled him to take action was, however, one thing, whether Grenville had actually stated—unequivocally and in writing—that Mitchell's expenses would be reimbursed by the state was another. According to Mitchell himself, the agreement from 1795 had been confirmed by Foreign Secretary Lord Hawkesbury in a letter dated 2 March 1802, in which Hawkesbury was supposed to have informed Mitchell that if he 'sent in the Accounts with Vouchers Your Lordship would transmit them to the Lords Commissioners of the Treasury that they might take His Majesty's pleasure with regard to my reimbursement'.[57] Quite why it took Mitchell two years to produce these accounts is not clear, but the Foreign Office does not, at any rate, seem to have been convinced by the case he presented. In a letter Mitchell wrote to William Elliot, the Parliamentary under-secretary for Foreign Affairs four months after he had submitted his accounts, he admitted 'that I was not *specially* authorised to draw bills on His Majesty's secretary of State for the amount of my disbursements exprest [*sic*] in the accounts in question, is certainly true'. Since he was 'repeatedly enjoined to persevere in the measures' he had adopted, however, he still felt that he 'might without impropriety request a reimbursement. If I have done that in an improper manner I am heartily sorry for it.' Furthermore, he would be content 'if the assignment per £1600 could be discharged: the other two are of less importance' (by then, Mitchell had already paid Kielland and Höyer for their outlay).[58] Mitchell followed up the case with another letter to Elliot in which he tried to argue for financial compensation based on the utility of the system he had adopted:

> I ask nothing for my twenty years personal service, nor for the extraordinary expense to which the office of Consul expose me; but I am persuaded His Majesty's ministers will allow me a reimbursement for the money which I have directly laid out for the good of the public service.[59]

The officials at the Foreign Office were still, however, reluctant to grant the money. 'I have received your two letters of the 21: August', Elliot wrote in reply, but although 'Every possible search has been made … in the Correspondence of the office for the letters from you' concerning the outlay on the intelligence system in Norway, none had been found, and the search 'for the Draft of any letter from the Secretary of State authorising you to continue the measures which caused the Expence [sic]' had been 'equally fruitless'. Elliot therefore asked if Mitchell could provide copies of these letters 'as a means of assisting us in our endeavours to find the originals'.[60] A few weeks later, another letter from Elliot addressed Mitchell's utility argument. Quoting a passage from Mitchell's second letter, where Mitchell had wondered 'whether such disbursements as shall be shewn to have been of real utility to the public Service, will, when properly authenticated, be allowed?', Elliot concluded that,

> in Cases which do not press in point of Time and in which therefore the Sanction of His Majesty's Government might previously be obtained for the

> Disbursement of Public Money by any Agent resident abroad, it does not appear to be a sufficient Justification of that Agent that he shall be afterwards enabled to prove that public Benefit resulted from the expence [*sic*] incurred.[61]

Claiming that his system was of great 'public Benefit' was not, in other words, sufficient grounds for reimbursement when an official approval of the outlay had not been given in advance. Mitchell's great initiative in service had thus come up against the formal rules for expenditure, and no payment was ever made. Evidence of this only emerged at the very end of Mitchell's life when a case was being built against him by his creditors because, keeping his finances in order does not appear to have been Mitchell's strongest quality, and over time he accumulated considerable debts. In one of the reports from the creditors' meetings it transpires that Mitchell had:

> A claim on the Foreign office for sums expended in the service of Government to the extent of about £ 3030. It is proper to observe that the success of this claim is very doubtful indeed having been frequently under the consideration of Government and by no means favorably [*sic*] entertained.[62]

Mitchell died on 10 October 1823 before the proceedings had been concluded.[63]

Mitchell was not, however, the only British consul in Denmark-Norway who faced problems because of the expenditure his service inevitably led to. A partially analogous case emerged when Consul Alexander Brown in Trondheim died in 1804. The story of Brown's consulship was told by his son-in-law Richard Hand, and touched upon some of the same issues as Mitchell had faced. After 'near thirty years' of service in the Royal Navy, Hand wrote, Lieutenant Brown had been appointed 'by his Majesty Consul for Drontheim' in 1786, where 'he continued 18 years in a Cold Northern climate', expending his entire savings on the service, 'in confidence that Government would refund the money laid out in the *Necessary duties of his office*, and in his Old age reward him for his long faithful and most zealous services'. Similarly to Mitchell, Brown had not received a salary, nor had he earned any consulage of note, and just before he died, he had been preparing a petition to the British government for a reimbursement of his outlay, Richard Hand explained. This money would clearly not be of any use to Brown now, but Hand hoped that it could be given to his daughter instead.[64] Another letter from Hand, sent several months later to George Hammond, the under-secretary at the Foreign Office in charge of the Northern department, suggested that the case was making its way through the system, and that Hand's claim had support. No evidence of the eventual decision has, however, been found, and it consequently remains unclear if a payment was made.[65] Hand may not, however, have been entirely on top of his brief, since Brown had, in fact, sent a petition to Foreign Secretary, the Duke of Leeds, already in 1789, asking for financial support, and his appointment as consul had taken place in 1773 (1786 related to a different matter, concerning the return of three British subjects from Norway to Britain). Otherwise, however, Hand's account seemed to be correct. Upon his arrival in Norway, Brown wrote in his petition, he had 'found to his great Surprize and disappointment that the Merchants and Factors there, Objected to the usual Emoluments of Consulage, or any other compensation whatever'. Since the British trade on the port was considerable, this meant that Brown had to 'Expend considerable Sums of his own property, in Unavoidable necessaries; for the Advantage of the Publick [*sic*] Service', and after 16 years, it had left him impoverished. He therefore hoped that he could be awarded a salary to compensate for his ongoing expenses.[66] Unable to obtain this, however, he proceeded to send another petition in 1793, this time to Lord Grenville, outlining his predicament once again. This time he hoped that at least 'the Balance' of his 'just-Account may be paid; being only for postage of Letters, Information relating to Trade, and Rent for a Consul Office held in Drontheim', but he also appealed to Grenville, 'that Your Lordship's Clemency may be extended to Petitioner in granting a Salary to enable him to exist in the Appointment'.[67] Brown made yet another attempt three months later,[68] and this time he also received the backing of the Lord Mayor of London, Sir James Sanderson, who wrote on behalf of 'some Connections in the City', merchants whose support Brown had solicited.[69] There are also indications that Brown may have submitted an account of his expenses to Grenville in May 1796, at which point they amounted to £718, but the circumstances are not fully clear and, as Hand's letters confirmed, none of Brown's requests were met.[70] The case of Consul Brown concerned consular expenses in general. Alexander Grieg in Bergen, however, faced a more specific problem when he took over the consulship from John Wallace in 1797, and this was related to the return of British seamen who had been landed in the port by French privateers.

The Case of Alexander Grieg in Bergen

Alexander Grieg was another Scotsman in Norway. He had emigrated from Fraserburgh to Bergen sometime between 1760 and 1770 in order to work for John Wallace (also of Scottish descent) at the consul office there, and had made his fortune in town as a fish merchant. Shortly after, in 1779, he had become a subject of the Danish-Norwegian Crown, and by the time Wallace died on 22 March 1797, Grieg was a close friend of the Wallace family.[71] This put him in a particular situation, which would create problems both for him and for the consulate office in Bergen. According to Grieg himself, Wallace had 'consulted and appointed' him British vice consul in Bergen just before he died, so that Grieg might 'take care of the affairs of the Nation until His Majesty shall be graciously pleased to appoint a Consul to supply the Vacancy'. Since he was 'the only British born subject here fit for this purpose', Grieg claimed, he was prepared to take on the consulship on a permanent basis, but only if one condition was met: he would have to be paid 'a Yearly Salary'. Having observed the 'detriment' the 'private affairs' of the Wallace family had suffered because of the lack of a fixed salary, Grieg explained, he was reluctant to 'subject myself & Family to the trouble and expences [*sic*] incurred by the Consulship' without proper payment, and he asked Fitzgerald to support him in this.[72] Fitzgerald, however, simply forwarded the request to Grenville, leaving it to the foreign secretary to decide: 'As I have no sort of acquaintance with, or knowledge of Mr Grieg' he wrote, he would 'immediately make every necessary Enquiry into the Character of Mr. Grieg' so that Grenville might 'determine on the Expediency of complying with or rejecting his Request'.[73] A few weeks later, he could confirm that the 'Information which I have been able to collect on Mr. A Grieg … is sufficiently satisfactory'. He was well-placed to become the British consul in a port which was 'always in Time of War, a rendez-vous for Privateers, and a Depôt for such Prizes as they make on the British Trades', and which required 'a Person who can stand perfectly independant [*sic*] of, and indifferent to the frowns or smiles of Danish Governors and Magistrates, as well as of commercial Concerns and Gains in the Country where he acts'. Whether 'these Considerations should induce your Lordship to grant him the Salary he requires', however, Fitzgerald did not know, but there is little doubt that he viewed the post of British consul in Bergen to be a particularly important one.[74] By late June he restated his support for Grieg, claiming that 'there is no Person in Norway more capable conducting the Business with Zeal and Intelligence', but adding that Grieg was now prepared to forego his salary to the 'unfortunate' widow and children of the late Mr. Wallace 'provided, however, that his Commission as Consul, if granted, may be given gratis, and unattended with any fees'.[75] Whether this meant that is was not so critical for Grieg to receive a salary after all does not transpire from Fitzgerald's letter, but it soon became clear that London was not prepared to offer any kind of remuneration to Grieg, be that in the shape of either a fixed salary or reimbursement of actual consular expenses. By the end of July, Fitzgerald could report that Grieg was determined to give up 'his Pretensions to the office of Consul at Bergen ... unless the Fees usually paid on such Commissions are remitted, or a yearly Salary annexed to it'. Fitzgerald also felt that he bore some responsibility for this decision since he had told Grieg that 'his Proposition for a Salary could not be admitted, on account of the Precedent which it would establish'.[76] Grieg continued to argue his case, both to Fitzgerald and directly to Grenville, threatening to refuse to become the British consul in Bergen on a permanent basis unless his demands were met, but to no avail.[77] In January 1798 he finally informed Grenville that:

> as I find the functions of the Office since my appointment to be so intricate, troublesome & expensive, taking up so much of my time, injuring my health & family, that unless recompence [*sic*] is allowed me, I cannot with justice to myself and Family continue longer in Office.[78]

Formally speaking, Grieg had now tendered his resignation, yet in practice, he would continue to perform the very same consular function that had caused him so much trouble and expense, not just until his resignation was accepted in May the same year, but all the way until his death in November 1803. He would also try to be reinstated as consul, with a salary. Why?[79] The main issues at stake were those of 'British prisoners'—of whom there were many in Bergen—and Grieg's own trade. We will look at prisoners first.

Grieg explained the problem he faced to Grenville shortly after he took on the job of British vice consul. Early in April, a French privateer had come into Bergen with 60 British sailors as prisoners on board. These men had been 'delivered over to me', Grieg wrote, and he had felt obliged to find lodgings for them, 'provisions being so dear' however, he had only been able to 'effectuate this with greatest difficulty'. Part of the problem appears to have been that the French and Dutch were driving up the prices of accommodation by paying 'full double' of what Grieg felt he could pay when lodging *their* men, but Grieg also faced other difficulties relative to these British sailors he was left to care for:

> I have almost every day trouble & vexation from disputes and disturbances that happen both in their Lodgings & in the Streets, where the Officers of the Police interfers and lodge severall [*sic*] at a time in Jail, this occasions a Court of Police to be called, where I or one for me must attend & pay the expences [*sic*] attending this whole before they are discharged.

Grieg had also had to provide clothing 'out of my own pocket to some of the Prisoners who were half naked', and was faced with the task of organising the transportation of these sailors back to Britain—all of it without financial support from the British government. It was an impossible situation, he claimed, and meant that 'in no place of Norway has His Majesty's Consuls more trouble and chicanery than here'. Surely, when this was the case, Grieg could be given a reasonable 'reward' for his efforts?[80] The 60 sailors who arrived in April were, however, just the beginning of Grieg's problems. French privateers kept bringing prize vessels and their crews into Bergen, and Grieg had to deal with accommodation and food for the British sailors who were brought ashore, as well as the task of organising their return to Britain. By early September he could report to Grenville that 'since the death of the late Consul Wallace', he had 'sent home upwards of 260 British Seamen', as well as provided care for those who were sick or wounded. Moreover, he had 'paid Pilotages' for British warships which had come into Bergen, and wondered if His Lordship would 'be pleased to inform me, how I am to reimburse myself' for this and other expenses he had run up, such as postage for his correspondence with London.[81]'I presume it is upon the Navy Office' to provide such reimbursements, Grieg wrote to Evan Nepean at the Admiralty just over a month later, 'but as there lyes [*sic*] two small Bills there, drawn by my predecessor unpaid & which is refused to be paid' he was not sure if applying to the Navy Office was the right approach, and therefore sought Nepean's advice on the matter too.[82] By mid-November the number of seamen returned to Britain had reached nearly 400, and Grieg was getting increasingly desperate: 'Can there exist a greater hardship?'he wrote in a letter to Grenville, pointing out that his expenses in office now exceeded his income by 'one forth or one third'. Yet, he continued to emphasise his loyalty to Britain and his desire to serve as consul, stating that 'all I wish is to be exempted from extra expence [*sic*] to the detriment of my family'.[83] Following his resignation in early 1798, Grieg provided detailed lists of the British prisoners who had been left in his care by the French Consul in Bergen, Jean Etienne de Chezaulx, awaiting a formal agreement between Britain and France on an exchange of prisoners of war. A list of 213 men, sailors, officers and others was submitted on 27 January 1798, and another list with a further 116 was presented by 31 May the same year.[84] In the heading for the second list, Grieg had changed his own title from 'British Consul' to 'Acting British Consul', a phrase which is revealing with respect to the complications Grieg's resignation from office created. As Fitzgerald pointed out in a letter to Grenville in August the same year, Grieg's resignation was most unfortunate, partly because the 'Services of a Person' so 'warmly attached' to the 'Interests of the British Nation'—as he held Grieg to be—were 'at this time particularly requisite and of real Consequence in that Post', and partly because the current lack of an official British consul in Bergen created problems. In the absence of a consul, it 'falls to the office of the Civil Governor at that Place to provide for the Care of the Prisoners', Fitzgerald explained, adding that 'such a Person' would be 'under no controul [*sic*]', and merely concerned

> to make a profitable Job of it while the unhappy sufferers left destitute of Protection and every Necessary, would be unable to resist the Temptations held out to them of enlisting on board French Privateers and neutral Merchantmen.[85]

As it turned out, Governor Fredrik Hauch in Bergen had no desire to act as British consul and was, according to Grieg, 'very anxious' that a someone else be appointed so that he might 'be exempted from a trouble His ignorance of the Language renders him unfitt [*sic*] for'.[86] Grieg now tried a new twist, which was to propose that his brother James could take over as consul, and this appears to have been approved of by Hauch, but it did not prove a lasting solution, and the eventual result was that Grieg had to step in and continue as 'acting' British consul.[87] This meant receiving and returning British prisoners, assisting crews from British vessels that had been shipwrecked nearby Bergen with food and accommodation, as well as other consular tasks. Much of this he did, Grieg claimed, out of necessity, duty and sheer compassion. In May 1802, for example, he reported that:

> Several distressed British Seamen cast away upon this Coast are here at present waiting an opportunity to be sent home to their Country, who for want of a Consul to whom they could apply, were left destitute in the Streets, until I got notice thereof, had pity upon them and took them under my care.[88]

The appointment of a new foreign secretary, Lord Hawkesbury, in 1801 presented Grieg with the opportunity to argue his case once again, and in a long letter he explained the development from the death of Consul Wallace until 1801—by which time Grieg estimated that he had he had seen to the return of a total of 1100 British prisoners of war. Once again he proposed to become the British consul at Bergen 'with a yearly Salary', arguing for the great necessity of a consul there, and pointing out that the French consul at the same place was paid £350 a year to sustain himself and a secretary. Grieg also, however, explained the other main reason why he had stepped down as vice consul in 1798. Although the lack of financial support from the British government had made it difficult to carry out his consular tasks, Grieg wrote, 'my naturall [*sic*] regard for the Nation made me continue my Services, until the French Consul … thought proper to refuse the necessary Passports for Vessels or Goods I had any concern with'. Vessels carrying Grieg's goods were now stopped by French privateers and brought into port.[89] In fact, Grieg had first raised this issue in a letter to Grenville in April 1798, at which point he had presented the case slightly differently: having first tendered his resignation in early January, 'one unexpected circumstance has happened which intirely [*sic*] alters the whole' he wrote. The 'French and Spaniards' had begun to intercept Grieg's 'property at Sea, upon the ground that I act as British Consul' and—short of a government salary—Grieg therefore found himself with no other choice than to give up the consulship in order to retain his income from trade.[90] Although Grieg had first seemed prepared to give up the post of consul because of the lack of salary alone, this attack on his single source of income must undoubtedly have made it even more pressing to do so. The problem, of course, was that Grieg continued to act as British consul all the same, and Chezaulx was not going to let that pass. By the end of July the same year, Grieg wrote to Fitzgerald that 'I have untill [*sic*] now continued under hand to support & take care of the Prisoners of War sent in here, as well as to attend to the Interest of the Nation', but the continuation of such 'underhand' practices on his part had been 'put a Stop too [sic]' by Chezaulx who had written to the Directory in France and received 'orders not to grant a Certificate to any Vessel I am concerned with as Owner, nor any Vessel having goods onboard belonging to me'. A Directory decree had made such certificates 'absolutely necessary' for all vessels leaving Bergen, Grieg wrote, and, as a consequence, a vessel of his carrying stockfish had recently been detained by the French because of Chezaulx''obstinacy in refusing the requisite Certificate'. The fact that Grieg was a 'Danish Burgher' was of no help as long as he acted as a servant of the British Crown.[91] Grieg does not seem to have raised the issue of French certificates again until he did so in his letter to Hawkesbury in 1801, nor does it feature in his correspondence thereafter. Whether this means that it was not so much of a problem thereafter is difficult to say based on the surviving evidence, but it may have played a role in his attempt to have his brother James established as consul in 1798.[92]

Grieg's position as 'acting' British consul created other problems too. Since he had no 'Authority to Act as Consul', he complained in a letter to Hawkesbury in October 1802, 'no British Shipmaster will submit to any Orders, I in a private capacity, might exact him to comply with', and much the same could be said for the local authorities in Bergen: 'knowing I am not invested with the proper Powers', Grieg stated, they simply ignored claims he put forward, and in several recent 'cases of Shipwreck', the consequence of this had been to deprive 'Individuals of that Support they have a right to claim'. In the same letter, Grieg expressed his disappointment over yet another refusal to be appointed consul with a salary,[93] and less than a month later, a now disillusioned Grieg summed up the situation in a succinct manner in a letter to his solicitor in London:

> Notwithstanding my having declined to transact any business respecting the British Consulate here, yet I still find myself subjected to its drudgery, every one applies to me in necessity & having no authority to act Officially, I cannot give them the assistance adapted to their several cases.[94]

Giving up the consulship was, in other words, easier said than done, or at least for someone like Grieg, who found it difficult to refuse helping people who knocked on his door. Moreover, in addition to those consular tasks mentioned so far, Grieg also took care of intelligence gathering for the Royal Navy, and played a central role in one of the most complicated and controversial cases of the entire period from 1793 to 1807, that of the prize ship the *Bell & Ann*, which we will return to in Chap. 4. Although his time in 'office' brought Grieg praise from many quarters, none of it seems to have been sufficient to make the British government reimburse his expenses.[95] No new consul was appointed upon Grieg's death on 13 November 1803, but it is possible that his son John later became acting consul.[96] At least he and his uncle James wrote a letter to Hawkesbury in April 1804 stressing 'the necessity of an English Consul being appointed here', taking the liberty 'to recommend ourselves to Your Lordship's notice'.[97] The case of Grieg thus bears some similarity to that of Mitchell and his system of intelligence gathering. Great initiative and 'agency' in carrying out important consular tasks at a time of war was not enough to make the Foreign Office open the purse. Or was it? A report written by James Craufurd, the former British chargés d'affaires in Copenhagen, in December 1798 revealed that Grenville had concerns about the British consular service in the Northern countries, and that he was prepared to look into several aspects of this, including the financial.[98] Moreover, as far as the return of British seamen is concerned, indications are that Mitchell *was* able to obtain reimbursements for his expenses in the Kristiansand district. We will look at Mitchell first, before addressing the content of Craufurd's report.

Mitchell and the Return of Seamen

It was only to be expected, perhaps, that the return of British seamen brought in by privateers would be as much of an issue for Mitchell in Kristiansand as it was for Grieg in Bergen. Yet, as was the case for his intelligence system, this was not an issue Mitchell raised very often in his running correspondence with the Foreign Office. Instead, evidence of it only emerged later when he tried to have his outlay reimbursed.[99] In 1804, for example, Mitchell produced a detailed account of the expenses he had run up when providing for the 'subsistence and passage' of '58 Distressed British Seamen ... who had been Captured by the Enemy or otherwise landed in Norway' over the short period of January and February 1799. His outlay involved the actual 'subsistence' of these sailors while under his care, thus food and shelter; extra provisions for those men who had 'landed in Norway almost naked, the French Sailors having pillaged them of their Clothes Linen & Shoes'; 'Boathire' to transport some of the men from Arendal and Flekkefjord to Kristiansand; and finally the 'Passage, with Provisions on the Passage' from Norway to London; all-in-all amounting to a grand total of £348.12. Calculations for each 'post' showed how the figures had been arrived at, and in a set of 'Observations' added at the end by officers at the Navy Office, it was stated that the 'accounts are very particular in their form', in that they provided great detail, and were supported by the testimony of the 'first respectable Merchants & Ship Owners' in Kristiansand.[100] In other words, it was all very properly done, and this was important. There is evidence to suggest that Mitchell sent numerous such accounts relating to the return of seamen, but as I have not been able to trace them, it is unclear how many British sailors Mitchell saw to the return of, and at what cost.[101] The issue re-emerged, however, in 1822 when Mitchell's creditors were building their case against him. By now, Mitchell's total claims on the Navy Board was calculated to be £19 000, but again it was not made clear if all of this related to the return of seamen during the period under investigation here. It was stated at one point that Mitchell's 'disbursements ... for the relief of distressed Seamen in the year 1807' had amounted to £1210.8, but no aggregate figure was presented.[102] What was made clear, however, was that Mitchell had kept close and accurate accounts of all prize ships brought into the ports in his 'district', making notes of all sorts of details such as the cargoes they carried, the point of capture, original destination and the crews landed in port. This thoroughness on Mitchell's part meant that he had been able to authenticate all his claims, and this seems to have been decisive. As the agent of the creditors reported from one of his many meetings with the Board of Commissioners of the Navy (the Navy Board),'the Board are most sincerely desirous to pay the amount of Mr. Mitchell's claims if *reasonable* ground can be shewn for their doing so'.[103] The critical point was in other words if accurate and verifiable accounts could be presented. In August 1823, after more than a year of negotiations with the commissioners, the agent could finally report that he had reached 'a compromise under which the Navy Board agreed to pay £11 000 in full of all demands in respect of these accounts under deduction of £3708.9. paid to Mitchell in imprest many years ago leaving £7291.11. to be received by him'.[104] The case now appears to have been resolved, and two important points arguably emerge from the passage cited here. First that Mitchell had already received some sort of reimbursement for at least a part of his expenses and, second, that the Navy Board acknowledged the rightfulness of his remaining claims, and was prepared to pay the creditors.[105] Although this evidence is no doubt patchy and not fully conclusive, indications are that there existed a system of sorts for the reimbursement of expenses relating to the return of seamen, and that a consul's outlay could be covered as long as accurate and verifiable accounts were presented. Returning seamen was but one of many consular tasks that needed funding, however, and Craufurd's report from 1798 addressed the wider picture of the British consular service and its financing.

Reforming the Consular Service?

As Craufurd stated in the opening passage of his report, he had been 'commanded' by Grenville to investigate and write a report on five individual points relating to the consuls in 'Denmark and Sweden'. They were:

> 1. The situation and character of the persons at present acting as His Majesty's Consuls or Vice Consuls in the posts of those Countries. 2. The nature of the emolument which they are supposed to derive either from Salaries or Fees of Consulage. 3. The places where it may be proper to have Vice Consuls resident in future. 4. The allowances which it may be necessary to make to them supporting them not to be engaged in trade on their own account. 5. The assistance which could be derived from the execution of this plan from the present Consular Fees or emoluments.

There were, in other words, two main issues at stake: *where* it would be useful to have a consular representation (and thereby also how *many* consuls and vice consuls that were needed), and how these consulates were to be sustained *financially*. Whether this investigation was spurred on by the case of Alexander Grieg does not transpire from the document itself, but point 4 certainly suggests that it may have played a role. Craufurd, however, addressed all the five points systematically, and on the first issue he stated that Consul Fenwick at Elsinore was 'the only one in all Denmark. His situation and character are I believe sufficiently known to your Lordship', while the 'only surviving' consul in Norway was Mitchell,'a Man of very good character, active and intelligent and in very decent circumstances'. Similarly, there was just one consul in Sweden, 'Mr. Erskine', at Gothenburg 'whom I do not know personally but who is I understand a Man of ability good character and easy fortune'. The comment on the 'known' character of Fenwick may have been a reference to the complaints Fitzgerald had put forward the previous year, while the reference to Mitchell's 'decent circumstances' suggests that Mitchell was not suffering from the same kind of financial troubles as were Grieg and Brown—the fact that he was accumulating debts due to his intelligence system on the southern coast of Norway notwithstanding. The state of affairs with respect to point 2 can be summarised quite quickly: there were no salaries 'annexed to the Consulships in the North' with the exception of Lower Saxony, and the 'prescriptive right which exists in the South of Europe of requiring fees of Consulage does not exist in the North'. Craufurd found this to be 'remarkable', but could not say why it was so. The income of the northern consuls was therefore 'very inconsiderable', and arose

> principally from Commissions charged to Shipmasters on different business done for them on repair of their Ships, on the purchase of articles of which they may stand in need, on certificate on bonded Goods of which however very few are landed in Denmark.

In fact, the meagre possibilities of 'deriving any advantage from the appointment' as consul at Copenhagen had led a 'respectable English Merchant of that city' to decline the offer Craufurd had made him of putting forward his name for the post. By contrast, Nicholas Fenwick at Elsinore enjoyed a grant from 'the Russian Company', but this was 'merely personal' having been issued because Fenwick's wife was 'the daughter of a very respectable member of the Russia Company', and would therefore 'probably not be continued to future Consuls'. The consul at Elsinore, however, enjoyed the possibility of earning an income from the commission he would charge for 'clearing' British vessels going through the Sound, that is, to administer the payment of the Sound duties, but since 'nothing obliges a British Shipmaster or Merchant to have his vessels cleared by the Consul and there is now a great number of Mercantile houses at Elsineur amongst whom this business is divided', this kind of income was 'various & fluctuating in its nature'. Craufurd's findings thus seemed to confirm the complaints put forward by Grieg, Brown and Mitchell. Consulship in the North was none too lucrative, and the current situation was, generally speaking, not satisfactory. Craufurd therefore proceeded to outline a comprehensive plan for the whole of the Baltic Sea region and Norway.

With respect to point 3, the allocation of consuls and vice consuls, Craufurd's recommendation was for a continuation of the current system in Norway, as 'I do not believe that a more convenient arrangement could be adopted, then that which at present exists; for instance a Vice Consul at Dronthein [*sic*] one at Bergen one at Christiansand', while a considerable expansion was needed in Denmark. In addition to the consul at Elsinore, Craufurd proposed the appointment of vice consuls at Tonningen

(Tønning) and Flensberg (Flensburg) in Schleswig-Holstein; Aalborg; the island of Bornholm; as well as in Copenhagen. The latter was 'wanted notwithstanding its proximity to Elsineur'. Craufurd's presentation of the arrangement in Norway was, however, a little opaque: did 'for instance' mean that consuls in these three port towns was already an established arrangement, or was this what he thought would be sufficient for the future? If he meant the former, one could argue that he did not give a fully accurate description of the current situation, as he made no mention of the vice consul at Stavanger (Schancke), Grieg as 'acting' consul at Bergen or, indeed, the particular arrangement which had been adopted for Kristiansand/Christiania with a consul and vice consul, alternating between the two towns. Furthermore, Craufurd's use of the terms consul and vice consul was arguably inconsistent or unclear. The consul at Elsinore was now referred to as the 'Consul General for Denmark & Sweden', and in his proposal for Sweden, he suggested the appointment of 'Consuls or Vice Consuls' at Gothenburg, Karlskrona, Stockholm and Abo. For the Russian part of the Baltic Sea he proposed the appointment of four vice consuls to 'be under the direction of the Consul residing at Petersburg', which he also denoted as the 'Consul General in Russia'. These inconsistencies aside, however, it may seem as if what Craufurd envisaged was a system of three consuls general—one for Denmark-Norway and Sweden at Elsinore, one for Russia at St Petersburg and one for Prussia at Memel (currently Klaipėda in Lithuania)—with all the others denoted as vice consuls. In total, there would be 25 vice consuls in the Baltic Sea region and Norway if Craufurd's plan were to be implemented. This was arguably quite a high number of appointments, but Craufurd thought it was justified on the grounds of the dangerous seas in the area. 'In pointing out the places where it may be necessary [to] have Consuls or Vice Consuls resident in future', he wrote, 'I shall not always be guided by the importance of the British trade carried on with those places but in many instances by a consideration of the frequent Shipwrecks which happen on the Danish Swedish and Norwegian Coasts'. In 'the interest of humanity' it was necessary to have 'Agents' at hand who could assist in such cases of shipwrecks. How was this to be paid for? Craufurd argued that the arrangement could not be sustained unless the vice consuls were given 'sufficient Salaries to render them independent of trade', and set up what he thought was the minimum amount to be paid annually for each vice consulship. This varied from £200 for most of the stations including all three in Norway, to £400 for Stockholm and £500 for Copenhagen. All together, the annual outlay would amount to £5700. Craufurd was 'aware' that Grenville 'might perhaps not deem it expedient to add the additional charge of salaries to the Consuls to the expences [*sic*] of your department', and knew that there was no chance of covering these expenses from the 'present Consular emoluments' in the North. For that reason, he proposed the introduction of a 'certain Fee on all Ships passing the Sound or touching at the Ports where they reside', which 'would be exactly what is practised in the South'. If a fee of 'four pence per Ton' was levied on all 'British Shipping annually cleared out for the Baltic and Ports of Norway', it would amount to £8333, and cover the costs of both the vice consuls and consul general at Elsinore and 'certainly be no hardship on the Trade'. Alternatively, the vice consuls could be allowed to do trade to support themselves, but Craufurd thought a salary was a better option as it 'would of course tend to render them more attentive to the duties of their situation'. Whichever solution was adopted, Craufurd was of the decided opinion that all the 'appointments ought to be made'.[106]

It is not clear if any of Craufurd's recommendations on appointments and finance were actually implemented before diplomatic relations between Britain and Denmark-Norway were suspended in 1807, but it seems most likely that nothing much was done until a uniform system of salaries and pensions was introduced through the Consular Act of 1825.[107] No new appointment as consul in Bergen or Trondheim appears to have been made for the remainder of the period when Denmark-Norway was neutral and, as we know, neither Mitchell nor Grieg was ever awarded a salary as consul. The consuls in Denmark-Norway remained underfunded, the importance of the work they did notwithstanding. While the consuls seem to have carried out their varied tasks mostly to the satisfaction of their superiors in London, however, there were also some problems. We have already seen how Nicholas Fenwick became an embarrassment in his later years, but greater difficulties were caused by John Mitchell's many activities and meant that, from time to time, he pushed the limits of his consular authority.

Was Mitchell Reliable?

It began with a Christmas party in Christiania in 1792. Mitchell was known to socialise with wealthy Norwegian merchants and other senior members of society there, and together with a number of notable figures—magistrates, officers and merchants—he had attended a party at a central location in town. Present at the party was also a junior member of the influential Anker-family-one of the wealthiest timber-merchants in Christiania—Jess Anker. Jess was known as a hothead with a reputation for initiating fights, and particularly so when he had had a few drinks. At the Christiania party, alcohol was in free flow, and none of Jess' family members was there to stagger him. Trouble began at the point when a series of toasts were proposed, and Mitchell proceeded to present his toast in favour of 'Liberty, Freedom and Unanimity'. He also handed out a couple of handbills, the exact content of which has never been ascertained. Jess Anker reacted negatively to this, arguing that it was 'impertinent' of an 'Englishman' to propose such toasts in Norway, and in the company of men 'who loved their King and Constitution'. This did not deter Mitchell and his companions at the party, however, who continued to propose toasts in favour of the French General Dumouriez, of the progress of French arms in the war and of the National Convention in France. Enraged by this, Jess Anker attacked Mitchell, man-handling him so badly that he had still 'not been seen' by the time one of the participants at the party, the governor of the Akershus region Fredrik Julius Kaas, reported on the event in early January 1793. There were even rumours that Mitchell would challenge Jess Anker to a duel, but nothing came of that, and the two of them appear to have been reconciled.[108]

News of this episode also reached Hailes in Copenhagen, who had been informed by Bernstorff at one of their weekly meetings in February 1793 of a 'serious complaint against Mr. Mitchell the British Consul at Christiania in Norway'. By now, the story had developed to the point where Mitchell had supposedly 'established a Jacobin Club for the propagation of democratical [*sic*] principles in Norway', and 'having gained over some persons to his new doctrine', Hailes wrote, 'he openly awaits to the success of the French Revolution'. Moreover, the Christmas party in Christiania had become 'one of his Meetings', and the scuffle with Jess Anker had ensued because the 'violence' of Mitchell's 'language' had given 'so much offence to a Mr. Anker a friend of the established Government, that after some altercation the disputants came to blows, and occasioned a scene of great Scandal'. Bernstorff had then demonstrated that he was well acquainted with the state of affairs in Britain at the time when he proceeded to point out to Hailes that 'as we did not tolerate such principles and conduct at home, there was every reason to hope that we should give every discouragement to them abroad'. This was fair enough, but Hailes nevertheless felt that Bernstorff had little reason to seize the moral high ground, as long as the Danish diplomatic representative 'M de Blome is still in Paris', and 'M de Framery a sort of French Charge d'Affaires sees Count Bernstorff in private occasionally'. He did, however, find reason to believe that the story could be true, as it was consistent with Mitchell's 'character', as he had come to know it. Bernstorff had also asked Hailes to report the incident in his dispatches to the Foreign Office, but instead Hailes had chosen to send a private letter to a friend in London since, 'out of delicacy to Mr. Mitchell I prefer the transmitting it to you in this less official manner, entreating you however to lay it before Lord Grenville'.[109] This seems to have been the end of the matter. There are no indications that Hailes ever raised the issue again, or that Grenville or anyone else in the government apparatus acted on the basis of the information they had obtained, and Mitchell—always one to defend his actions—never referred to the incident himself. In some way, this is a bit odd, not the least because Bernstorff's observations were so perceptive. The year 1792 was marked by increasing alarm about the influence of French revolutionary ideology in Britain, and the British government had already issued two Royal Proclamations against seditious writings by the time the Christiania party went ahead. The following year saw a clamp down on political radicalism, where several leading radicals were brought before the law courts on charges of sedition and, in some cases, were convicted and sentenced to severe punishments.[110] Proposing toasts in favour of the French Revolution and handing out handbills with French revolutionary ideas—if that was what Mitchell had actually done at the party in Christiania—were in other words unlikely to have earned him any friends in high places. So why was there no reaction? There is, of course, the possibility that the information contained in Hailes' letter never actually reached Grenville, but more likely, perhaps, that it was dismissed as based on rumours referring to a singular event of no particular consequence—nothing more than a drunken brawl. Mitchell was, in any case, not in Britain, and if he had indeed proposed a few toasts at a private party in Norway, that would have no effect at home. Nevertheless, some concern about Mitchell and his reliability seems to have lingered thereafter, at least on the part of Hailes. When Bernstorff insisted in June 1793 that the Danish government had no intentions of permitting the sale of the captured British vessel the *Hope* of Lyme Regis, as Mitchell had reported, Hailes found that the 'language of the Danish Minister is so directly opposite to what Mr Mitchell his Majesty's Consul at Christiania writes to me, that I confess it embarrasses me extremely'.[111] The next month, he wrote to Grenville about intelligence he had received from Mitchell that 'lest his information should not be good, I have desired the Chevalier de Souza, the Portuguese Minister who is just gone to make a Tour in Norway, to procure for me what lights he can upon these matters'.[112] Two weeks later, Hailes could report that de Souza had been able to confirm most, if not all, of the intelligence provided by Mitchell, suggesting that the information Mitchell had procured was largely sound.[113] Moreover, if the Christmas bash in Christiania had left a poor first impression, Mitchell's subsequent work as consul proved, of course, beyond any doubt that he was loyal to the British government, and concerned to promote British interests as best he could. In fact, the concerns which arose with respect to Mitchell thereafter were linked precisely to his eagerness in service, rather than to any suspicion of pro-French views on his part (as Craufurd's comments to Mitchell's exchange with Governor Levetzow in the *Christiansand Weekly Gazette* in the autumn of 1795 demonstrated so adamantly).[114] This was to become a more serious problem during Mitchell's time in Hamburg from 1797 onwards.

Mitchell's decision to move to Hamburg is clouded in a degree of mystery. At the time he moved, he only explained somewhat cryptically to Grenville that 'Domestic Concerns having obliged me to leave Norway for a few weeks', he had left Christian Höyer, his long-standing vice consul, 'in charge of my office as far as Relates to the Consulship'.[115] A few days later, Robert Fitzgerald confirmed that Mitchell had left Norway, stating that he 'is at Hamburg on private business'.[116] Exactly what this 'business' entailed was not clarified by Fitzgerald, either then or later, and although Mitchell came to remain in Hamburg, not just a few weeks, but several years, he never explained it himself either. Once in Hamburg, however, Mitchell began to operate as if he was a government representative there, sending a series of reports on current affairs, and establishing contact with Prince Charles of Hesse, the father-in-law of Crown Prince Frederick, the Danish Regent. This turn of events has led some scholars to assume that Mitchell was appointed British consul at Hamburg, but there is no evidence to suggest that this was the case.[117] No royal commission was ever issued for this purpose and, in a letter to Lord Hawkesbury from 1801, Mitchell confirmed that his 'acquaintance upon the Continent is merely Personal'. He had no 'Pretention' of 'Consular official Consequence' there, he explained. Moreover, he stressed that his reasons for sending 'Notes' with intelligence to Hawkesbury was merely the 'good of his Majesty's Service', adding that 'although they are Perhaps of little importance I trust they can do no harm'.[118] Clearly, Mitchell did not claim to hold any kind of official post in Hamburg, but why did he feel this need to excuse the provision of what was probably useful information to the Foreign Office? The reason was that, by now, his dealings with Charles of Hesse had earned him reproach from London.

What Mitchell had done was to set about negotiating with this senior member of the Danish Royal family in a way that made it seem as if he was acting *on behalf* of the British government. The opportunity had presented itself in the autumn of 1798, when it had become clear that Prince Charles sought 'Anxiously to have the leading influence in the Copenhagen Cabinet', Mitchell argued.[119] This ambition was coupled with a strong dislike on the part of Hesse of what he held to be Christian Bernstorff's sympathies with the French republicans, and presented Mitchell—who claimed to 'have Known' Hesse 'Personally these many years'—with a chance to work for a British-Danish collaboration. Hesse had 'sent to me one of His Confidential Gentlemen', Mitchell wrote in a letter to Grenville,

> who, in an indirect manner, proposed, that I should State to the Kings Ministers, that Prince Charles and the Prince Royal were so disgusted with the insulting Tyranny of the French Republicans ... that if they could depend upon the firm support of His Britannick Majesty, Denmark would instantaneously brake [*sic*] off all intercourse with France, and enter into a Close Connection with Great Britain.

Although Mitchell's personal acquaintance with Hesse convinced him that the proposal was genuine, he nevertheless felt the need to have it ascertained, and particularly to make sure that it was supported by the 'Prince Royal', Crown Prince Frederick. For that purpose he instructed his own agent, one 'Marquis de Pellport', to investigate, and 'endeavour by every decent means to bring the Prince to Speak as plain as possible upon the Principles of His Son in Law'.[120] Pellport was furnished with a set of instructions which underlined how central Prince Charles—in the view of Mitchell—now was to the government of Denmark. It was he 'who now guides in all essential matters the politics of His Royal Highness', Mitchell claimed, and Pellport was therefore to 'Consider the Prince Charles as the Person who leads the Danish Government; and Regulate your Conversation with him accordingly'.[121] Pellport met with Hesse, and submitted his report on 22 November, concluding that a three-hour-long conversation had confirmed that 'the attitudes of Prince Charles are such that the alliance with England is a dominant passion within him'.[122] The following day, Mitchell penned a letter to Grenville which was styled as 'A Proposition made by Prince Charles of Hess father in Law to the Prince Royal of Denmark, for Connecting Denmark with Great Britain against the present Government of France; the Prince Royal being privy to this Overture'. The document did not state explicitly that Denmark-Norway should join the war on the side of Britain, but the gist of the argument presented pointed in that direction. In one central passage it was, for example, held that the 'Prince Royal of Denmark … is fully determined, to contribute with all the Efforts his Country can make towards the Reestablishment of Europe's Independency'. It was Republican France Europe was in need of being freed from, and the two princes—who 'pride themselves of both being descended of English Blood'—saw a 'Connection between Great Britain & Denmark' as one important step to achieve that goal.[123] Had Mitchell, through his contact with Charles of Hesse, secured the preliminaries to a Danish entry into the war on the side of Britain? London was not convinced. In fact, the government did not take kindly to either Mitchell's initiative, or the scheme he had devised, and issued a stern rebuke, the bluntness of which makes it worth quoting at length:

> Sir, I am directed by Lord Grenville to acknowledge that receipt of your letters of the 24 – 27 – & 30th of November, and 4th of December, relative to a correspondence into which you have entered With the Prince Charles of Hesse, on the subject of establishing a closer connection between this Country & Denmark; Lord Grenville has no doubt that your intentions on this occasion have been such as you represent them, but as it is highly improper that negotiations of this nature should be commenced and carried on by persons unauthorised & holding Subordinate Situations in his Majesty's Service, His Lordship desires that you will by no means continue that correspondence, and that you will for the future confine yourself more strictly within the limits of the employment which you hold in his Majesty's Service.[124]

Mitchell had clearly overstepped his mark, and nothing further was heard of the proposal for a British-Danish 'connection'. Of course, as long as Mitchell had no official appointment at Hamburg, or had been sent on a special mission to conduct negotiations on behalf of the British government, his activities could hardly be seen as a natural part of his consular responsibilities, and he seems to have realised this himself. As he admitted in a letter to Grenville, written well before he received the official reprimand: 'I have assumed no diplomatique [*sic*] Character, nor official authority from your Lordship' and, instead, it was 'my attachment for the good of His Majesty's Service, which ever forms the Criterion of my Conduct'.[125] As with the intelligence system he had built up on the southern coast of Norway, Mitchell had pursued his role as consul based on what he thought would be of use for the government and the war effort, and his personal acquaintance with Charles of Hesse had simply provided him with an opportunity too good to be missed. Furthermore, while Mitchell never seems to have entered into unauthorised negotiations of this kind again, the reprimand did not deter him from carrying out further investigations and operations on his own initiative. In the summer of 1801, for example, he had investigated the 'Projects & Preparations of Bonaparte' in Holland and Flanders and, based on the intelligence he had procured from this, he collated a document entitled 'Plan or Project of Bonaparte to invade England'. This he then proceeded to dispatch to London with one of his own couriers, justifying his actions with a familiar argument: 'I have no Orders, nor have I any other Motive', he stated in a letter to Evan Nepean at the Admiralty, 'but merely the Advancement of His Majesty's Service in General'.[126] It is not clear how the Admiralty responded to this initiative. Once in Hamburg, however, Mitchell also worked to promote his own career, and in ways which appear to have raised a few eyebrows.

Shortly after he had established himself in Hamburg, Mitchell wrote to Grenville on the occasion of the recent death of Consul Wallace in Bergen, stating that 'if your Lordship will be pleased to appoint me Consul in Norway, I shall be as attentive to the Service as possible'.[127] One month later, Fitzgerald could confirm Mitchell's 'application', giving him his support in a letter to Grenville:

> Mr. Mitchell, My Lord, is desirous of obtaining the Appointment of Consul General for Norway, and if his wishes should meet with your Lordship's approbation, I can speak with Confidence in favor [*sic*] of his local Knowledge, Zeal, and activity, and so far recommend him to your Lordship's notice and good offices.[128]

But Mitchell was not, of course, appointed to the consulship in Bergen, and instead Alexander Grieg was offered the post. Whether there was any connection between this outcome and Grieg's later claim that 'a Colleague in [the] Office of Mr. Mitchell' had 'misrepresented' him to Admiral

Duncan, the Commander-in-Chief of the North Sea Fleet, 'as a Man much in the French Interest' cannot be said for certain, but at least Mitchell seems to have changed his mind with respect to further employment in Norway, for a while at any rate.[129] When the British consul for Lower Saxony (who resided at Hamburg), 'Mr. Hunbury', died on 10 November 1798, Mitchell applied for the position, stating that 'Norway is not a Country wherein a Person would wish to live and die, if they had a free choice'. One could be excused for suspecting that hard feelings on Mitchell's part played a part in this, though, in the end, he did not give up his post in Kristiansand.[130] All-in-all, Mitchell's activities in Hamburg led James Craufurd in Copenhagen—the man who had praised Mitchell in his report on the consular arrangements in Denmark-Norway and Sweden—to wonder what he was really up to. In a private letter to George Hammond, the under-secretary at the Foreign Office, he stated in a revealing passage that: 'May I ask also what Mitchell the Consul at Christiansand is employed about here. I have long known that he is about something, but not exactly what. He is I believe a man of some intrigue'.[131] In April 1799, Mitchell was instructed by London to 'proceed without Delay to Your Station at Christiansand' in order to provide intelligence to the new British representative in Copenhagen, Anthony Merry, but it is not clear if he actually did so, and *if* he did, he certainly returned to Denmark and the Duchies later.[132] By January 1800 he was in Copenhagen,[133] and as late as by the end of July 1807—shortly before the Battle of Copenhagen brought Denmark-Norway into the war on the side of Napoleon—he was reporting from Schleswig, while Höyer continued as his 'acting Consul in Norway'.[134] Mitchell thus proceeded to operate as consul *in absentia* and, a man of intrigue or not, it can at least be held that he approached consulship in an unorthodox manner.

Conclusion

The overall experience of the British consuls in Denmark-Norway during the period 1793–1807 is one that seems to support D. C. M. Platt's view of a service that was still in the making. No clear provisions or instructions had yet been worked out with respect to how consuls in neutral countries were meant to operate at a time Britain was at war. Their consular tasks and responsibilities remained less than well-defined, and the question of finance was—as we have seen—unresolved in many respects. The British government seems to have realised that the situation was unsatisfactory, and that these problems needed to be addressed, but although James Craufurd was commissioned to come up with a plan for the improvement of the consular arrangements in the North of Europe, few, if any, of his proposals appear to have been implemented by 1807. Moreover, Craufurd had not been asked to look at those issues which related specifically to a wartime situation—such as the return of British seamen set ashore in a neutral port—and his plan was devised accordingly; it concerned the ordinary peacetime activities of consuls relating to British trade first and foremost. No mention was made of privateering. Admittedly, a more regular salary—such as that proposed by Craufurd—would have been of great use for consuls at a time of war also, but what about the system of intelligence gathering which Mitchell had built up? Was this to be seen as a natural part of a consul's responsibilities at a time of war, or not? On this, Craufurd was silent.

These problems notwithstanding, in practice, the consuls no doubt carried out crucial wartime work, and it can be argued that they were vital not only for the operation of Britain's diplomatic service but also for the Royal Navy in the Northern waters, as we will see in the next chapter. This state of affairs was not unique for the British consuls. The French and Dutch consuls seem to have performed similar tasks to the British in support of the war effort of their countries. As Mitchell stated in February 1794, 'A French Consul is lately formally appointed; and Acknowledged at this Port to care for the Rights & Privileges of his Privateering CountryMen on this Coast'. A few months later he could confirm that the system was in operation: 'Prizes must inevitably be made by these French [privateers] especially as they have their Agents at Elsinore and every other Port in Denmark & Norway who gives them the minutes information'.[135] None of this was, of course, part of the peacetime responsibilities of French consuls.[136] In the next chapter, we will look further into the role played by the British consuls with respect to privateering in practice.

Notes

1. D. B. Horn, *The British Diplomatic Service 1689–1789* (Clarendon Press, Oxford, 1961), pp. 5–6.
2. Horn, *Diplomatic Service*, pp. 16, 29–30, 42–45. Ambassadors would normally be appointed to countries which had an ambassador in Britain only. *Ibid.*, p. 72.

3. S. T. Bindoff, *British Diplomatic Representatives (1789–1852)* (The Royal Historical Society, London, 1934; reprint by: Facsimile Publisher, Delhi, 2017). Representatives to Denmark are covered on pp. 40–43 [quote p. 42].
4. See Chap. 2, p. **nn**.
5. Mitchell had, for example, appointed his own vice consuls at the towns of Farsund, Arendal, Risør and Mandal. See: National Archives [NA], FO 22/50, Foreign Office Correspondence, Denmark, fos. 12–17, John Mitchell to Robert Ward Esq., British Consulate Office Christiansand, 10 February 1806. See also: Sverre Steen, *Kristiansands Historie 1641–1814* (Grøndahl, Oslo, 1941), pp. 386–387.
6. D. C. M. Platt, *The Cinderella Service: British Consuls since 1825* (Longman, London, 1971), p. 10.
7. Horn, *Diplomatic Service*, p. 234.
8. NA, FO 211/4, Foreign Office and predecessor, Embassy, Consulate and Legation, Denmark: General Correspondence; or the same letter FO 22/16, fos. 3–7, 'George R—Instructions for Our Trusty and Wellbeloved Daniel Hailes Esq. whom We have appointed Our Envoy Extraordinary to the Court of Our Good Brother The King of Denmark. Given at Our Court at St. James's the Twentieth Day of January 1792 in the Thirty Second Year of Our Reign'.
9. Platt, *Cinderella Service*, p. 7. On the concept of 'consul', see: Halvard Leira and Iver B. Neumann, 'The Many Past Lives of the Consul', in Jan Melissen and Ana Mar Fernández (eds.), *Consular Affairs and Diplomacy* (Martinus Nijhoff Publishers, Boston, 2011), pp. 231–232.
10. Platt, *Cinderella Service*, p. 1.
11. This piece of information transpires from Norwegian primary sources consulted by Bård Frydenlund for his work on one of the leading members of the influential Anker-family in Christiania, Peder Anker. It is not mentioned in any of Mitchell's own correspondence, or in other sources on the British side. See: Bård Frydenlund, *Stormannen Peder Anker: En biografi* (Aschehoug, Oslo, 2009), p. 81.
12. As far as British consuls were concerned, all those who were appointed for service in the North African so-called Barbary states received regular salaries from 1754 onwards. See: Horn, *Diplomatic Service*, p. 246.
13. *Ibid.*, pp. 50–51, 243–247; Platt, *Cinderella Service*, 10–14. See also: Violet Barbour, 'Consular Service in the Reign of Charles II', in *The American Historical Review*, Vol. 33, No. 3 (1928), pp. 553–578.
14. NA, FO 22/28, Foreign Office Correspondence, Denmark, fos. 13–15, Robt Steph Fitzgerald to Lord Grenville, Copenhagen 13 May 1797 [quote fo. 15].

15. NA, FO, 22/29, fos. 46–47, Robt Steph Fitzgerald to Lord Grenville, Copenhagen 9 September 1797 [quote fo. 46].
16. The official appointment of Charles Fenwick by a king's letter did not take place until five years later, in 1802, and he was referred to as 'Deputy Consul' before that. See, for example: NA, FO 22/34, fos. 459–460. 'Extract of a Letter from Chs. Fenwick Esq His Majesty's Deputy Consul at Elsineur to Lord Robert Fitz-Gerald His Majesty's Envoy Extraordinary at the Court of Denmark, dated Elseneur 23d May 1799'. For the appointment: NA, FO 90/11, Foreign Office: King's Letter books. Denmark, pp. 31–34, 'Georgius Tertius', 26 March 1802, [signed by 'Hawkesbury', the Foreign Secretary at the time]; and H. S. K. Kent, 'The Background to Anglo-Norwegian Relations', in *The Norseman* 11 (1953), p. 152.
17. See: Ulrik Langen, *Revolutionens skygger: Franske emigranter og andre folk i København 1789–1814* (Lindhardt og Ringhof, Copenhagen, 2005), pp. 43–45, 187–198, 216–219, 272–274, 304–305, 362.
18. Bindoff, *Diplomatic Representatives*, pp. 41, 148.
19. It is the view of D. C. M. Platt that the British consular 'service' did not really begin to resemble a service proper until the Canning reforms of 1825. See: Platt, *Cinderella Service*, Preface and Introduction.
20. Horn, *Diplomatic Service*, pp. 239–241.
21. NA, FO 22/31, fos. 69–70, Alex Grieg to Geo Hammond Esq., Bergen 9 June 1798 [quote fo. 70v].
22. NA, FO 90/10, Foreign Office: King's Letter Books. Denmark, pp. 11–13, 'Georgius Tertius etc.', St James' Palace, 20 February 1761 [signed by 'Holdernesse', the Secretary of the Northern Department at the time]; and FO 90/10, pp. 14–16, 'Georgius Tertius etc.', St James' Palace, 20 February 1761 [signed by Holdernesse]. These are the earliest royal commissions of this sort which I have been able to trace, but that does not preclude, of course, the possibility that similar type letters could have been issued earlier. For the development of consular representation in Norway before the eighteenth century, see: Halvard Leira and Iver Neumann, 'Consular Representation in an Emerging State: The Case of Norway', *The Hague Journal of Diplomacy*, 3 (2008), pp. 1–19.
23. FO 90/10, pp. 11–13 [quotes translated from Latin].
24. *Ibid.*, pp. 14–16.
25. *Ibid.*, pp. 142–144, 'Georgius Tertius', 10 May 1773 [signed by 'Suffolk', the Secretary of the Northern Department at the time]; and *ibid.*, pp. 159–161, 'Georgius Tertius', 17 July 1775 [signed by Suffolk].
26. *Ibid.*, pp. 196–197, 'Georgius Tertius', 9 July 1784 [signed by 'Carmarthen', meaning the Duke of Leeds, who was the Foreign Secretary at the time]. Christiania (present-day Oslo) was the main town in the

province of Akershus, though the name Akershus could also refer to the fortress of Christiania itself.

27. *Ibid.*, 261–263, 'Georgius Tertius', 20 June 1797 [signed by Grenville, the Foreign Secretary]; and FO 90/11, pp. 31–34, 'Georgius Tertius', 26 March 1802 [signed by Hawkesbury, the Foreign Secretary].
28. Bindoff, *Diplomatic Representatives*, 41; and Horn, *Diplomatic Service*, pp. 241–242.
29. See Chap. 2, pp. 28–37.
30. Horn, *Diplomatic Service*, p. 253.
31. Jan Melissen, 'The Consular Dimension of Diplomacy', in Jan Melissen, and Ana Mar Fernández (eds.) *Consular Affairs and Diplomacy* (Martinus Nijhoff Publishers, Leiden, 2011), p. 2.
32. This correspondence is contained in the 'Letters from British Consuls'-series of the Admiralty papers held by the National Archives, see: NA, ADM 1/3841–3845.
33. Mitchell admitted as much in a letter from 1790, concerning his own business interests. National Archives of Norway, RA/EA-4025/G/L0088b/0010, John Mitchell to Justits-Raad Hagerup, [place illegible], 19 April 1790.
34. NA, FO 22/18, fos. 17–18, John Mitchell to Lord Grenville, Christiansand 31 January 1794 [quote, fo. 17v].
35. *Ibid.*, fos. 34–35, John Mitchell to Lord Grenville, Christiansand 15 February 1794 [quote, fo. 34].
36. *Ibid.*, fos. 17–18, John Mitchell to Lord Grenville, Christiansand 31 January 1794 [quote, fos. 17–17v].
37. *Ibid.*, fo. 99, Henry Dundas to the Lords Commissioners of the Admiralty, Whitehall, 8 March 1794.
38. NA, FO 22/16, fos. 68–69, John Mitchell to Lord Grenville, Christiania 23 March 1793 [quote, fo. 68].
39. NA, FO 22/44, fos. 222–245, '*Norway*, British Consulate Office Christiansand. Accounts of Sundry disbursement on His Majesty's service amounting to the sum of £ 1600' [quotes, fos. 222, 225–225v].
40. By an edict of 5 March 1725, all ships entering or leaving a port in Norway had to employ a pilot. See: H. S. K. Kent, *War and Trade in Northern Seas: Anglo-Scandinavian economic relations in the mid-eighteenth century*, pp. 14–15, footnote 4.
41. NA, FO 22/44, fos. 226–228v.
42. *Ibid.*, fos. 234v.
43. *Ibid.*, fos. 229v–235. Later, however, it appears that Mitchell had been able to recruit a local merchant, Jochum Brink Lund, as his agent at Farsund. See: NA, FO 22/50, fos. 12–17.

44. NA, FO 22/44, fos. 274–275, 'Norway, Department of the British Vice-Consulship of Stavanger', signed by 'John Mitchell Consul'.
45. *Ibid.*, fos. 317–318, John Mitchell to Lord Hawkesbury, Hamburgh, 1 May 1804 [quote fo. 317v].
46. All the towns included on the map are denoted by their modern Norwegian names.
47. *Ibid.*, fos. 252–253, 'Norway, British Consulate Office Christiansand', signed: 'John Mitchell Consul' [quote fos. 252v–253]. Höyer's accounts are covered in: *ibid.*, fos. 254–259. The arrangements supervised by Kielland at Stavanger were also wound down in 1800, see: *ibid.*, fos. 276–277, 'G M Kielland, British Vice Consul by Permission of His Danish Majesty, Extraordinaire Disbursements on His Britannic Majesty's Service', Stavanger 31 December 1800.
48. NA, FO 22/36, fos. 271–274, John Mitchell to Lord Grenville, Copenhagen 29 April 1800 [quote fo. 274].
49. The general rule was that consuls in British service were British, while vice consuls were natives. See: Horn, *Diplomatic Service*, p. 248.
50. NA, FO 22/44, fo. 244v, 'Given under our hands at Christiansand this thirty first day of December 1796. Ole Clausen Mørch, Johannes Nyrop'. All the accounts Mitchell submitted were signed by witnesses.
51. On the French and Dutch hiring of pilots, see: *ibid.*, fo. 234. We will return to the issue of Norwegian commissioners for the French and Dutch in Chap. 4, pp. 173–176.
52. *Ibid.*, fo. 228v.
53. *Ibid.*, fo. 220, John Mitchell to Lord Hawkesbury, British Consulate Office, Christiansand, 5 April 1804.
54. Leos Müller and Jari Ojala have divided these consular tasks into three main categories: 'General assistance to citizens of the country they represented', 'notary functions' and the promotion of 'commercial exchange', which included 'gathering information' on issues such as ships coming to, and leaving the port. See Müller and Ojala, 'Consular Services of the Nordic Countries during the Eighteenth and Nineteenth Centuries: Did They Really Work?', in Gordon Boyce and Richard Gorski (eds.), *Resources and Infrastructures in the Maritime Economy, 1500–2000* (Liverpool University Press, Liverpool, 2002), p. 29.
55. Platt, *Cinderella Service*, p. 2.
56. NA, FO 22/44, fos. 248–249, James Craufurd to Mr. Consul Mitchell, Copenhagen 24 October 1795 [with comment by Mitchell; quotes fos. 249–249v].
57. *Ibid.*, fos. 279–280, John Mitchell to Lord Hawkesbury, British Consulate Office Christiansand, 5 April 1804 [quote fo. 280].
58. NA, FO 22/45, fos. 122–123, John Mitchell to William Elliot, Hamburgh, 21 August 1804 [quote fo. 122v; original emphasis].

59. *Ibid.*, fos. 124–125, John Mitchell to William Elliot, Hamburgh, 21 August 1804 [quote fo. 125].
60. *Ibid.*, fos. 171–172, 'Draft to Mr. Mitchell', and 'Mr. Eliot to Mr. Mitchell', Downing Street, 18 September 1804.
61. *Ibid.*, fos. 191–192, 'Draft to Mr. Mitchell', Downing Street, 1 October 1804 [quote fo. 191v; it transpires from the content of the letter that it was written by Elliot].
62. National Records of Scotland [NRS], CS 96/4726, Court of Session Records, 'John Mitchell in Edinburgh, formerly Hamburg, Creditors' minute book, 1821–1824', pp. 3–4.
63. See: Stuart E. Fleming (ed.), *Edinburgh monumental inscriptions (Pre 1855). Vol. 2, Canongate Churchyard Holyrood Chapel Royal*, compiled by John F. Mitchell, C.I.E. (The Scottish Genealogy Society, Edinburgh, 2003), p. 6.
64. NA, FO 22/45, fos. 284–286, Rich Hand to Earl of Camden, 12 upper Belgrave place, Pimlico, 3 December 1804 [quote fo. 284; original emphasis; the source states 'Pimlico', although 12 Upper Belgrave Place is in Belgravia].
65. NA, FO 22/46, fos. 181–182, Rich Hand to Geo Hammond Esq, No. 12 upper Belgrave place Pimlico 10 April 1805.
66. NA, FO 22/11, fos. 398–399, 'To His Grace the Duke of Leeds. The Petition of Alexander Brown British Consul', 1 October 1789 [quote fo. 398].
67. NA, FO 97/117, Foreign Office and predecessors: Political and Other Departments: Supplements to General Correspondence before 1906. Denmark, fo. 45, 'To the Right Honorable Lord Grenville. The humble Petition of Alexander Brown, British Consul', London 1 May 1793.
68. NA, FO 95/1/4, Foreign Office and predecessors: Political and Other Departments: Miscellanea, Series 1. Supplementary Correspondence. Denmark, fos. 250–251, 'To the Right Honourable Lord Grenville. The humble Petition of Alexander Brown', London 22 July 1793.
69. NA, FO 95/1/4, fos. 248–249, Sir James Sanderson to Evan Nepean Esq., Mansion House 8 August 1793 [quote fo. 248].
70. NA, FO 97/117, fos. 383–384, Alexander Brown to Lord Grenville, Dover 30 May 1796.
71. J. Russel Greig, 'Grieg and his Scottish Ancestry', *The Music Book*, Vol VII, edited by Max Hinrichsen (1952), pp. 510–523. Grieg changed his surname from the Scottish Greig to Grieg at the time he became a Danish subject, apparently to make the Norwegians pronounce it correctly. Usage was, however, inconsistent at the time, with both forms used. See also: R P Fereday, *Saint-Faust in the North 1803–1804: Orkney and Shetland in Danger, An Abortive Raid and its Consequences* (Tempvs Reparatvm, Oxford, 1995), pp. 24–26.

72. NA, FO 22/27, fos. 205–206, Alex Grieg to Lord Rt Steph Fitzgerald, Bergen 25 March 1797 [quotes fos. 205–205v].
73. *Ibid.*, fos. 203–204, Robt Steph Fitzgerald to Lord Grenville, Copenhagen 8 April 1797 [quotes fo. 203]. See also Grieg's letter to Grenville: NA FO 97/117, fos. 434–435, Alex Grieg to Lord Grenville, Bergen 18 April 1797.
74. NA, FO 22/27, fos. 219–221, Robt Steph Fitzgerald to Lord Grenville, Copenhagen 22 April 1797 [quotes, fo. 220].
75. NA, FO 22/28, fos. 114–115, Robt Steph Fitzgerald to Lord Grenville, Copenhagen 27 June 1797 [quotes fo 114].
76. *Ibid.*, fos. 179–180, Robt Steph Fitzgerald to Lord Grenville, Copenhagen 29 July 1797 [quotes 179–179v].
77. See for example: *ibid.*, fos. 231–232, Alex Grieg to 'the Right Honbl', Bergen 19 August 1797; and NA, 22/29, fos. 176–177. Alex Grieg to Lord Grenville, Bergen 18 November 1797.
78. NA, FO 22/30, fos. 55–56, Alex Grieg to Lord Grenville, Bergen 27 January 1798 [quote fo. 56].
79. On the acceptance of Grieg's resignation, see: NA, FO 22/29, fos. 69–70, Alex Grieg to Geo Hammond, Esq., Bergen 9 June 1798. On the time of death, see: J. Russell Greig, *Grieg and his Scottish Ancestry.* Grieg was, of course, appointed consul by a royal commission, dated 20 June 1797, but in this document, the words 'not used' have at some point been added in the margin. See: FO 90/10, p. 261.
80. NA, FO 97/117, fos. 434–435, Alex Grieg to Lord Grenville, Bergen 18 April 1797 [quotes fos. 434–434v].
81. NA, FO 22/29, fos. 54–55, Alex Grieg to Lord Grenville, Bergen 9 September 1797 [quote, fo. 54].
82. NA, ADM, 1/3843, Alex Grieg to Evan Nepean Esq., Bergen 21 October 1797. This statement may not have been fully correct as Wallace appears to have received a compensation of 'Nine Pence per Day Allowance provided by Parliament, for distressed British Seamen' by the Commissioners of the Navy the year before. Wallace had argued that this was not enough to cover his expenses, however, and had supplied accounts to support his case. It is possible that this is what Grieg referred to. See: NA, FO 97/117, fo. 374, John Wallace to Lord Grenville, Bergen 5 March 1796; *ibid.*, fos. 376–377, 'An Account of such Seamen as were Subsisted by John Wallace British Consul at Bergen…', J. Wallace 5 March 1796; and *ibid.*, fo. 378, John Wallace to 'Honbl Sirs' [Commissioners of the Navy], Bergen 5 March 1796.
83. NA, FO 22/29, fos. 176–177, Alex Grieg to Lord Grenville, Bergen 18 November 1797 [quote fo. 177].
84. See: NA, FO 22/30, fos. 57–59, 'List of British Prisoners of War liberate [*sic*] by the French National Consul Chezaulx residing here in Bergen

delivered to the Underwritten British Consul upon condition that a like number of French Prisoners and of the same Quality shall be liberate in Britain when the Cartel for the Exchange of Maritime Prisoners shall be admitted between Great Britain and France'; and NA FO 22/32, ff. 34–35. 'List of British Prisoners of War, liberate here in Bergen by the French National Consul Chezaulx residing here and delivered to me the undersigned Acting as British Consul on condition that a like Number of French Prisoners and of the same quality shall be liberate in Great Britain as soon as the Cartel for the Exchange of Maritime Prisoners shall be settled between Great Britain and France'.

85. NA, FO 22/31, fos. 197–198, Robt Steph Fitzgerald to Lord Grenville, Copenhagen 11 August 1798 [quote fo. 198v].
86. NA, FO 22/32, fo. 99, Alex Grieg to Lord Grenville, Bergen, 1 September 1798. Although referred to as 'von Hauch' by Grieg, the Governor's name was Fredrik Hauch, see: Tor Weidling, *Eneveldets menn i Norge: Sivile sentralorganer og embetsmenn 1660–1814* (Messel Forlag a/s, Oslo, 2000), p. 35.
87. See: NA, FO 22/32, fos. 216–217, James Grieg Snr to Evan Nepean Esq., Bergen 2 October 1798; NA, FO 22/41, fos. 400–401, Alex Grieg to Lord Hawkesbury, Bergen 15 November 1801; NA, ADM 1/3842, James Greig Snr. To Evan Nepean, Bergen, 2 October 1798; and NA, ADM 1/3842, Alex Grieg to Evan Nepean Esq., Bergen 6 June 1799.
88. NA, FO 22/42, fos. 136–137, Alex Grieg to Lord Hawkesbury, Bergen 1 May 1802 [quote fo. 136]. For other examples, see: NA, FO 22/33, fos. 106–107, Robt Steph FitzGerald to Lord Grenville, Copenhagen 17 November 1798; FO 22/43, fos. 33–34, Alex Grieg to Lord Hawkesbury, Bergen 29 January 1803; and *ibid.*, fos. 260–261, Alex Grieg to Lord Hawkesbury, Bergen 5 September 1803.
89. NA, FO 22/41, fos. 400–401, Alex Grieg to Lord Hawkesbury, Bergen 15 November 1801 [quote fo. 400]. French consuls in the 'northern countries' had enjoyed a fixed salary since 1755. See: Jörg Ulbert, 'A History of the French Consular Services', in Jan Melissen and Ana Mar Fernández (eds.), *Consular Affairs and Diplomacy* (Martinus Nijhoff Publishers, Leiden, 2011), p. 317.
90. NA, FO 22/30, fos. 174–175, Alex Grieg to Lord Grenville, Bergen 7 April 1798 [quote fo. 174].
91. NA, FO 22/32, fos. 58–59, Alex Grieg to Lord FitzGerald, Bergen 29 July 1798—Copy [quotes fo. 58]. The decree was publicised in Norway. See: National Library of Norway [NLN], *Christiansand Weekly Gazette*, No. 6, 9 February 1798 [*Christiansand Weekly Gazette* was John Mitchell's translation of the original: *Kristiansands Adresse Kontors Efterretninger*].
92. Presumably, it was not an issue while the Peace of Amiens was in force from 25 March 1802 until 18 May 1803.

93. NA, FO 22/42, fos. 380–381, Alex Grieg to Lord Hawkesbury, Bergen 23 October 1802 [quote fo. 380].
94. *Ibid.*, fo. 400, Alex Grieg to Kinloch & Sons, Bergen 13 November 1802.
95. On praise, see, for example: NA, FO 22/31, fo. 71, Testimony by Charles Webb, Commander, 'Given onboard His Maj's [Majesty's] Armed Cutter the *Cobourg* at Bergen', 9 June 1798. There are indications that a smaller claim Grieg made on 120 'Rixdollers', the equivalent of £25, may have been reimbursed. See: Caird Library [CL], ADM/B/202, Admiralty, A Duncan to Evan Nepean Esq., Navy Office 29 August 1801.
96. Hinrichsen, *Grieg*.
97. NA, FO, 22/44, fo. 306, James Grieg Senior and John Grieg to Lord Hawkesbury, Bergen, 21 April 1804. There is clear evidence that no new appointment had been made by September the same year at least. See: NA, FO 22/45, fos. 167–168, Chas Adam to Rear Admiral Vashon. 'Extract of a letter from Captain Adam to Rear Admiral Vashon dated La Chiffonne Leith Roads 6th September 1804'.
98. Although Craufurd ceased to be chargés d'affaires when Fitzgerald arrived in May 1796 as the new envoy extraordinary, he continued as the British secretary of legation at Copenhagen. See: Bindoff, *British Diplomatic Representatives*, pp. 41, 66.
99. Mitchell raised the issue in one letter to Grenville from 1794, where he addressed the problem of British Seamen who 'are daily cast destitute in my hands', and the expenses he ran up because of this. NA, FO 22/20, fos. 40–42, John Mitchell to Lord Grenville, Christiania 28 June 1794 [quote, fo. 40v].
100. CL, ADM/216, 'State of the Disbursements of John Mitchell Esq. His Majesty's Consul at Christiansand in the Months of January & February 1799 for the Subsistence and Passage of British Seamen'. These accounts were enclosed with a letter to William Marsden, dated: Navy Office 10 July 1804 [three illegible signatures; one is possibly 'Palmer'].
101. Another letter to Marsden referred to a 'Statement' on the 'Subsistence of distressed British Seamen between the 12th April 1794 and 31 Decr. 1797' but, unfortunately, the statement itself appears to have gone missing: CL, ADM/223, Hamilton [and two illegible signatures] to William Marsden Esq., Navy Office 14 July 1806. See also a letter from Mitchell concerning a forthcoming 'Statement of all the Disbursements made on His Majesty's Naval Service on this coast down to the 31st December 1804'; the statement itself is not included: CL, ADM/221/160, John Mitchell to The Hon'ble Commrs of His Majesty's Navy, British Consulate office Norway, Christiansand 6 September 1805.
102. NRS, CS 96/4726, pp. 25–26.
103. *Ibid.*, p. 41 [original emphasis].

104. *Ibid.*, p. 53.
105. The term 'imprest' suggests that Mitchell may have administered a small fund of cash he could spend on his service, and that when he was running short of cash, he could request a 'replenishment' of the fund up to a certain predetermined level (called the *imprest balance* in modern accountancy terminology). In order to receive this top-up of the fund, however, he would have needed to submit accounts of the money spent. It is not clear what the imprest balance of Mitchell's fund may have been or, indeed, precisely how this system was organised at the time.
106. NA, FO 33/17, Foreign Office and predecessor: Political and Other Departments: General Correspondence before 1906, Bremen, Hamburg and Lubeck. Sir James Craufurd to John Mitchell, fos. 2–33, James Craufurd to Lord Grenville, Hamburgh, 18 December 1798. The consul at Gothernburg was Thomas Erskine, see: NA, FO, 73/7, Foreign Office and predecessor: Political and Other Departments: General Correspondence before 1906, Sweden [from 1788].
107. This also meant that consuls were no longer required to rely on fees for their income. See: Platt, *Cinderella Service*, pp. 14–15, 30–48.
108. Ludvig Daae, *Af Geheimeraad Johan v. Bülows Papirer* (Johan Dahls Forlag, Christiania, 1864), pp. 120–128, Letter from Kaas to Bülow, Christiania 5 January 1793 [translated from Danish]; and Frydenlund, *Stormannen Peder Anker*, pp. 80–81.
109. NA, FO 22/16, fos. 39–40. Daniel Hailes to Geo Aust Esq., Copenhagen 16 February 1793, marked 'Private'.
110. In a couple of highly publicised and arguably notorious cases, the High Court in Edinburgh sentenced a few leading radicals to 14 years transportation to Australia; a sentence second only to capital punishment under Scots Law. Sentences in English courts were generally far less severe. See: Atle L. Wold, *Scotland and the French Revolutionary War, 1792–1802* (Edinburgh University Press, Edinburgh, 2015), Chap. 2, 'Political Trials'. The two Royal Proclamations were issued on 21 May and 1 December, see: *ibid.*, p. 17.
111. NA, FO 22/16, fo. 187, D. Hailes to Lord Grenville, Copenhagen 29 June 1793.
112. NA, FO 22/17, fos. 27–28, Daniel Hailes to Lord Grenville, Copenhagen 13 July 1793 [quote fo. 28].
113. *Ibid.*, fos. 51–52. Daniel Hailes to Lord Grenville, No. 38, Extract sent to Admiralty, Copenhagen 27 July 1793. The information de Souza could not confirm was a plan of sending out armed fishing vessels under French colours from Norway in order to attack the British Baltic Sea trade, but this may just have been a rumour Mitchell had picked up on. Bernstorff had 'strenously' denied it. FO 22/17, fo. 28.
114. See Chap. 2, p. 44.

115. NA, FO 22/27, fos. 197–198, John Mitchell to Lord Grenville, Hamburg 4 April 1797 [quote fo. 197v].
116. *Ibid.*, fos. 203–204, Robt Steph Fitzgerald to Lord Grenville, Copenhagen 8 April 1797 [quote fo. 203].
117. See: Halvard Leira and Iver B. Neumann, 'Fremmede konsuler i Norge ca. 1660–1905' in *Historisk Tidsskrift*, 106 (Copenhagen, 2006), p. 468. One possible reason for this confusion is that the front page set up by archivists for each volume in the Foreign Office Correspondence-series, in several cases gives the impression that Mitchell was consul at Hamburg. So for example volume 41: 'Letters and Papers from Mr. Consul Mitchell at Christiansand and at Hamburgh': NA, FO 22/41, fo. 1.
118. NA, FO 22/41, fos. 309–310, John Mitchell to Lord Hawkesbury, Hamburg 30 [?] June 1801.
119. NA, FO 22/33, fos. 102–103, John Mitchell to Lord Grenville, Hamburg 16 November 1798 [quote fo. 102].
120. *Ibid.*, fos. 136–139, John Mitchell to Lord Grenville, Hamburg 24 November 1798 [quotes fos. 136–137v].
121. *Ibid.*, fos. 140–144, 'Note No. 1. My Instructions to Mr. de Pellport'. John Mitchell, Hamburg 12 November 1798 [quote fo. 140v].
122. *Ibid.*, fos. 145–151, 'Note No. 2, M de Pellports conversation with Prince Charles', Le M'is de Pelleport to M. Mitchell, Hamburg 22 November 1798 [quote fo. 152; translated from French].
123. NA, FO 22/33, fos. 122–125, John Mitchell to Lord Grenville, Hamburg 23 November 1798.
124. *Ibid.*, fos. 180–181, 'To Mr. Mitchell', Downing Street, December 1798.
125. *Ibid.*, fos. 165–169. John Mitchell to Lord Grenville, Hamburg 27 November 1798 [quote fo. 165v].
126. NA, ADM 1/3843, John Mitchell to Evan Nepean Esq., Hamburg 14 August 1801. The 'Plan or Project' was submitted with a previous letter: *ibid.*, John Mitchell to Evan Nepean Esq., Hamburg 14 July 1801.
127. NA, FO 22/27, fo. 217, John Mitchell to Lord Grenville Hamburg 18 April 1797.
128. NA, FO 22/28, fos. 13–15, Robt Steph Fitzgerald to Lord Grenville, Copenhagen 13 May 1797 [quote fo. 15].
129. NA, FO, 22/32, fos. 58–59, Alex Grieg to Lord Fitzgerald, Bergen 29 July 1798, Copy [quote fo. 58v].
130. NA, FO, 22/33, fos. 86–87, John Mitchell to George Hammond, Esq., Hamburg 13 November 1798. See also: *ibid.*, fos. 102–103, John Mitchell to Lord Grenville, Hamburg 16 November 1798 [quotes fos. 86–86v].
131. NA, FO 33/18, fos. 67–68.James Craufurd to George Hammond Esq., Hamburg 19 April 1799, Private [quotes fos. 67–67v].

132. NA, FO 22/34, fo. 342, 'to Mr. Mitchell', Downing Street, 26 April 1799.
133. NA, ADM 1/3843, John Mitchell to Evan Nepean, Copenhagen 11 January 1800. See also NA, FO 22/36, fos. 94–95, John Mitchell to George Hammond Esq., Copenhagen 11 February 1800.
134. NA, ADM 1/3845, John Mitchell to William Marsden Esq., Sleswick 27 July 1807.
135. NA, FO 22/18, fos. 34–35, John Mitchell to Lord Grenville, Christiansand 15 February 1794 [quote fo. 34v]; and FO 22/19, fos. 56–57, John Mitchell to Lord Grenville, Christiania 3 May 1794 [quote fo. 56v]. All the French 'chambers of commerce' were abolished in 1791, but consulates were reestablished under the Ministry of Foreign Affairs in 1793. Ulbert, 'French Consular Services', pp. 305–306. A French vice consulate had first been established at Kristiansand in 1756. Leira og Neumann 'Consular Representation in an Emerging State': p. 9, note 43.
136. For an account of the responsibilities of French consuls, see: Ulbert, 'French Consular Services'.

CHAPTER 4

Privateering in Practice

The diplomatic debate on privateering and neutral ports, which was carried out between the British and Danish governments in the summer of 1793—as we stated in Chap. 2—was focused on the *principled* aspect of this particular question. It concerned the rules of privateering as they could be deduced from British-Danish treatises specifically, as well as from the Law of Nations more in general. Although an uneasy agreement had been reached, whereby privateers were to be admitted into the ports of Norway on certain conditions, it remained to apply this accord in practice. Doing so presented at least two distinct challenges. One was the actual policing of the agreement. How was one to make sure that all parties adhered to the specific rules that had been set out? Mitchell's reports had, for example, indicated that the local authorities in the Norwegian port towns permitted the sale of both non-perishable goods and prize vessels, which, if it was true, was clearly in breach of the agreement. The other challenge was the application of general rules in individual cases. Laws and rules need to be interpreted or applied, and it might not always be immediately obvious who was in the right and who was in the wrong in a particular case of dispute. Over the course of 1793–1799, a series of practical issues related to privateering were up for debate, and a handful of individual cases caused difficulties and disagreements, which, in some cases, it took years to resolve. This chapter addresses both the more general issues—such as the use of false flags, sale of contraband goods to privateers, transgressions of Danish-Norwegian neutral waters and the sale of

A. L. Wold, *Privateering and Diplomacy, 1793–1807*,
https://doi.org/10.1007/978-3-030-45186-8_4

prizes in Norway—and those individual cases that attracted particular attention. Most of these cases concerned, precisely, violations of neutral waters in one way or another, and have been addressed under that heading. The British response to privateering in practice centred, however, as much as anything on its *military* strategy to counter the problem, and it is to the British war on privateering that we will turn first. In this, as in all other aspects of the British response to privateering in practice, the consuls in Denmark-Norway played a central role.

The British War on Privateering

The policy adopted by the British government to counter the threat posed to Britain's trade by enemy privateers and warships centred on the adoption of a convoy system, combined with a strategy of 'harassment' of such enemy ships by the Royal Navy. Neither was new by the 1790s, and particularly the use of convoys had a long history, going possibly as far back as the thirteenth century. It took time for this protection of trade to become a well-organised system, however, and even as late as by the end of the seventeenth century it was arguably still not working very effectively.[1] The problem became very apparent during the War of the Spanish Succession, when public demand caused by severe losses to the French in the summer of 1707 led to the introduction of the 'Convoys and Cruizers Act' of 1708. This Act provided details on how convoys were to be formed at 'cruising stations', included instructions to commanders of escort ships and addressed other practical issues related to convoying. A certain number of warships were now reserved for convoy duty, and Parliament was to receive an 'annual report on the working of the Act'.[2] In the view of one historian, the 'twin ideas of protecting the country's own trade while "annoying" that of the enemy' had now been put 'firmly in place'.[3] The escort duty of Royal Navy warships was crucial to this system, and through the revised version of the 'Articles of War' Act issued in 1749, the rules which applied for convoy duty—with concomitant penalties for negligence—were specified in detail for the first time.[4] At the outbreak of war in 1793, therefore, the Royal Navy already had long experience in the protection of seaways trade, and a ready-made convoy system it could activate. As far as the Baltic Sea trade was concerned, the consuls in Denmark-Norway had an important role to play, both with respect to the organisation of convoys and the 'harassment' of enemy privateers, while their assistance to the Archangel trade was largely 'limited' to the harassment part of the strategy. We will look at convoys first.

A worldwide British system of convoys was introduced at the outbreak of war in 1793, but it remained voluntary for merchant vessels to join a convoy.[5] If they chose to sail without protection, they were in other words free to do so. The escalation of the French war on trade in 1797, however, rendered the need for the protection of British trade more pressing, and led to the passing of the Convoy Act of 1798. Convoys were now made compulsory for most trades, and the importance of this policy is further underlined by the fact that the Act was renewed in 1803, at the end of the short-lived Peace of Amiens. It was possible to obtain a licence to sail without convoy for faster-going vessels, and some trades, such as the East India and Hudson Bay Companies' routes, were exempted from the general rule. For all other merchant ships, however, convoys were mandatory and convoy discipline was upheld by a set of severe penalties. £1000 would be forfeited by the master of any ship who 'desert or wilfully separate or depart from such Convoy without Leave obtained from the Captain or other Officer in his Majesty's Navy, entrusted with the Charge of such Convoy', and if the ship was carrying 'Naval or Military Stores', the penalty would be hiked up to £1500.[6] Convoys bound for the Baltic Sea came from various ports in Britain, and differed markedly in size. The larger ones were typically assembled at the Nore at the mouth of the Thames Estuary, reflecting the central position of London to the Baltic trade, and would sometimes count as many as a 1000 ships by the end of the Napoleonic War. From the Nore, these larger convoys sailed via Hull to the Skagerrak, and then through the Sound. The logistics involved in assembling, organising and escorting such large numbers of sailing ships were significant and, once underway, there were bound to be 'stragglers' from the convoy, ships which were either not able to keep up or which were separated from the others due to bad weather. For the French privateers on the Norwegian coast, these slower-moving vessels made up a main target alongside so-called runners—ships whose captain took the chance of sailing independently (with a licence after 1798)—and they therefore tried to monitor the movements of British convoys, large or small. Once through the Sound, however, the merchant ships were generally safe from privateers, and the convoy was disbanded.[7] The same logic applied to ships returning from the Baltic. Until they reached the Sound, they sailed independently, and convoys for the return-leg were formed at the Sound. This meant that the British consul at Elsinore sat the hub of much convoy-related activity, and while he does not seem to have had any kind of formalised role in the disbanding and assembling of convoys, he did function as a main provider of intelligence for the Admiralty, and a point of call for merchants asking for protection through convoys.

Neither Nicholas Fenwick, nor his son Charles from 1797 onwards, seem to have carried out any kind of systematic monitoring of convoys coming into, or leaving the Sound, but their reports and letters nevertheless provide good examples of the many issues which were at stake. For one thing, their correspondence with the Admiralty demonstrates how convoys came from different parts of Britain, and that they were of varying size. In a letter written on 10 September 1793, for example, Nicholas Fenwick asked the Secretary of the Admiralty, Philip Stevens, to inform 'my Lords Commissioners of the Admiralty' that a small convoy of 10 ships had arrived safely from Hull three days earlier.[8] Similarly, in August 1795, Fenwick could report that a convoy of '16 Sail' had arrived from Newcastle, while a letter from the same month two years later referred to a convoy of 40 ships 'from the Humber' and another small one of 16 'from the Nore'. A somewhat larger convoy of 73 ships arrived from 'Shields & Leith' in June 1798, while '24 Vessels under convoy from the Orkneys', as well as another 40 from the Nore, came in in May 1799.[9] Such references to incoming convoys were, however, relatively few and seemingly quite random, and the main task the consul at Elsinore performed in relation to both convoys and individual merchant ships arriving at the Sound from Britain was arguably to convey the intelligence they provided on French privateering activity. Thus in April 1796, Nicholas Fenwick could report that 'some' of the British merchantmen who had recently 'passed for the Baltic', gave accounts of 'more small Privateers, being on the Norway Coast'. In other cases, his reports referred to individual ships, such as the *Cyrus* of Sunderland whose master could inform him 'that he narrowly escaped being captured ... by 2 French Privateers, which took 2 of his consorts' as prizes.[10] Letters concerning merchant vessels sailing from the Baltic to Britain were more numerous and related to several issues. The most basic one before 1798 was the question of convoy or not. While most masters of merchant vessels appreciated the security the adoption of convoys provided for them, others seemed oblivious to the danger of sailing without convoy, chose to ignore it or were unhappy about the often significant delay convoying imposed upon their journey. In some cases, merchants who were exasperated by long waits took the risk of sailing independently, rather than continuing the wait. As Nicholas

Fenwick complained in October 1795, despite recent 'very alarming' news of French captures off the Naze, 'I still find the greatest Difficulty, in making near 40 Sail, of British Merchantmen here, waiting Convoy, sensible of the Danger, attending their passages'. Although the North Sea had 'become very precarious again', Fenwick wrote in another letter, he still experienced that 'Several British Merchantmen, are Running it Daily from Hence', while others 'are Stopping here, in hopes, of a Speedy relief by Convoy'.[11] A similar case from 1797 sheds further light on the dilemma facing the merchants: 90 merchantmen, 'despairing ... Relief of a Convoy', Fenwick wrote, 'have run it hence yesterday, notwithstanding their imminent danger ... from the daily Risk reported from Cattegat [*sic*]'.[12] James Craufurd in Copenhagen also commented on this problem, though in his case not to the Admiralty, but to the Foreign Office. Recent news held that the 'crews of the French Ships of War, upon the Coast of Norway, are so sickly, that many of those vessels have been obliged to go into Port', and for that reason, Craufurd hoped that a group of 'English Merchant Ships, which sailed without Convoy, which some of them from impatience, thought proper to do, will have arrived safe'.[13] If the wait for a convoy proved too lengthy, in other words, many masters of merchant vessels took the chance of sailing home on their own. Of course, exactly when convoy protection was available for ships that arrived at Elsinore from the Baltic Sea depended on a number of factors outside of their control. One thing was whether there were any warships available for convoy duty there and then, another the state of the weather. Moreover, there would also need to be a sufficient number of merchant vessels on site to form an actual convoy of ships. Sometimes the wait could be quite short, such as when the vessel the *Freedom* belonging to the London firm Michael Henley & Son arrived at Elsinore on 27 July 1794, and was able to join a convoy of 100 ships which left on 1 August.[14] Other times, the wait was clearly much longer, but indications are at least that the escorting warships lost little time in 'exchanging' convoys if there were sufficient ships in waiting when they reached Elsinore with an outwards-going convoy. In late July 1797, for example, a convoy of 30 ships from the Nore, escorted by the frigate *Garland* and sloop-of-war *Martin*, had arrived at Elsinore, and 'finding as many waiting Convoy here', the commander had informed these merchantmen that he would 'carry them under his Care at first fair Wind', Fenwick reported. In fact, as we have 'Ships dropping in hourly from the Baltic', Fenwick wrote in the same letter, he was pleased to learn that 'another Convoy is about leaving Hull soon'.[15] Such quick turnovers certainly helped. In many cases, the departure of convoys seems to have gone ahead without any problems, and Fenwick simply reported on the fact. In early September 1793, for example, he could state that 'Captain Laforey' had sailed for 'the Nore yesterday, with about 30 Sail of British Merchantmen, & will, I hope, soon arrive safe with them all!'[16] Although convoys were organised from the start of the war in February 1793, the need for even more convoys was emphasised by Fenwick at an early stage. In July 1793, he wrote to the Admiralty that—with the threat of privateers looming, and many British merchant ships sailing independently off the shores of Southern Norway—'it would be a great comfort & relief, to them, if their Lordships judged proper, to order more frequent Convoys, for their protection, hither, & some Cruisers for the Norway Coast, before the Evil, strikes too deep a root'.[17] Another issue related to the convoys assembled at Elsinore was the presence of the Russian squadron, which sailed with Admiral Duncan's North Sea Fleet from 1795 until 1800. The availability of this substantial naval unit to relieve Duncan's hard-pressed ships meant that some convoys were escorted by Russian warships.[18] In early November 1796, for example, a convoy of 30 British merchant ships sailed from Elsinore under the command of Admiral Peter Makaroff. While this was clearly better than no convoy, there was still some concern about the quality of the Russian escort, and for the next time around, the merchants 'will be wishing for a real English Convoy', Fenwick stated. The fact that Makaroff had taken a whole two weeks to procure provisions for his own ships, all the while the merchantmen were waiting, did not make the Russian escort more popular. Fenwick had, however, made sure to inform the Russian Admiral of 'alarming News of Privateers, expecting to Cruize in the Cattegat [*sic*]', which he had obtained from John Mitchell.[19] He was, in other words, providing the Russians with the same kind of intelligence as he submitted to the Admiralty and to the commanders of British escort vessels. Fenwick also reported on 'smaller' issues such as the delay of convoys due to adverse weather. In August 1793, for example, he informed the Admiralty that the commander of a convoy assembled at Elsinore, Captain Williams, was simply awaiting 'a fair Wind' before he could 'carry home near 60 Sail of British Merchantmen', while in October the same year, he could report that 'a strong Gale' had forced another convoy 'to take shelter in Norway'. The continuation of the bad weather off the Norwegian coast meant that, as far as Fenwick was aware, the British ships were still stuck in port at the time of writing.[20] The introduction of the Convoy Act in 1798 obviously created a new situation, and left Charles Fenwick wondering exactly which tasks he was now meant to perform. In a letter to Evan Nepean, the secretary to the Admiralty, written in late November that year, he asked if the secretary could present two queries to the Lord Commissioners of the Admiralty on his behalf. The first was related to the organisation of the convoys, and Fenwick's role in that. As the recent departure of a convoy of 320 vessels from Elsinore had 'nearly emptied the Baltic of British Ships', Fenwick wrote, he felt that 'it would be of great Service to the Trade which still may be expected from the Baltic, if their Lordships would be pleased to acquaint me when the last convoy for the Sound this Season will Sail'.[21] Since the inlets to the Baltic Sea tended to freeze over in winter, there was no trade there during that part of the year, and—when convoys were now meant to be made mandatory for all British merchant vessels involved in the Baltic trade—the timing of the last convoy of the season was clearly of great importance for many. It was information Fenwick, as the British consul at Elsinore, simply needed to have. As it turned out, he was to play an important role with respect to the timing of, particularly, the first convoy of the season, since he could observe directly when the ice broke up again, and report on this to London.[22] The second query related to the system of licences included in the Convoy Act, and on this Fenwick wondered 'if their Lordships would be pleased to empower me to grant Licenses to Ships to Sail from hence without convoy, and in what cases such Licenses may be granted'. The second point was, of course, outlined in the Act itself, but it is not clear if the Admiralty ever gave Fenwick the authority to issue licenses. However that may have turned out, Fenwick did at least continue to submit reports of recently departed convoys for some time thereafter.[23]

The other part of the British policy for the defence of trade, the harassment of the enemy, gave greater room for consular involvement. Since there was little French trade on the Baltic Sea in our period, harassment was primarily a matter of targeting the, at times, numerous French privateers operating out of Norwegian waters, as well as the less numerous French warships, which also appeared off the coasts of Denmark and Norway from time to time. This was not as much of a logistical undertaking as the organisation of convoys, and essentially consisted in the deployment of British warships to those seas where the privateers were likely to be operating. Although the coastal waters just outside Kristiansand and Bergen were obvious areas to patrol, the fact that French and Dutch privateers utilised numerous outports, creeks and bays along the entire length of the southern and western Norwegian coastline meant that updated intelligence on recent sightings of privateers was of great use for the Navy. Apart from Brown in Trondheim, all the British consuls in Denmark-Norway provided regular intelligence on the movements of French and Dutch privateers to the Admiralty. This included information on which privateers had been sighted—thus the name and other information about the ship, such as armament—where the sighting had taken place and details on captured merchant ships. If the prizes in question had been brought into a Norwegian port, this would usually be specified too. Mitchell's pilots on the coast played a central role in providing information of this kind, and altogether this meant that the Admiralty was kept well informed about the development of the privateering menace. A typical example of the many reports that were sent was that written by John Wallace on 22 June 1793 on the capture of the *Janet* of Leith. Here Wallace stated that 'the Brig the *Janet of Leith* James Spittle late Master' had been brought into Bergen on 16 June 'a Prize to the *Sansparielle* Privateer of Dunkirk, Mulenair Commander', following the capture of the vessel on 11 June 'about seven Leagues off Buchaness on his Voyage from Corsöer in Denmark, load with Barley and Oats for Leith'. Wallace expected the *Sansparielle* to be out on 'another Cruize' very shortly, and added that it was 'a Cutter Brig of 16 Guns and Seventy two men'.[24] Fenwick followed up with further reports on the movements of the *Sansparielle*, based partly on information he had received from Wallace. By July, it was clear that the privateer was intending to 'extend her Cruise, towards the Naze of Norway, where she no doubt will also do more mischief' given the higher number of British vessels in that area, Fenwick wrote, and less than two weeks later, pilot reports suggested that six British ships had been captured and carried into Farsund. By November, the *Sansparielle* was still at large, and—together with the smaller privateer the *Pandeur* of 14 guns—she had captured 'a dozen of British Merchantmen, & some Dutch & Prussians, betwixt the Dogger Bank & Naze'.[25] Thereafter she appears to have disappeared from Norwegian waters for a while only to return in January 1794 under a new name, the *Subtile*. Another two British and two Dutch merchantmen were captured but, in this case, the prizes were 'sent home to France'.[26] The *Sansparielle/Subtile* continued to operate in Norwegian waters for several years thereafter, capturing a number of ships, and Fenwick, Wallace and Mitchell all reported on her movements, as they did for other French privateers.[27] The consuls also reported on the capture of privateers by British warships. Thus in September 1794, Wallace was pleased to inform the Admiralty that the *Narcissus* privateer had been taken, stating that 'it should rejoice me to see that all Privateers who have infested the North Sea met the same fate'.[28] From time to time, the consuls submitted lists of 'recent captures' brought into ports in Norway and—if the relevant information could be procured—whether the French were planning to send these prizes home to France, or to dispose of them in Norway. In early December 1794, for example, John Wallace could report from Bergen that the French were putting 12 British, 2 Dutch and 1 'German' prize 'in a Sailing condition' in order so that they could be sent home to France. Most of the prizes in question came from the Archangel trade, such as the *Susana* of Hull and the *Princess Royal* of London, both carrying tar, but there were also a couple of ships from the Baltic trade, among them the *Charles* of Borrowstounness, which carried hemp from St Petersburg.[29] The forwarding of information about forthcoming French departures of this kind no doubt increased the chances of recapturing the prize vessels in question, and was therefore valuable.

Providing the Admiralty with useful intelligence on privateering activity was, however, one thing. Another was the actual deployment of British warships to hunt for privateers, and this presented challenges of its own. The first was, of course, the immense length of the Norwegian coastline, which required a substantial number of ships in order to be patrolled effectively. The second was that this kind of 'patrol duty' competed with the other responsibilities the Navy had to meet. As Patrick Crowhurst has pointed out, the later eighteenth century was a period of rapid growth in British trade, and this meant that, in the 1790s, the Navy had 'a greater number of merchant ships to protect than in any previous war'.[30] Patrol duty thus competed with convoy duty, but on top of that came the other wartime tasks the Navy had to fulfil, such as the blockading of French ports. The resources of the North Sea Fleet were stretched to breaking point, but this state of affairs did not stop the consuls in Denmark-Norway from making repeated requests for a greater naval presence off Norway.[31] As we saw, Nicholas Fenwick's request for 'more frequent Convoys' from July 1793 had also included one for 'Cruisers', and this was a point he returned to very shortly. In August the same year, he stressed that it was 'a pity we seem to have no Cruisers at all, in the No Sea, nor the Dutch either, except perhaps, off the Texel'.[32] Similar requests were put forward by Mitchell, Wallace and Grieg also and, judging from their correspondence on the matter, it would seem as if the naval presence off Bergen was particularly inadequate. In late May 1796, for example, Wallace reported to Mitchell that, as far as he knew, there were no British warships on the western coast, and when seen in light of the recent captures, this was a cause of worry. About four months later, he could report on the capture of five Archangel ships by two Dutch frigates, the *Scipio* and *Venus*, stressing that as soon as 'the prises are arrived they will proceed with the first fair wind on another Cruize', and being 'indifferently manned', he was convinced that 'a single Thirty Gun Frigate would take them both'. Mitchell passed the information on to the Admiralty, but it is not clear if any action was taken, and the situation does not seem to have improved much by the time Grieg took over as consul at Bergen.[33] In July 1797, he reported on the recent captures of the *Vengeur* privateer—a 'very fast' schooner which was due to depart on a new cruise shortly—pointing out that 'Was a good fast Sailing Cruizer to be Stanioned [*sic*] of [*sic*] the inlets to the Port, few Prizes could escape being retaken'. Little seems to have happened in the next few weeks, and in mid-August, Grieg complained that 'I hear of no British Cruizers being off the inlets of this Coast'. By early September, however, the situation was in the process of being addressed. A Royal Navy cutter or sloop, the *Cygnet*, had arrived in Bergen with requests for full information on 'the Enemy Cruizers', including lists of 'Prizes taken by them & sent into this Port of late', and Grieg assured Nepean that he would provide 'the fullest information in my power'. Still, there was room for improvement Grieg thought, and in the wake of the defeat of the Dutch Fleet at Camperdown on 11 October 1797, he wondered if 'the Lords Commissioners will now have it in their power to adopt a model of Protection upon the coast of Norway that will prevent the Ennemys [*sic*] considerable Depredations, such as I have formerly hinted'?[34] The situation on the southern coast was somewhat better, with what appears to have been a more regular deployment of British warships, based in the waters outside the port town of Mandal. Mandal had been chosen because 'ships from England generally make the Norway Coast about Mandahl' giving them the 'advantage of falling in with our Ships of War' stationed there. A local representative, Giert Torreson, was even meant to act as a liaison between the warships and Fenwick at Elsinore, but it is not clear if this arrangement ever materialised.[35] Moreover, the southern coast was, of course, Mitchell's area of responsibility, and as could have been expected, perhaps, he played a more central role in the coordination of naval resources on the coast of Norway than either of the other consuls. What Mitchell did was initiate a collaboration between himself and his informants and pilots on the one hand, and the warships on patrol or 'cruising' duty on the other, so that the commanders of the warships could be kept abreast of the most recent intelligence on privateers, and thereby directed to the areas of the greatest need. He outlined his ideas on this in a letter to Evan Nepean in September 1795 where he stated that 'I presume it might be beneficial to the Service were One of His Majesty's Cruisers which are Stationed on or near this Coast to call sometimes here on me for Intelligence'. The Admiralty concurred and instructed Admiral Duncan to send 'his Cruizers on the Northern Stations' into Kristiansand for intelligence updates.[36] While this was useful, there were also occasions when Mitchell needed to contact the commanders of the patrolling vessels directly without waiting for them to arrive in port, and for this purpose, he employed his pilots. In October 1796, for example, he reported that he had sent out a pilot boat to look for the frigate *Phœnix* and its companion the cutter *Cobourg*, both under the command of Captain Lawrence William Halsted. The two warships were believed to be cruising 'about, or to the westward of the Naze', but there was now an urgent need to deploy them further east, to the seas off Kristiansand, Mitchell wrote, and this was the reason he had decided to send a boat in search of Halsted's ships. The cause of urgency was the confirmed presence of the small French privateer the *l'Epervier*, a 'Lugger of 4 guns & 30 Men', which had been reported to be 'lurking amongst the Creeks to the Eastward' of Kristiansand. This had prevented 'several British Baltick [*sic*] Ships' which were hiding away in 'the Ports of Mardøe, Helligland & Fleckerø' from leaving port, and Mitchell thought that they would not risk doing so 'until Some of His Majesty's Ships Relieve them'. The problem was made worse by rumours of another four, probably Dutch, privateers, which were believed to be operating in the area disguised as 'Swedish Fishing Boats'. At the time of writing, Mitchell had not yet heard from his pilots, or from Halsted, and he had therefore 'informed Captain Wray of the Sea-Gull that the Epervier & her Companions are on this Coast'. The 16-gun sloop *Seagull* was then in port at Farsund.[37] While Mitchell thus used his informants and pilots to direct those British cruisers which were already in Norwegian waters, he also stressed the need for an increased naval presence from time to time. Such requests were sent to both the Admiralty and the Foreign Office. In February 1794, for example, he wrote to Grenville that, as the number of French privateers on the coast was expected to rise, it was his 'opinion that one or Two Sloops of War, & two Cutters of 16. or 18. Guns each, immediately Stationed on this Coast would be of infinite Service to the Trade. Large Frigates are not so well calculated for this Station.'[38] Similarly, early in December 1795, he reported to the Admiralty on three Dutch privateers, which he believed were about to sail for 'Holland with the most valuable of their Prizes', adding that 'I am Sorry we have no British Cruisers on this Coast' to intercept them.[39] In the end, however, the Admiralty does seem to have tried to answer the calls for warships as far as the available resources would allow, and as early as in September 1793, Nicholas Fenwick could write with satisfaction that 'the precautions My Lords Commissioners, of the Admiralty, took, of sending out Cruisers, to scour the No. Sea, of the Enemy's Privateers, has had the good effect, that, I have not heard of any more there'.[40] The problem would, of course, return with a vengeance thereafter, but the key point was that the strategy worked.

Finally, the task of providing the Admiralty with intelligence on privateering also involved the investigation of rumours and the clarification of misunderstandings. In early August 1793, a 'foolish report' had landed on Fenwick's desk concerning a 'Fleet' of British merchant vessels, which was supposed to have left Mandal just under a month earlier. Most of the ships in question were then believed to have been captured by 'French Men of War', but this could 'only be a Danish misconstruction of the Word, *Privateers*, for *Ships of War*', Fenwick thought. Investigations appear to have been set in train, and two weeks later Fenwick could report that the 'news of the French Men of War, in the No Sea, Happily proved false; And on the Contrary, Two of His Majesty's Frigates & a Sloop of War, have been seen Cruising there, lately'.[41] Nothing more was heard of the ships that were meant to have been captured, so, presumably, this was also a misunderstanding. An analogous case appeared in August 1796, when rumours of a 'French Fleet' in the North Sea turned out to be the work of a 'Danish Mercht. Man' who had 'deceived' the captain of a British warship on convoy duty into believing that French warships were in the area. No clear motive for the deception seems to have been discovered, and Fenwick simply referred to the perpetrator as 'nothing but an Impostor'.[42]

The impression formed on the basis of this evidence is therefore that the British consuls in Denmark-Norway cooperated closely with the Admiralty and the Navy on many aspect of the protection of British trade, and this cooperation was, if anything, only more comprehensive with respect to the more difficult individual cases we will return to later. Moreover, as the wartime situation changed, so did the tasks the consuls were expected to perform. When the Baltic Sea became more of a war zone after Denmark-Norway's entry into the war in 1807, and Britain deployed a Baltic Sea Fleet under the command of Admiral James Saumarez from 1808, the British consuls in the Baltic Sea region could add victualing or 'sea provisions'—the supply of food and drink to the fleet—to their existing job list. By then, however, Fenwick had moved across the Sound to Helsingborg in Sweden, and operated in an informal capacity only.[43] Although the British system for the defence of trade probably did much to reduce losses to privateers, it did not prevent them altogether, or stop the privateers from evading the rules set out in the British-Danish agreement of 1793. Alongside the sighting of privateers, however, the consuls also reported on the presence of French warships in Norwegian waters, and we will turn to the threat posed by French naval units next.

French Warships

The *la guerre de course*, which the French had adopted as their main naval strategy in the eighteenth century, did not just mean a strong focus on privateering.[44] It also meant that 'commerce raiding' took precedence over more conventional naval operations and, for that reason, French naval units were deployed specifically to attack the enemy's trade. While the British naval strategy also involved an element of commerce raiding through the policy of 'harassment', attacking the enemy's trade was arguably never as important to the British as it was to the French. Since the French perception was that the British economy relied more heavily on trade and commerce than that of France, and that this made it particularly vulnerable, it was thought that 'Britain could be driven out of the war through attacks on its trade'.[45] Commerce raiding was therefore a deliberate war strategy, not just the fallback position of an inferior naval power. Moreover, because of the possibilities it offered of seizing prizes, commerce raiding was generally popular with commanders, and while the French navy had its problems in the 1790s, the French men-of-war were still better armed and manned than most privateers, and therefore potentially more dangerous.[46] For that reason, sightings of French naval units caused considerable concern.

The situation in the North Sea, with French privateers operating out of Norwegian ports, was somewhat unusual and meant that French warships were not simply sent out to hunt for the enemy's trading vessels, but also to assist the privateers. This supporting function was particularly important in the first year of the war when the French government required that all prizes be sent home to France, and meant that naval vessels were dispatched to escort 'convoys' of prize vessels, which had been assembled in

Norwegian ports.[47] The policy is exemplified by one particular series of events in the summer and autumn of 1794, which also demonstrates the practical operations of Mitchell's system of pilots and informants. It began in August, when John Wallace in Bergen conveyed news he had received from the 'East of Norway' that 'Seven Frigates and two Cutter French are most certainly Cruizing in the North Sea; by whom a great mischief will undoubtedly be done'.[48] Two months later, he could report that four French warships had arrived at Bergen in order to escort prize vessels to France.[49] By then, Mitchell had also reported on these ships: 'By an Express arrived this moment from Mr. Kielland my Agent at Stavanger', he wrote to Lord Grenville on 1 October,

> I am informed that the 24th September there past that Port 5 large French Frigates & a Cutter Brigg Steering for the Fiord or Bay of Bergen. And as all the Prizes that were laid between the Naze & Bergen have been lately ordered to that Port, I suppose these frigates are intended to Convoy them to France.

At this point, Mitchell was at Mandal, and he had already 'dispatched Two experienced Pilots from the Naze, & ordered Mr. Kielland to dispatch Two from Stavanger', in order to find and inform the British warships that were on patrol in the area.[50] By November, the 'greater part of the French Squadron' was still in Bergen, and a month later, Craufurd could report that the French seemed to have 'abandoned the idea of taking their Prizes to France and that they have begun to unrig them at Bergen'.[51] In the end, however, there was no need for British naval vessels to intervene, as the French warships and prize vessels in question were frozen up in port and unable to leave.[52] A similar series of events began in the summer of 1796, but this time it concerned warships on commerce raiding.

'It is with much pain that I now inform you', Mitchell wrote to Evan Nepean on 3 June, 'that Captain Le Bozee in la Republicaine French Frigate with 7 other Frigates & Strong Armed Vessels under his orders sailed lately from Flushing to cruise on our Northern and East Country Trade'. Bozee had already captured 16 British Baltic sea vessels, one of which had been brought into Egersund, and Mitchell had grave concerns about a homewards-bound convoy of '70 or 80 Sail of Merchantmen' escorted by the three naval vessels the *Garland, Greyhound* and *Weazle*, which had passed by Kristiansand the day before. He was convinced that the convoy was the French captain's 'Object', and thought that 'there is

Scarce a possibility of their escaping Bozee'.[53] Mitchell was concerned to get hold of a vessel that could be dispatched to the convoy to warn the commander of the escort, and four days later he reported that he had hired a Norwegian ship and provided its 'master', one 'Mr. Anders Hansen with a Letter to the Commander or Commanders of any of His Majestys Ships or Vessels which he might fall in with at Sea'. Moreover, by 'An Express' he had received from Skudeneshavn the same morning, Mitchell had been informed that the *Jason*, a vessel of 300 tons from Liverpool, had been carried into Bergen by the French squadron. 'Here are none of His Majestys Ships, nor do I know where any of them are Stationed', Mitchell complained, adding that 'I have heard nothing of the Garlands Convoy since they past here the 2nd instant', but since 'none of them have been get chaced [*sic*] in on the Coast about the Naze I would fain hope that they have escaped Bozee'.[54] The French squadron continued to hunt for merchant ships thereafter, and on 15 July, the *Republicaine* was damaged in a clash with the converted British Indiaman the *Glatton* off the coast of Flanders, but later returned to commerce raiding.[55] In October 1797, Alexander Grieg reported that she had carried 13 British merchant vessels into Bergen as prizes, information which was later confirmed by the British envoy at Copenhagen, Robert Stephen Fitzgerald. It was expected that she would be 'joined by two other Frigates of equal or superior Force', and then make her way to Brest via north of Scotland and St. George's Channel.[56] Thereafter, nothing more was heard of her on the Norwegian coast and, eventually, on 25 August 1799, both the ship and Captain Bozee were captured off the coast of Surinam by the British frigate *Tamar*.[57] Although the presence of Bozee's squadron in the North Sea no doubt constituted a serious threat to the British Baltic Sea trade, French privateers were far more numerous than French warships, and therefore presented the greater challenge. Although the British-Danish agreement from 1793 meant that the British side accepted the presence of French privateers in the neutral waters of Norway, and that the privateers might bring their prizes into Norwegian ports temporarily, it remained to be seen if these privateers would adhere to the more general rules of privateering. As it turned out, this was not always the case, and in the following sections, we will look at different types of 'transgressions' on the part of these privateers. We start with the adoption of 'false flags' and the purchase of contraband goods, before moving on to the question of whether the privateers respected the prohibition against belligerent activities in the territorial waters of Denmark-Norway. On this final point, however, we will see that the privateers were not alone in committing transgressions against the sanctity of neutral waters.

The False Flag Issue

The adoption of a 'false flag' essentially meant one out of two things: it could be either that a *privateer* would fly the flag of a neutral country, and then quickly change to the French standard before challenging an enemy merchant vessels (and possibly also changing back to neutral colours afterwards in order to avoid detection by enemy warships); or that a *merchant* vessel from one of the belligerents, or a *prize* ship, would be equipped with a neutral flag in order to disguise its real identity. The point in either case was to create a deception. Mitchell suspected that a French-Norwegian collaboration on the use of false flags was in the making as early as in June 1793. In a letter to Grenville he wrote that 'I am informed by unquestionable Authority that an association is formed of French & Norway Merchants to carry on the French East-India Trade during the present War under Danish Colors [*sic*]'.[58] The British did not, of course, accept that neutral countries moved into the colonial trade of France (from which they were barred in peacetime), but as far as the use of Danish colours was concerned, this would only be matter of adopting false flags if the vessels flying them were French, not Norwegian. In that sense, it was not yet fully clear that a transgression was in the making, but Mitchell suspected that there was more to it.[59] In August the same year, he reported that the magistrates at Kristiansand were 'granting the King of Denmarks passports and neutral Colors [sic] to the ships and seafaring Citizens of France'. He had also sent a letter directly to Bernstorff, asking two principled and rhetorical questions. First if it was really the case that a 'Citizen of France' residing in Norway could obtain 'the Privileges of a Danish Citizen, during the present War', merely by paying a 'simple tax' and, second, if ships which were the property of the French (i.e. prizes) could 'be taken under Danish Colors' [*sic*] and given Danish passports, by a 'formal Transfer to Danish Citizens'? If so, it would be inconsistent with recent Danish practice since in 'the late War between Russia & Sweden, the Danish Government from a professed Principle of Neutrality forbid their Subjects to purchase Ships from Powers Actually at War', and the Danish government had, after all, stated that it would 'Act upon the same Principles of strict neutrality in the present War'. The argument presented in the letter to Bernstorff was perhaps rather technical, but the overall point Mitchell seemed to make was that the Danish government was prepared to assist the French in an underhand manner, while simultaneously making sure that the formalities of neutrality were upheld.[60] An analogous case emerged later in the year, when Mitchell could report that the 'French Agents' in Kristiansand had received orders from Paris to send all prizes to Bergen in order for them to await convoy to Dunkirk. Again, he suspected that this was an attempt to circumvent the prohibition of sales:

> I rather believe that they intend to put them under Danish Colors [*sic*] there, as they argue that if the Vessels have been once at Sea, and then comes into any Port in Norway under French or other Colors they cannot be longer considered as Prizes and consequently may be sold or transferred to any Danish Subject &c. They have lately obtained Permission from the court of Denmark to purchase Ships at pleasure from the Subjects of any of the Powers at War.[61]

Nicholas Fenwick at Elsinore also suspected that the French were planning to adopt a false flags policy more in general. As he wrote to Philip Stevens at the Admiralty in July 1793, 'There are reports prevailing that, the French intend procuring Danish Flags for many of their own Vessels, & Prizes' and, for that reason, 'His Majesty's Ships will do well, to examine all Similar Vessels, & their Papers'.[62] Fenwick's and Mitchell's suspicions were soon confirmed. In January the next year, an exasperated Mitchell wrote to Grenville about the problems involved in preventing the use of false flags:

> It is Remarkable that Several Vessels actually French Property, & Commanded by French Citizens … have been taken by His Majestys Cruisers, & afterwards Released with extraordinary Damages because they had Danish Papers onboard. To Release such Vessels & allow them Damages strengthens the Enemys Confidence in neutral Papers, induces the neutral Merchants to grant their names & Passports to French Property & makes His Majesty's Officers more than otherwise necessarily Cautious what Vessels they inform, or detain.

Unless 'effectual measures' were found to prevent this kind of collusion, France would be better supplied than in any previous war, Mitchell thought.[63] No effective way of dealing with the problem appears to have been found, however, and Mitchell kept returning to the issue in subsequent letters, as did others.[64]

In December 1797, the commander of the Royal Navy sloop the *Hound* reported to Fitzgerald that the *William* of Liverpool 'a valuable Ship of Six or Seven hundred Tons Burthen' had been brought into Farsund as a prize. There, Jacob Lund, a 'native of the place and French Consul' had ensured that she was sent to Flekkerøy 'under the Danish Flag, navigated entirely by Danes'. At Flekkerøy, the Danish flag had been lowered and the 'St. George's Ensign' hoisted when Wood passed by (on Lund's orders) in order to 'distinguish her being a Prize'. The deception had been easily detected, however, as the Royal Navy flag had been raised 'Union downwards', or upside down. 'I shall submit to Your Lordship's superior judgement' the commander concluded, 'whether the navigating of French Prizes from one Port of Norway to another by the King of Denmark's Subjects and under His Flag in presence of his Forts and Garrisons is not a Violation of the Laws subsisting between the two Courts'.[65] Such imaginative uses of false flags could just have been the result of individual initiatives, but the policy of adopting neutral flags appears to have been authorised at the highest level in France at the beginning of the war. In late June 1793, the French chargés d'affaires in Copenhagen, P. Framery, responded to a dispatch he had received from the 'Minister of Public Contributions' in Paris earlier the same month, requesting him to organise the purchase of saltpetre in Denmark-Norway. Since saltpetre was contraband, Framery wrote in response, 'the most secure and perhaps the only method of entering saltpetre into the ports of the Republic is to load it onto Danish ships as Danish property with a false destination for neutral ports in the Mediterranean'. The captain of such ships would then be furnished with a 'private contract' whereby he committed himself to deliver the cargo in a French port. 'It will not be difficult to find safe ships and intelligent captains here for such an expedition', Framery concluded. The scheme received full backing from Paris, and while this particular case was not directly related to privateering, it did demonstrate a readiness to use false flags as a wartime strategy.[66] Moreover, the purchase of contraband goods in a neutral state was an issue that was of relevance for privateering too.

Supplying Contraband Goods to Privateers

The question of which goods constituted contraband, and not, was, as we saw in Chap. 2, a contested one in the eighteenth century generally, and in the 1790s specifically. Although Britain was a nation which tended to promote a comprehensive understanding of contraband, and consequently promoted 'long' lists of contraband goods, the British government had vacillated on the question of whether food should be seen as contraband. The general perception of the Norwegians as, on balance, pro-French and prone to support French privateers meant that the British side suspected them of supplying these privateers with contraband goods. The lack of an agreement on what constituted contraband, however, made this challenging to assess in practice. It was generally accepted that vessels from the belligerent powers could seek refuge from adverse weather in the ports of a neutral nation, and even after the closure of the ports in 1799, the Danish government allowed privateers to enter Norwegian ports when pursued by enemy warships. The question was what they could purchase once in port because, presumably, a ship that had been damaged in a storm might need to be refitted and repaired if it was ever to leave the port again, and much the same could be the case for a privateer vessel which had sustained battle damage. Yet, the 1780 addition to the British-Danish Treaty of 1670 had stated that all 'naval stores' were contraband, and both sides had insisted that this agreement still applied (though the on-and-off British attempt to make food contraband suggests that the British side was happy enough to disregard those aspects of the accord which did not suit their interests).[67] Thus, according to the 1780 agreement repairs of privateer vessels were problematic, but provisions for the crew were fine. How did this work out in practice? There was, no doubt, considerable *concern* about the issue on the British side, but actually confirmed cases of contraband goods supplied to privateers in Norwegian ports were not that many. Sometimes, rumours turned out to be unfounded, as was the case for an incident which took place in the autumn of 1794.

It had come to Craufurd's attention that 'the French Squadron', which 'had assembled in the Port of Bergen' in order to convoy prizes home to France, had 'armed their Prizes' there, and he made sure to raise the issue in his next meeting with Bernstorff. Unfamiliar with this particular case, Bernstorff stated that 'he could not answer for their not having obtained any arms from the people of the country', but suggested that perhaps the French had simply 'removed some of their own guns from their Frigates into the Prizes', a course of action 'the Danish Government could not prevent'. He promised to look further into the matter, however, to make sure that 'no improper assistance had been afforded to the French'. Nothing more was heard of this case, which suggests that Bernstorff was probably right.[68] Two years later, however, Mitchell claimed that the

French privateer *le Petit Diable* had received 'additional' guns while it was being repaired and refitted at Farsund, and in March 1797, Robert Stephen Fitzgerald in Copenhagen was instructed by Downing Street to raise the issue of certain 'practices' in Kristiansand with the Danish government. One of these concerned a place of 'Rendezvous' which the French consul had opened in town for the enlistment of seamen to man French privateers, the other, that the privateer *Le Vengeur*, 'having lost her guns in a gale of wind has been furnished with others from the port of Christiansand'. Fitzgerald was to 'make the most serious and forcible representation upon the subject to the Danish Minister and, in the event of their professing upon this as on former occasions an ignorance of the particulars which I have mentioned', he 'should immediately direct Mr. Mitchell to furnish you with the necessary evidence, by which they may be substantiated'.[69] Fitzgerald raised the issue in a note to Bernstorff, but it is not clear what the response was.[70] Two years later, however, Fitzgerald claimed that this particular privateer vessel had been 'fitted out in Norway where she wintered and cost 12000 Rix-dollars or 2400 Pounds Sterling in Repairs', and that 'her Case is not single and that immense numbers of vessels of the same description have, during this War, received similar assistance in the Ports of that Kingdom'. He did not provide any examples of these supposedly numerous cases, or state exactly what the repairs of the *Le Vengeur* had amounted to—if, indeed, she had been supplied with guns—but the indications were, at least, that French privateers were able to obtain naval stores in the Norwegian port towns.[71] A case from 1804 confirms this. The captain of a Royal Navy vessel, Charles Adam, had 'discovered that the Squadron of Enemy's vessels lately at Bergen were actually supplied with Grape shot or Langrage by the Inhabitants of that place', and he felt the need to convey this information to his superior, not the least because he thought it could 'in all probability … have been prevented if a British Consul could have interfered'. There was, of course, no British consul in Bergen at the time, but grape shot was unquestionably contraband.[72]

French privateers or men-of-war purchasing contraband goods in neutral ports were arguably of less concern for the British than the supply of contraband goods to France on Danish keels, however, and on this latter issue, there was a more considerable correspondence between the British diplomatic and consular representatives in Denmark-Norway and London. One issue was, of course, the export of grain to France, which we looked at in Chap. 2. More serious was the supply of saltpetre, a main ingredient in the production of gunpowder. As mentioned earlier, there was a French plan to purchase saltpetre in Denmark under way in the summer of 1793, and by February the next year, Mitchell had detected that something was in the making. Reporting from Kristiansand, he stated that there 'is here at present a Danish Galiass ... loaded with Powder, Salpetre &c. & cleared out from Copenhagen for Genoa; but certainly bound for France; perhaps Toulon'.[73] By December, it was clear that the export was up and running. As James Craufurd reported to Grenville:

> I learnt yesterday, that Saltpetre, which has been purchased here on account of the French, is to be taken from hence to Norway, where it is to be put on board the French Frigate, and other armed vessels, which have been for some time upon that Coast, in order to be conveyed to France. A part of it is already gone. The whole quantity which is to be thus sent is to the amount of about a Million Sterling.[74]

Craufurd raised the issue of this 'illicit Trade in Saltpetre' at his next meeting with Bernstorff, but the Danish minister dismissed the complaint, stating that 'the Danish Government could not prevent its Subjects from exporting Saltpetre from hence to Norway', as long as the normal 'Regulations' for this were being upheld. In other words, he does not seem to have accepted that the trade was conducted on behalf of the French. Craufurd was not convinced that these regulations were 'very rigorously enforced', however, 'Certain it is that they are eluded, and that the Saltpetre has been constantly sent without interruption'. The export of saltpetre also seemed to fit into a broader picture of contraband goods being supplied to France, as 'Great quantities of Naval Stores have been lately contracted for here by the French'. A little over a year later, Craufurd could again report that 'I have just been informed from authority on which I can depend, that several vessels are on the point of sailing from the Ports of Norway', carrying 'Gun Powder & Naval Stores for France'.[75] This traffic in saltpetre and naval stores was not directly related to privateering, of course, but for the British it seemed to confirm their suspicion that both the Danish authorities centrally and the local officials in Norway were all too ready to assist the French and, in this too, the Norwegian ports played a central role. Although the use of false flags and the supply of contraband goods to privateers were serious issues, the main concern on the British side was arguably the fate of the merchant vessels that were captured by French or Dutch privateers and brought into the ports of

Norway. The remainder of this chapter will focus primarily on the issue of prizes and prize-taking, and we start by looking at the various attempts that were made from time to time to retrieve prize vessels and goods.

Attempting to Recover Prizes

Before the British and Danish governments reached their agreement on privateering and neutral ports in August 1793, the British position was that it was incompatible with neutrality to allow privateers to bring prizes into the ports of a neutral country. Daniel Hailes in Copenhagen therefore protested against such practices whenever he obtained information about individual cases from the consuls in Norway but, as he stated to Grenville, without much hope of achieving any kind of cooperation on the part of the Danish government: 'Applications are made to me by His Majestys Consuls to obtain the release of those [prizes] which remain in Norway, but the principles professed here leave me without the smallest prospect of Succeeding in any such solicitations'.[76] This did not, however, stop the owners or insurers of individual vessels that had been captured from attempting to recover them, and they often did this by presenting a petition to Grenville at the Foreign Office. One of the very first such individual cases to emerge was that of that of the *Peggy* of Leith, a brig carrying a 'Cargo of Oak Plank', which had been separated from its convoy on the return leg to Britain from the Baltic Sea, and captured by the French privateer the *Vrai Patriote* on 1 July 1793. The ship had then been 'carried into Fahrsund in Norway' as a prize, and a petition was subsequently presented to Grenville by a number of people who had an interest in the vessel and its cargo. Since 'there is an existing Edict of the court of Denmark which prevents the confiscation within the Danish dominions of property belonging to the Subjects of a Nation at Peace with themselves', the petitioners argued, both ship and cargo should be restored to them, and they asked Grenville to assist them in this.[77] An analogous case was that of the *Janet* of Spittal—a vessel carrying grain from Denmark to Leith—which had been captured off Buchanness by the French privateer *Nonsuch* around the same time as the *Peggy*, and 'carried into Bergen'. The *Janet* belonged to Kingston-upon-Hull, and the MP for the constituency, Sam Thornton, raised the issue directly with Grenville on behalf of the owners and insurers in late July. Grenville reacted promptly, instructing Hailes to

> represent this Case to the Danish Ministers, in addition to those which have before occurred, and that you will express, in the strongest and most unequivocal Terms, His Majesty's confident Expectation, that the Court of Copenhagen will give immediate orders for the Restoration of all the Vessels in question to their respective Owners in conformity to the those Principles of Neutrality which the Danish Government profess to observe in the present War.[78]

The Danish government, however, thought differently as to what conformed to its 'principles of neutrality', and there are no indications that the *Janet* and its cargo were ever returned to Britain. By October 1794, Mitchell could report that those vessels which had been captured and sent into Norway the year before had now been sold, together with their cargos.[79] Paradoxically, perhaps, just as the British tried to recover vessels that had been captured by the French and brought into Norway, so the Danish side made attempt to have ships which had been arrested by the British—typically at sea by the Royal Navy, and on accusations of being involved in illicit trade with France—released on the grounds that the arrest was 'illegal' and a violation of Danish neutrality.[80]

Once the agreement of August 1793 was in place, however, it made little sense to object, solely on the grounds of prizes being brought into port in Norway, since the British government had now accepted that kind of practice.[81] Instead, focus came to be on two issues: whether any sales of prizes that took place in Norway were in line with the agreement, or not, and *where* had the capture of a given merchant vessel taken place. The second point concerned what might be termed Danish-Norwegian neutral waters, and this was clearly a two-sided issue, since it concerned British warships pursuing French and Dutch privateers as much as it did privateers chasing and capturing merchant vessels. Any such belligerent action that took place within the neutral waters of Denmark-Norway would constitute a violation of neutrality, and both the British and the French were quick to protest whenever they thought the other side had transgressed upon this. The question was how neutral waters were to be defined.

Respecting Neutral Territorial Waters

The sanctity of neutral territory, understood as the actual land area of a neutral state, had been undisputed for a long time by the end of the eighteenth century. It was a duty of belligerent powers to abstain from military action on neutral soil. Less clear was the status of the sea, or of water immediately adjacent to this land (in the case of coastal nations). Should this be seen as part of the territory of a neutral sovereign also and, if so, how far out would these neutral waters extend before one reached the international or 'open' sea? Any supposed 'line' to mark the end of territorial waters would, of course, be arbitrary and invisible in a way the coastline or land borders were not, so should all of the sea, going all the way up to the shoreline itself, be seen as international? It seemed reasonable to think that vessels from a belligerent nation could not be attacked while they lay at anchor in neutral ports, at least if they were in actual contact with the pier, but what if a vessel was sailing close to the shore of the neutral nation (as sometimes happened)? Could it then be attacked by an enemy vessel, even though that involved the risk of cannon shot landing on (neutral) ground, and thus violating neutral territory? A variety of solutions to this problem of territorial waters, or not, had been presented historically, but by the eighteenth century, two main alternative 'principles' had emerged. The dominant principle throughout the century was that of the 'cannon shot rule', the essence of which was that territorial waters extended as far as the maximum firing range of a cannon. The rationale behind this rule was, as Wyndham L. Walker has stated, that 'provided a State can exercise a sufficient degree of control over the sea adjacent to land to amount to occupation, it is justified in treating that sea as under its dominion'.[82] It followed from this line of reasoning that the cannon shot rule was not meant to apply generally, in the sense that the waters up to a certain distance from the shore—and all along the coastline—were part of the territory of the nation in question. The rule only applied where there were actual cannon in position, on a fort for example, and the territorial waters were made up the area or 'zone' covered by these cannon. Exactly how far out into the sea the territorial waters extended therefore depended on the range of the cannon *in situ*, and where there were no cannon to cover the sea, there were no territorial waters either. Under the cannon shot rule, vessels from belligerent nations could seek the protection of neutral shore-based guns, and while they remained within the range of these guns, enemy vessels could not attack them without violating the neutrality of the host country. Similar to the rules for blockade, one might therefore say, only those parts of the seas adjacent to the coast of a neutral nation which were effectively policed could be regarded as territorial waters.[83] In this sense, it was a very practically oriented rule, and it was also one that had developed more out of practice than out of legal reasoning. In the eighteenth century, both Britain and France adhered to the cannon shot rule as their main principle for territorial waters, and the French monarchy had even incorporated the rule into French law.[84] The alternative principle was to see territorial waters as a continuous 'belt' going all along the coastline, where the width of the belt was decided by the 'limit of view'. The range of eyesight was held to be about four leagues, where one league equalled four modern nautical miles, and this was undoubtedly much further than the range of eighteenth-century guns. According to the continuous belt-principle, there was no requirement of actual cannon on the coast to enforce the sovereignty of the neutral country over its territorial waters. They 'belonged' to the country on the basis of their proximity to land. In the seventeenth and eighteenth centuries, Denmark-Norway was the main proponent of the continuous belt-principle, but was joined by Sweden during the Seven Years' War. This Scandinavian preference for a continuous belt created friction with the likes of Britain, France and other countries that adhered to the cannon shot rule, and pressure from various quarters led the Danish government to reduce the belt to one league in 1745. Thereafter, however, the French seemed to be content with the situation—particularly as this narrower belt benefitted their privateers who could now hunt for merchant vessels relatively close to the Norwegian coast, while at the same time enjoying the possibility of escaping from Royal Navy vessels all along that same coast—and by the end of the Seven Years' War in 1763, both France and Britain had accepted that the one-league continuous belt applied for Denmark-Norway.[85] Successive Danish governments were less clear, however, on the question of whether the belt should be measured from the shore, or from the outermost islands and rocks, and this issue was not fully decided until 1812, when a royal ordinance decreed in favour of the latter.[86] By 1793, therefore, there was no disagreement on which rule applied for the territorial waters around Norway, but there was potential for debate on how to measure the belt. The continuous 4-mile neutral 'belt' along the Norwegian coast, which all parties had agreed on, gave rise to both practical problems and individual cases of dispute, however.[87]

One central issue was the departure of vessels from ports in Norway. Although the threat of French privateers operating along the Norwegian coast made it dangerous for British merchant vessels to call upon Norwegian ports in the 1790s, many still did, either because they had trade to conduct there or because they had been forced to take shelter from adverse weather. Once in port, however, they often faced the risk of being followed by privateers out of port, and attacked as soon as they were out of neutral waters (or even before). The *Success* of Peterhead, for example, was taken by a Dutchman three hours after sailing from Kristiansand in May 1796, and the masters of 26 vessels at Trondheim petitioned Consul Brown for protection against Dutch warships around the same time. The governor at Trondheim tried to address the problem by giving the merchantmen a head start on the privateers, but as D. H. Reid has pointed out this 'handicapping system was unsuccessful'. Similarly, the French and Dutch sometimes struggled to get safely out of port because there were British naval vessels watching the entrance to the harbour, or even laying besides them at anchor, waiting for them to depart.[88] While not exactly a blockade in the traditional sense, this British approach could certainly be said to hamper the traffic in and out of these neutral ports, even if the warships did not actually attack the privateers before they were out in the open sea. In September 1796, however, Mitchell found his own solution to this particular problem. The occasion was the arrival of the privateer *l'Epervier*, which had taken up 'her station at Helligsund where several loaded British ships' were laying, waiting for favourable winds. Since Governor Levetzow in Kristiansand had recently held back the British cutter *Princess Royal* in port for 24 hours after the *Augustine* privateer had sailed in pursuit of British merchantmen, Mitchell claimed, he had now written an 'Official Note' to the governor requesting him to likewise 'order the Epervier to be detained in Port, 24 hours after the Sailing of the Merchant vessels which were in the neighbourhood of where the Privateer lay'. Levetzow was not forthcoming on this, however, and Mitchell then decided to detain the British vessels himself, pending the arrival of a British warship to escort them. Two weeks later, the merchantmen sailed under protection of the cutter *Cobourg*, while the privateer remained in port. A couple of days after that, Mitchell observed that the 'Privateer got underway' to attack a British ship which was 'passing along shore'. Flying 'English Colours' the privateer 'ran close alongside of the English vessel intending to board her, but the Master suspecting her to be an Enemy, discharged several large Cannonade shot into the Privateer, when she bore away, and has not since been heard of'.[89] The *l'Epervier* was thus unsuccessful on this particular occasion, but at other times, both French and Dutch privateers caught prizes within the neutral belt.

One of the earliest cases of this appeared in April 1793. Three British vessels had been taken by the *Sansparielle* privateer and carried into Kristiansand, and Mitchell had found that 'Upon investigation' the third vessel, the *Syron Hugh* of Carnawn, had been 'taken so near the Norway Land' that 'she could not be considered a Lawful Prize'. He consequently raised the issue with the governor of Kristiansand, who agreed with Mitchell's assessment and ordered the vessel to be released, notwithstanding 'violent opposition' to this from the French consul and 'numerous Friends' of his.[90] The decision reached by the governor was an indication of the attitude adopted to violations of neutral waters by the Danish authorities thereafter. As a main rule, both the Danish government and the local officials in Norway were determined in their defence of the dual-monarchy's territorial waters, and non-acceptance of violations, but they could also be pragmatic in individual cases. Sometimes, this meant that it could take very long to settle an individual case. One example was the British merchant vessel the *Nancy* of Ayr, which had been captured in Norwegian waters at some point in 1795. Three years later, the vessel was still being detained, although it had been 'declared an unlawful prize by the Courts of this Kingdom', Fitzgerald complained to Grenville. Ostensibly, the 'difficulty in the process of liberating' the ship rested with the Danish government's inability to 'determine to which Department of State it belongs to do so', which sounded decidedly odd.[91] Another vessel, the *Industry* of Leith, 'had been taken from her Anchorage on the Coast of Jutland, within the neutral Limits of Denmark', and then brought into Larvik in Norway. Although Fitzgerald had raised the issue with Bernstorff, 'who seemed perfectly satisfied with the Illegality of the Capture', the ship was not immediately restored. On this occasion, the problem seems to have been resistance from the French, who demanded a tit for tat. The French consul at Larvik would only let the *Industry* of Leith go, if the British released the French privateer *le Petit Diable*, which had been captured in neutral Norwegian waters by British warships. The Danish government functioned as an intermediary, brokering a deal, whereby this 'exchange' could take place.[92] We will return to the case of the *Diable* later.

British transgressions of neutral waters attracted even greater attention, and they were often linked to the pursuit of privateers who were trying to escape British warships by heading for a Norwegian port or outport. It is not difficult to understand that the commander of a British naval vessel would be reluctant to break off the chase if he was gaining on a privateer he had engaged, and thus tempted to continue the pursuit, even to the point where there was no doubt that he had entered neutral waters. One argument even held that a vessel could be legally chased into neutral waters and captured there if the 'initial contact had been made outside neutral jurisdiction'.[93] The question then, however, was how the point of 'initial contact' was to be ascertained, and even if one accepted this argument on the original place of engagement, outright combat close to the shore would quickly become problematic if any third parties were affected by it. An incident that illustrates this problem occurred in August 1795, when a 'Small Squadron' of Royal Navy vessels attacked three Dutch warships, two frigates and a cutter, which were on their way to Bergen to convoy a group of East India ships home. The British ships were able to capture the frigate *Alliance* off the Naze, but the other frigate, named the *Argo*, and the cutter escaped into the port of Hidra. The chase continued until the Dutch vessels were 'within about one English Mile of the Norway Land', and a subsequent report from the 'Pilots & Fishermen in the Neighbourhood of Liester' to Governor Levetzow in Kristiansand stated that 'several shot fell in & about their Houses'. Because of this event, Mitchell reported, 'Governor Levetzow (who like the most of his Countrymen is by no means well disposed towards Great Britain) has dispatched an Express to Copenhagen with a Circumstantial Detail of this according to Mr. Levetzow very Serious insult'. Mitchell was not, perhaps, on the best of terms with Levetzow to start with, but in this case, the Norwegian governor's complaint seemed reasonable enough: cannon shots whizzing past the windows of residential houses were just not acceptable.[94] In response to this violation of its neutrality, the Danish government dispatched two warships, the frigate *Mermaid* of 44 guns and cutter *Defence* of 16 guns, to Norway in order to give the 'appearance of maintaining the Neutrality of the coast', Craufurd reported. As became clear in the early stages of the British-Danish debates on privateering and neutral ports in 1793, the Danish government did not have sufficient naval resources to patrol the length of the Norwegian coast in full, and Craufurd's comment seems to suggest that he thought this small force was of limited use.[95] Coincidentally, Mitchell would later claim that the *Mermaid* had done little to prevent the capture of 14 British merchant ships in her immediate vicinity, when they 'were all captured by two Dutch Privateers within musket shot of the muzzles of the Mermaid's Guns'. The British ships had sailed without convoy, and they were all taken in Norwegian waters.[96] A second case, the capture of the French privateer *Vrai Patriote* in August 1793, reveals, however, that the Danish government could be prepared to let violations of neutral waters pass in the interest of an amicable settlement.

While patrolling off the southern coast of Norway, Captain Sir Charles Hamilton in the frigate *Dido* had detected and laid chase to the *Vrai Patriote*, pursuing her until she was driven ashore. Before Hamilton and his crew could seize control of the privateer, however, the French crew had set fire to their ship, and then escaped on land. Incensed by what they saw as an attempt to deprive them of a valuable prize, Hamilton and his men had pursued the French sailors inland, and arrested some of them. As soon as the situation had been brought under control, the fire extinguished and the prize secured, Hamilton sailed to Copenhagen for repairs, and while the ship was in dock, news of the capture reached the Danish capital. Workmanship in the dockyard was first-class, and Daniel Hailes decided to introduce Hamilton to Bernstorff, in order to 'give him an opportunity of expressing his sense of the attention which had been paid to him'. While at the reception, however, 'the Danish Minister took me aside', Hailes wrote, and said that

> he was willing to overlook, altogether, the manner in which the French Privateer, the Vrai Patriote, had been captured by Sir Charles, so near to the Norway Coast; but it was impossible for him not to take some notice of the violation of Territory, committed by a part of the Crew of the Dido, in following the French up the Country, in firing on them, and taking some of them Prisoners.

Bernstorff stated that 'he had kept back the Reports of these Transactions', and that he was prepared to let the whole incident pass into 'oblivion' as long as 'Sir Charles would give up Seven Men whom he had made Prisoners on the Norway shore'. Hamilton immediately consented to this, and the matter appears to have been resolved.[97] A third case, the capture of the erstwhile successful French privateer *le Petit Diable* in the spring of 1796, illustrates the wider complications that sometime arose because of belligerent actions in neutral waters. The story was as follows.

The American captain of this small French privateer—a cutter of eight guns—William Ripner, had gone to the unusual step of taking up his 'station' in the small harbour of 'Lyshaven' (probably Loshavn near Farsund), and from this position he had armed and sent out the ship's boats 'to seize on British vessels, whenever he perceived any, *at the mouth of it*'.[98] Ripner was thus not just hiding out in this outport—from where he could observe, and then sail out to attack British vessels passing by in the open sea—but literally attacked them just outside the harbour. In order to bring an end to these depredations, the commander of the North Sea Fleet, Admiral Adam Duncan, ordered one of his commanding officers, Captain Halsted, to search out and seize the Frenchman in early April 1796. Halsted commanded the frigate *Phœnix* and cutter *Kite*, and on 22 April, he saw an opportunity to carry out his mission. Informed by Norwegian pilots that the *Diable* was presently at its station together with a Dutch cutter named the *Vlugheid*—having sent two recently captured prizes into Farsund—Halsted ordered the captain of the *Kite*, Mirajah Malbon, to 'proceed in & take possession of them', following closely behind in the *Phœnix* as a show of strength. Both the French and Dutch ships were taken in an 'active & officer like manner', Halsted reported, as were the two prizes, the merchantmen *Farina* and *Master*.[99] Malbon then sailed to Britain, arriving at the Nore on 4 May with all four captured ships.[100] As if he was expecting trouble, Admiral Duncan defended his order to Halsted in the report he sent to the Admiralty shortly after. In light of the 'shameful way these small Privateers have gone on', capturing ships, but never going home 'to their Own Port to Victual', or ever venturing out into the open sea, Duncan wrote, he thought there was 'no possibility of putting an end to their Depredations without taking them out of those Inlets wherein they take shelter'.[101] The capture of the *le Petit Diable* led to a dispute between the British and Danish authorities, in which Duncan's point formed the basis of the British line of argument. Craufurd found that there was 'nothing of which the Danish Government can with any justice complain' in this case, as it 'cannot be denied that if the Merchant Ships of His Majesty's Subjects are attacked within the Danish Territory his Ships of War must defend them there, as elsewhere'. Confronted with this argument, Bernstorff had 'denied the fact of the French Privateer having armed his boats, made any Prizes, or attacked any English Ships in the Port', Craufurd wrote in his main report to London, but he had acknowledged that a privateer could not legally take up station in a port in the way the *Diable* had done. This was in 'direct opposition to the orders issued by the Danish Government', whereby 'they had declared to the French' than any privateer doing so would be considered a pirate. Therefore, 'if a representation had been made to the Governor of the district the Petit Diable would have been obliged to depart; but that did not authorize the step taken by Captain Malbon', Bernstorff insisted. Craufurd continued to press Bernstorff, however, stating that he had 'every reason to place confidence in the account' he had received, arguing that this 'justified' Malbon's actions, but to this Bernstorff simply 'observed, but with great good humour, that even if the French had made some Prizes' within the neutral belt, 'His Majesty's Ships had violated it in the like manner' when they captured the Dutch cutter. Since it seemed clear that the Dutch ship had not 'joined in any degree in the illegal conduct of the Frenchman', Craufurd had to admit that at least the capture of the *Vlugheid* was illegal.[102] The issue at stake was therefore if the capture of the *Diable* was acceptable in a situation where the Danish authorities seemed unable to police their own territorial waters. The British government appears to have been uncertain about this, and sought legal advice from the king's advocate-general, the government main legal adviser, Sir William Scott. Although Scott would become a strong and famous supporter of the British position on issues such as visitation rights in his later role as judge on the High Court of Admiralty, he was not in favour of the British side on this occasion.[103] In his view, 'the Act of capturing Vessels within a neutral Port is prima facie a high Misdemeanor [*sic*], and ought to be followed by a Restitution of the Vessels so illegally captured', even if 'the neutral Sovereign had afforded an undue and noxious Protection to accommodate in … his Ports the Cruizers of the Belligerent Party'. The British action could only have been condoned—or at least it would have served to 'diminish the Impropriety' of it—if 'Representations and Remonstrances' had been made to the Danish government first, and this had failed to result in any 'Correction of the Abuse'.[104] Since Captain Halsted had ordered the attack on the *Diable* without consulting Copenhagen first, or giving the Danish government any opportunity to address the problem, such extenuating circumstances could not be said to apply. Halsted may well have thought that it would have been pointless to ask the Danish authorities to intervene but, in legal terms, that was not good enough. It thus seemed clear that the capture of the *Diable* could not be justified in legal terms, and the British government consequently decided to restore all the four vessels Malbon had carried across to Britain.[105] This decision caused new problems, however. First, the original owner of the *Farina*, a Liverpool merchant by the name of Caleb Fletcher, tried to prevent the return of his vessel to Norway by means of a petition to the government, but without succeeding.[106] Then, the former captains of the *Diable* and *Vlugheid* protested at the state of repair of their ships, 'peremptorily' refusing to 'receive them until they are repaired and every thing replaced on board'. The officer in charge of returning the vessels to Norway, Captain Henry Wray, insisted that 'every thing is on board the Cutters that was delivered in my charge', except an anchor that was 'left hooked to the Moorings at Sheerness', and a boat towed by the Dutch cutter, which was lost 'in a heavy Sea', but the French and Dutch captains insisted that their ships were in a more general 'want of repair'. The 'Store and Provisions are very short of the original Quality', they claimed, with a 'great part having been Embezzled and the remainder having suffered much through dampness and other causes'. The Danish officer who had been charged with the task of overseeing the return of the vessels, Captain Löwenörn, sided with the two captains and refused to accept the return of the vessels.[107] This turn of events sparked a fierce response from London, and Fitzgerald was instructed to make a 'formal complaint' to the Danish government on the actions of the Danish officer, stressing that:

> it is by no means His Majesty's wish to decline entering into a fair discussion with the Danish Government on any just representation that may be made to Him on the part of the His Danish Majesty respecting any difference between the former and present state or value of those ships, & the causes of such difference. But that it is the offensive intervention of His Majesty's Enemies in this proceeding, permitted by the Danish Officer, of which His Majesty complains.

Wray was to make another attempt to return the vessels, and should Lövenörn 'decline to receive them' yet again, he was simply to leave the ships at Farsund, and 'depart without delay'.[108] The intervention seems to have resolved the issue. All the ships were now restored, Wray returned to Britain and the *Diable* resumed its privateering career.[109]

Before his partaking in the capture of the *Diable*, Captain Malbon had been involved in another controversial case, the capture of the British vessel the *Prosperous Mary*. Although it was not directly related to privateering, this case also concerned violations of neutral waters, and took years to resolve. In the letter Malbon submitted to John Mitchell the day after the capture on 27 October 1795, he explained the incident in the following way: while on patrol duty off the southern tip of Norway, Malbon had detected an 'Armed Vessel' sailing close to the shore, and 'knowing that there were no British Armed Vessels on this Part of the Coast' apart from his own ships—the frigate *Dryad* and the *Kite*—he 'naturally concluded she was an Enemy under British Colours'. He therefore laid chase to the vessel, but as this Brigg was 'remarkably fast', the *Dryad* could not keep up and, instead, the *Kite* followed her towards Flekkerøy. Just as the *Kite* was about to catch up, the Brigg cast anchor and 'He who calls himself

Master', together with part of the crew, lowered a boat and absconded inland. When Captain Mackenzie of the *Kite* confronted the few remaining crewmembers on board the ship, they could not produce any papers to verify the identity of the ship, but claimed that she belonged to 'a Mr. Benjamin Douglass of Guernsey'. Upon inspecting the vessel, however, a 'parcel of Letters relating to Smuggling' was found, and it was clear that she was fully rigged as a warship, carrying 14 guns, as well as 4 in reserve. Because of these suspicious circumstances, and considering that she had been captured 'among the Norway Rocks', Malbon decided to bring the ship into Kristiansand in order 'to have the matter more fully investigated'. Hopefully, any complaints from the Danish government could then be avoided.[110] There was, of course, no doubt that the capture of the *Prosperous Mary* had taken place in neutral waters, but Malbon would later claim that the point of initial contact had been outside of the neutral belt—or more precisely—outside the range of the shore-based cannon, stating 'that when the Chace began she was between 10 & 12 English miles from the Danish Coast; Consequently not within Gunshot of the said Coast'.[111] Was this sufficient to make the capture legal? Mitchell tried to argue so in his subsequent discussions with Governor Levetzow. As an illegally 'Armed Smuggler Navigated by British Subjects … for the purpose of introducing Contraband Goods in Great Britain and Ireland', Mitchell stated, the ship was to be considered 'an acting Pirate by the Laws of England, & I presume by the Laws of all other European Maritime States'. For that reason, Malbon had been both 'fully authorized, and in manner obliged' to seize the vessel, but since the capture had taken place 'upon the Territories of the King of Denmark', he was nonetheless prepared to deliver her over to the governor for 'safe deposit'. Levetzow responded that since the vessel had been captured in neutral waters, it was for the King of Denmark to decide the matter, suggesting that they pass the whole question on to Bernstorff and Craufurd in Copenhagen. Mitchell, however, insisted that 'all such cases wherein British Subjects *only* are concerned, can only be tried in & decided upon by British Tribunals', and Levetzow did not find reason to contest this argument, as long as the ship remained in Kristiansand harbour for the time being. It was agreed that the 'Military Commander' in town should take the ship into 'safe Custody' to ensure that the crew did not try to escape with the vessel.[112] The case now moved on to Copenhagen where news of the incident appears to have reached Bernstorff before it came to the attention of Craufurd. At one of their regular 'conferences', the Danish minister raised the issue, though without 'the smallest appearance of ill humour', Craufurd reported. In fact,

> Count Bernstorff even indulged in some pleasantry on the singularity of their Coast having been violated by an English Frigate for the purpose of capturing an English vessel. The only instance of the kind, he said, he had ever known![113]

While Bernstorff and Craufurd were discussing the case, the owner of the *Prosperous Mary*—whose real name was Ninian Douglass—presented a petition to the Danish government for the restoration of his vessel. Admitting no misbehaviour whatsoever, Douglass simply stated that the *Prosperous Mary* had been on a 'Voyage' from Guernsey to 'Gottenburgh for a Cargo', and that her Captain Patrick Henvey had thought the approaching British warships 'Enemies', and therefore tried to 'Escape them' into the 'safety of Your Majesty's Harbour of Fleckery'. When the ship had been taken to Kristiansand by Malbon, Henvey had approached the 'Governor there and represented the Case to him', hoping for 'redress' against the British officers, whose 'behaviour was truely [*sic*] unwarrantable'. Douglass therefore hoped that the ship could be restored to him, and continue her 'intended Voyage to Gottenburgh'.[114] He also, however, decided to take legal action against Malbon and Mackenzie in England in order 'to recover the Value' of his ship, and as long as the case was before the law courts, nothing more was done about it on the part of either the British or the Danish authorities. The ship remained in detention in Kristiansand harbour for years thereafter. By April 1800, however, Douglass had 'relinquished' his legal action, and the British government moved to settle the affair.[115] The new British representative in Copenhagen, Anthony Merry, was instructed to 'acquaint the Danish Ministers, that His Majesty's Government consents to this Vessel, the Prosperous Mary being restored to her Owner, Mr. Douglas, or to any Person or Persons legally authorized by him to receive her'.[116] Thus, in this case also, the British government accepted that the capture had been unlawful, while the Danish government simply awaited the English court case. The most extraordinary of all the individual cases involving transgressions of neutral waters, however, was arguably that of the prize vessel the *Bell and Ann*, and we will address this in a separate section.

The *Bell & Ann* Case

'An unusual transaction hapned [*sic*] upon this River lately', Alexander Grieg, the British consul at Bergen, wrote to Grenville in late January 1798. The 'river' in question was the narrow passage between the island of Karmøy and the mainland, just north of Stavanger, and the transaction concerned the recapture of a prize vessel during the night from 22 to 23 December 1797. The circumstances of this recapture were, as Grieg stated, truly unusual. A British merchant ship, the sloop *Bell & Ann*, had been brought into the tiny harbour of Høyevarde on the eastern side of Karmøy, as a prize to the French privateer *L'Anacreon*, commanded by 'Capt. Fresson'. Lying in the harbour at the same time was also a British vessel, 'the *Favourite* of London commanded by Captain Robert Lawson', and during the night, the *Bell & Ann* had disappeared from the port. 'Six Seamen' who had deserted from the *Favorite* were suspected of being the 'perpetrators of this unlawfull [*sic*] transaction', and in the wake of this affair, the French consul at Bergen had 'instituted Examinations tending to Criminate Capt. Lawson'.[117] As far as Grieg had been able to determine, however, Lawson 'seems upon the whole to have been ignorant of the Desertion of the Six Seamen before the morning after the Prise Sloop was carried to sea' and, for that reason, appeared to be innocent. The recapture of the *Bell & Ann*, on the other hand, was undoubtedly unlawful, Grieg thought, and he had therefore informed the Admiralty of the incident so that they could take the 'necessary Steps to secure the Sloop if She arrived in any Port in Great Britain'. Since then, Grieg had received news that the *Bell & Ann* had made port in Harwich. All in all, he complained, the whole affair had 'created me excessive trouble, chicane & expence'.[118] After the *Bell & Ann* had departed from Høyevarde, Captain Lawson hired a few local pilots to make up for the deserted crewmembers, and set sail again. Poor weather, however, caused damage to the *Favorite*, and forced Lawson to take refuge in Bergen, where he was required to remain as the ship needed 'thorough Repair'.[119] It was this delay, which gave the French consul the opportunity to lodge a complaint on the capture of the *Bell & Ann* with the local authorities in Bergen, who in turn initiated formal legal hearings in preparation for a full-fledged court case. The hearings clarified most details of the incident at Høyevarde, but arguably not the central question of whether Lawson bore any responsibility for the recapture.

Since the recapture of the *Bell & Ann* had taken place at Karmøy, the case against Captain Lawson was due to be held before the magistrates' court of *Ryfylke*, the Stavanger region to which Karmøy belonged. The court was set at the house of an inn-keeper at Høyevarde, Magnus Gabrielsen, and the preliminary hearings were conducted on 23 January 1798. The purpose of the hearings was to 'shed further light', as it was as stated, on the 'criminal Act' which had taken place at Høyevarde port in December 1797, though as it emerged from the subsequent proceedings, the issue at stake was to determine whether there were sufficient grounds for charging Lawson. Had he ordered, accepted or at least been aware of the actions of those of his crewmembers who seized the prize ship *Bell & Ann?* For this, efforts had been made to find and call as many witnesses as possible, and the first witness to be questioned was the pilot Peder Endressen Mæland. Mæland had been present at Høyevarde when the *Favorite* arrived, and could provide a detailed account of events as they had unfolded. He had spotted the British ship arriving from his home at 2 pm on the 20th of December, and had immediately made his way out to the ship to offer his services as pilot. Since he spoke no English, however, he had returned home and called for a friend or acquaintance of his, Mathias Moxem, who did understand English, so that Moxem might accompany him, and present his offer to the captain. Moxem had arrived the next morning, and after he had spoken to the captain, Mæland was hired as pilot. This meant that Mæland was on board the *Favorite* when the prize ship was seized, and he had observed the arrival of that ship in port at dusk on Friday the 22nd. Mæland had dined on the *Favorite* the same evening, and slept on board the subsequent night, during which he had not heard any 'Noise or Alarm'. The next morning, everything was calm and quiet on board as the day before, but Mæland was told by Moxem that, during the night, a boatswain, constable and four other crewmembers had deserted from the ship. A Swedish sailor had then told him that the ship which had arrived the evening before was a French prize, and Mæland could observe for himself that it was now gone. This was as much as Mæland could state based on his own observations, but he added that he had since heard a rumour that 'some English people' had been on board the French prize ship, committed robbery there and then taken the ship away. Whether the captain of the British vessel, Robert Lawson, had been involved in this in any way was, however, 'unknown' to Mæland, notwithstanding the fact that he had piloted the ship to Bergen afterwards, and presumably would have had time and opportunity to investigate. Mathias Moxem was then called as witness, and he confirmed Mæland's testimony, but could not add much beyond that. A further six witnesses were called, of whom three refused to give testimony on the grounds that it had not been clarified what, if any, kind of financial compensation or pay they would receive for this, and the other three did not have anything substantial to add, with one exception. Magnus Gabrielssen, the owner of the inn, stated that in early January, a French privateer had arrived in port, and that he had turned out to be the privateer who had caught the *Bell & Ann* and sent *her* into port. The captain of the privateer was furious when he learnt about the 'abduction' of his prize, and had subsequently sailed on to Stavanger. In other words, the *Bell & Ann* had arrived at Høyevarde with nothing more than a small prize crew to protect her, and it seems likely that this was why some of the crewmembers on a British merchant vessel had taken the chance to board the ship. An unstated number of further witnesses did not meet, and the hearing was adjourned.[120]

A so-called extra court was then held at the same place on 20 March for the purpose of obtaining further testimonies from witnesses, as well as to prepare the case against Lawson. Both an official prosecutor and a defence lawyer were now appointed. Lawson himself was not present. Thirteen witnesses gave testimony over two days, and again, several witnesses who had been called did not meet. Only four witnesses gave testimonies on the first day, three of whom could not provide much of substance beyond the now common rumours which Mæland had referred to, and that there had, in fact, been considerable commotion and noise when the party of British sailors entered the prize ship at night. The fourth witness, however, the pilot Tormod Tormodsen, could provide more information on the cause of events. Although it is not fully clear from the court protocol, Tormodsen appears to have piloted the prize ship into port, and he was on the ship when the British party entered. He could therefore confirm that they had been armed; that he and others on board the prize ship had been threatened directly, 'Pistols aimed at his Chest'; that the French prize crew had been taken prisoners and then sent off the ship; that the French had been robbed of 'Money and Clothing' and that Tormodsen had been forced to pilot the ship out of the harbour in the middle of the night, while two 'Englishmen' who were both brandishing 'naked Sabers' had been positioned to 'look after him'. Most crucially, though, Tormodsen had received a note to Captain Lawson from the British mate on board the prize ship, but although the note was 'unsealed', he does not seem to have tried to read it, nor was he asked about its content during the examination. Unable to make his way to the *Favorite* as long as he was forced to pilot the prize ship out of port, however, he passed the note on to another pilot, Endre Endresen, so that he might do it for him. Moxem was now meant to have testified, but as it was too late in the day, the court was adjourned, upon which Moxem stated that he would not turn up the next day. He did not state why, but a general complaint made by many of the witnesses was that testifying constituted a considerable loss to them, both in terms of travel expenses and in terms of lost working time.[121] The remaining nine witnesses gave testimony the following day, and they could confirm many of the points already made, such as that Tormodsen had been threatened to pilot the prize ship, and that the British boarding party had stolen money and clothes from the French prize crew. One major new piece of information that emerged was, however, that both the prize ship and the *Favorite* had called upon the port of Kopervik (just north of Høyevarde) shortly before arriving at Høyevarde. The pilots on board the *Favorite*—who were the first two witnesses called—had then been given the task of taking Lawson over to the prize ship (presumably by small boat). Lawson had not actually entered the ship, but the British mate on board had appeared on deck, and the two of them had talked for a while. Since neither of the two witnesses knew any English, however, they could not say what the conversation had concerned. The British ship had then left Kopervik shortly before the prize ship, and the witnesses had observed Lawson speaking to his crew, but again they could not say about what. At this point, the prosecutor asked if the crew had seemed 'particularly cheerful' at this point, but the witnesses could not say. The following questioning of witnesses saw a greater focus on the central question: whether Lawson had been involved in the actions of those of his crew who seized the prize ship, but arguably without establishing much of substance. Halvor Johansen Kaalstöe, another witness who had been hired by Lawson for the journey out of Høyevarde, stated that upon their arrival at Bergen, he had been told by an 'easterner' (Norwegian from the eastern part of southern Norway) by the name of Conrad, that a sailor on board the *Favorite* had held that Lawson's claims of ignorance were not to be believed. Hans Birch, for the defence, then asked if this Conrad had said who the sailor in question was, but Kaalstöe could confirm that he had not. Mons Monsen Mæland—who had been on board the *Favorite* during the crucial hours because he had brought provisions to the ship in the shape of milk, and then been unable to leave when the crew refused to give him back his milk churn—could confirm that Lawson had been in his cabin all night. He did not know, however, if Lawson had ordered the seizure of the prize ship, or if it had 'happened with his knowledge'. The 11th witness called, Andreas Christian Friis, a Royal Customs officer at Kopervik, told the court that a sailor, who had been on board the *Favorite* on the journey from Høyevarde to Bergen, had told him that Captain Lawson had been 'fully aware' of the whole incident, and that the shackles, which had been used to chain up the French prize crew before the they were sent ashore, had been collected in Lawson's own cabin. Friis could not, however, produce the name of this sailor. The final two witnesses could not add anything of significance, and this led Hans Birch to sum up the proceedings of the day in dismissive terms. Having observed closely the statements made by the various witnesses, he found it to be 'as much unnecessary as superfluous' of him to uphold the court with any further 'contra questions' on his part. No evidence had so far been presented which incriminated Captain Lawson 'in the slightest way', he claimed, and those few witnesses who had argued otherwise had based their accusations on nothing but 'Rumours and Presumptions'. As with the preliminary hearings, however, there were also now witnesses who had failed to turn up. Some of them had valid reason, such as that they had been away on travel when the summons had been delivered at their home, but for three witnesses, Moxem, Mæland and another pilot, Rasmus Endresen Mæland, there was not such excuse. The three of them were now to be cautioned that, unless they turned up at a subsequent extra court on 20 April, they would be fined 10 rixdollars each.[122] A further seven witnesses gave testimony over two days for this second session of the 'extra court', including the brothers Peder and Rasmus Endresen Mæland, neither of whom could provide any new information. Endre Endresen—the pilot who had received the note to Lawson from Tormodsen—could, however, shed further light on this particular issue.[123] While he had not read the note himself, Endresen stated that he had heard it read out aloud by the British boatswain to the crew on board the prize ship, and could remember 'some of its content'; more specifically: 'that they had now left him, and were out in the open Sea, hoping to arrive happily in Scotland and wishing Cap. Lawson would soon join them'. If Endresen remembered correctly, indications were in other words that Lawson was involved, but this was hardly conclusive evidence, and he could not provide any other information to confirm the impression either. It was not made clear if the note ever reached Lawson. The following day only contained one testimony, that of the 20th witness Mathias Moxem.

Moxem's presence on the *Favorite* during the crucial hours and his knowledge of English arguably made him a central witness, but he was not able to provide much more information now than he had during the hearing in January. According to Moxem, Lawson had enquired after his missing crewmembers the morning after they had seized the *Bell & Ann*, to which his mate had replied that six men had deserted during the night. Moxem had subsequently asked Lawson if he had been involved in the capture of the prize ship, but Lawson had insisted that he was entirely 'ignorant' of the plans to seize and 'abduct' the vessel. The proceedings of the day ended with statements by the prosecution and defence, who argued alternatively that Lawson was undoubtedly guilty (prosecution) and that there was no case to answer (defence).[124] The defence won out, and the case was dropped.

Although Lawson had never actually been arrested and the charges against him were given up, his ship remained under detention in Bergen, and the question of its release was far from settled. Governor Fredrik Hauch had informed Grieg shortly after the extra court was adjourned that Lawson 'must not be allowed to Sail from hence before He has given full and sufficient Security for the every thing that can depend upon the affair, respecting the French Prise Bell & Ann', and the *Favorite* was in any case in such a 'wrecked state' that she could not sail, Grieg reported. Unable to leave Bergen, Lawson had contacted his 'Concerns in Britain' to send a vessel across to Bergen to carry the cargo of the *Favorite* home, but to this move Hauch reacted promptly. Lawson was to write to his contacts in Britain to call off the vessel, and Hauch now also threatened to arrest Lawson should he 'attempt to leave' Bergen. The problem was, of course, that although Lawson had been cleared—or at least his culpability could not be proved—the seizure and abduction of the *Bell & Ann* remained a serious violation of Danish-Norwegian neutrality. As Grieg stated, the crewmembers who had done this deserved punishment, 'first for deserting from their Ship and afterwards doing an Action tending to disturb the Harmony that had hitherto subsisted between the Courts of Great Britain & Denmark'.[125] The case was perhaps not *that* serious, but the Danish government nevertheless presented two demands to its British counterpart, both of which would have to be met if the *Favorite* was to be released: first that the *Bell & Ann* be returned to a port in Denmark or Norway and, second, that the perpetrators were given an 'exemplary punishment'. Lawson had provided a list of the names of the crewmembers who had deserted, which meant that they could be identified, but by the time the official Danish note was submitted by the ambassador to London, Count Wedel Jarlsberg, in late June 1798, it was clear that they had 'made themselves invisible', and had therefore not been apprehended.[126] According to the owners of the *Favorite*—who had taken upon themselves the task of investigating the case—the original owner of the *Bell & Ann*, a 'Mr David Cargill of Arbroath', had travelled down to Harwich himself and 'paid to the Sailors who had run away with this Ship from Norway, Three Hundred Pounds'. The sailors had then given up the ship to Cargill, who had brought it back with him to Arbroath. It was not clear, however, where the sailors had taken off to, or if they had been apprehended thereafter.[127] By the end of the year, the new Danish ambassador to London, G. H. Schönborn, submitted another note to 'remind' the British government of the previous note by Wedel Jarlsberg, and to request that the matter be brought 'to the conclusion that the Court of Denmark has every right to expect', but nothing much appears to have happened.[128] In February the next year, the owners of the *Favorite* made another attempt to have their vessel released, writing a petition to the Danish king and, by now, it was also clear that Lawson had been allowed to leave Bergen, and that he had travelled to London to discuss the matter with the owners. The petition made no mention of the Danish demand to have the *Bell & Ann* restored, however, simply arguing for the release of the *Favorite* on the grounds that 'Capt. Lawson and his remaining Crew' had been 'fully exculpated' of the charges brought against them.[129] The plan appears to have been to follow up on this by sending 'Mr Lawson to Copenhagen to pursue their claim, aided by his Government', as Anthony Merry stated in an official note to Bernstorff just under a year later, but nothing came of this either when Lawson turned seriously ill.[130] Merry proceeded to raise the issue with Bernstorff at one of their conferences, but the Danish minister responded in a predicable manner: the release of the *Favorite* was conditional on the restoration of the *Bell & Ann* to the French and, for that reason, 'the Affair' could only be resolved by the British government 'restoring the latter Vessel'.[131] It is not clear if the British government refused to restore the *Bell & Ann* or, indeed, if the British sailors who had taken her were ever caught, but the case seems to have remained unresolved. In November 1801, Alexander Grieg reported to the new Foreign Secretary Lord Hawkesbury that the *Favorite* was still 'detained here as a Reprisal for a French Prize', and that there was nothing he was allowed to do about it as long as the case was under dispute 'between His Majestys Court and that of Denmark'.[132]

As an example of a British crew, stealing back a British ship from a neutral port, the *Bell & Ann* case was probably unique in the history of privateering, but together with the other individual cases addressed here, it serves to demonstrate the many, and different, kinds of problems privateering out of neutral waters could and did result in. In most cases, however, captured British vessels were brought into Norwegian ports without such complications. What became of them, and was it correct as Mitchell had claimed that, by the end of 1795, the governor of Kristiansand was 'selling them daily'?[133] The local publication, the *Christiansand Weekly Gazette*, provides some answers to this question.

Auctions: The Case of the *Christiansand Weekly Gazette*

Under the British-Danish agreement reached in August 1793, only so-called perishable goods could be condemned and sold in Norwegian ports. Neither the prize vessels themselves, nor any other kind of cargo they might carry could be disposed of there, and the French privateers were instead obliged to bring both ships and non-perishable goods back to France. As we saw in Chap. 2, however, Mitchell discovered that such sales took place all the same, and raised the issue with governor Levetzow in Kristiansand, leading to the exchange between himself and the governor in the *Christiansand Weekly Gazette* in the late autumn of 1795. Although many of the sales which had taken place up till then were found to be in breach of the British-Danish agreement from 1793, evidence from the *Gazette* reveals that the problem persisted thereafter. It also sheds light on the extent and nature of sales in the area the newspaper covered, the coastline from Stavanger in the West to Risør in the East.[134]

As was normally the case for prizes condemned in the home country of privateers, those that were brought into neutral Norway and condemned there were also sold at auctions. Advertisements for such auctions were inserted in the *Gazette* throughout the period from 1793 until the closure of the ports in 1799, though there were few before 1795, and a marked increase from 1797 onwards. At least 60 individual auctions of prize vessels were advertised over the course of the whole period. Usually, the goods carried by the ships were sold together with the vessels themselves but, in a handful of cases, separate auctions were held for the sale of the cargo. In most cases, the auctions of prize vessels involved the sale of one or two ships, but there were also examples of multiple vessels being put up for sale. In May 1796, for example, Daniel Isaachsen, consul for the Dutch at Kristiansand, placed an advertisement for the auctioning of 11 prize vessels captured and brought into port by Dutch warships.[135] The total number of vessels put up for sale exceeded 80. Most advertisements were re-issued two, three or four times, which means that the first notification came well in advance of the auction, and sometimes quite a long time in advance too. The French consul at Kristiansand, Pierre Pauly, for example, re-issued the same advertisement for the auction of the *Hoop* and the *James* to be held at Farsund no fewer than seven times in the spring of 1797. The frequent re-issuing of advertisements also meant that most issues of the *Gazette* contained information about auctions, and that they took up a substantial amount of space in this small publication. The majority of the auctions were held at either Kristiansand or Farsund, but the port towns of Stavanger, Egersund, Flekkefjord, Mandal, Arendal and Risør all hosted auctions from time to time. The advertisements were inserted by either the French or Dutch consuls themselves, by the Norwegian 'commissioners' they had appointed to assist them in the various port towns or by commissioners acting on behalf of the privateer that had captured the merchantman or men in question. Thus in one advertisement from January 1796, the wealthy Kristiansand merchant Niels Moe entitled himself 'Commissioner for the Cutter la Vengence Capt. L'Eveille, and all its Prizes in this District', though at other times he acted as commissioner for Pauly directly. Although this meant that Moe was in charge of the auction, his role as commissioner was not enough to make the sale legal. It was important that the auction had been sanctioned by the appropriate authorities and, as Moe wrote in his advertisement, such approval had been given. The full text read:

> In the month of March forthcoming, I intend to sell by public Auction, the Prize Ship *Alexander the Hugh*, now at Farsund, together with its cargo of malt and oats; by permission of the appropriate Authorities and with the approval of the French Consul Pauly; which advertisement serves as a preliminary notification only, Time and Place to be decided. Kristiansand 29 January 1796.[136]

Other advertisements stated explicitly that the sale was 'legal', and the importance of the official sanction is borne out by a specific case from March 1797. Having discovered a 'Notification from Stavanger' of a forthcoming auction in the latest issue of the *Gazette*—for which 'no other Permission or Authority, than the Commissioner's, who calls himself Kielland' had been given—Consul Pauly found himself with no choice but to react, and to 'protest against such assertiveness on the part of a private Man'. Kielland could not claim ignorance, Pauly stated, of the unlawful nature of an auction that had not been given prior approval by the French consul and 'Permission by the Royal Danish Chancery'. For that reason, he concluded, the advertised auction could 'not take place'. Apparently, Kielland had applied to become commissioner for the French consul about six months earlier, but as he had not yet been appointed, he was in no position to advertise auctions.[137] In most cases, however, due authorisation appears to have been given for the auctions that were advertised, and the case of Kielland in Stavanger indicates that the French consuls were concerned to make sure that the correct procedure was upheld. It is important to note in this context also that none of the (very few) auctions that were advertised before 1795 were commissioned by a French consul, which of course is consistent with the French government's initial insistence that prizes be brought back to France, and the reference to the Danish Chancery suggests that, in this case at least, approval was granted from Copenhagen.

Moe's advertisement was very brief and did not contain any information about the prize vessel itself. More often than not, however, details about the ship, such as type, tonnage and age, would be included, as well as a more general assessment of its state of repair. Similar details about the quality of the cargo were also included in many cases, and both ship and cargo could normally be inspected at the place of auction 8 days in advance. Most of the vessels that were brought into port in Norway seem to have carried a fairly uniform cargo, but in some cases, the ship held a variety of goods, and the general rule then appears to have been that everything was put up for sale, perishable or not. The advertisement for the auction of the *Charlotte*—which was due to be held at the house of 'Sören & Jonas Lund' at Farsund on 8 June 1798—stated that the cargo consisted of a variety of clothes 'of different Colours and Qualities', shoes and hats, as well as 'Wine- Beer- and Dessert Glasses, Decanters etc.; English Beer in Bottles; Butter, Cheese, Beef, salted Pork, 237 Iron rods etc. etc.'[138] In one single case, the list of goods also included items which could arguably been seen as contraband (though as long as the goods were sold to neutral Norwegians, this was perhaps not a problem). The cargo of the *Lucinda*, which was due to be auctioned by Isaac Leth at Arendal in February 1798, included six 'Brass Muskets' and two 'Rifles'.[139] The sale of ship and cargo was not all, however. Many advertisements also stated that the ship's 'inventory' would be put up for sale at the same auction as the ship, and that 'lists' specifying the content of this inventory would be made available for inspection, typically at the place of the auction, as well as in one or two other port towns. In a few cases, however, copies of the list were made available in a number of places, and even beyond Norway. The inventory list for the *Guildford* of Hull—a ten-year-old 'Barque-Ship' of 194 tons, which was put up for sale at the house of Jacob Kielland & Son in Stavanger on 23 August 1799—could be seen at the residences of the 'Commissioners of the Armateurs' at Bergen, Trondheim, Kristiansand, Arendal, Mandal, Farsund, Flekkefjord, Hamburg, Copenhagen and Altona.[140] Indications were, in other words, that just about *anything* held on board a captured ship that *could* potentially be sold, *was* presented for sale at the auction.

These advertisements do not, of course, say anything directly about the actual sales at the subsequent auctions. Indirectly, however, a few things can be deduced from them nonetheless. First, it is unlikely that such auctions would have been held year after year if the sales were not good, suggesting that they must at least have been reasonably successful. Second, the advertisement of 'inventories' indicates that there was a market for a wide variety of objects. Moreover, there are a couple of examples of new auctions, which were held for the purpose of disposing of goods that had not been sold at the original auction. In September 1798, for example, Pierre Pauly inserted a notice stating that an auction would be held at Sören and Jonas Lund's in Farsund in order to sell the 'remaining' goods from the *Charlotte*.[141] In this particular case, it is clear that cargo, ship and most of the inventories had been sold at the original auction, but the advertisement of a new auction such as this one also suggests that 'left-overs' from auctions were the exception; that typically, everything was sold at the first attempt.

One of the last auctions to be advertised in the *Christiansand Weekly Gazette* was that of the brig the *Isabelle* of Banff, which had been captured by the French privateer *L'Adelle* and brought into Stavanger. The auction of ship and inventory was due to be held at the house of the notable Stavanger-merchant Peder Valentin Rosenkilde on 30 August the same year, by which time the ship's cargo of barley had already been sold at a separate auction on 22 June.[142] Before the auction could be held, however, the Danish declaration on the closure of the ports to privateers was published in the 9 August edition of the *Gazette*.[143] It is not clear if the auction of the *Isabelle*—or, indeed, a couple of other auctions that were due to be held around the same time—were ever carried through. What is clear though, is that no further advertisements of auctions were included in the *Gazette* thereafter, suggesting that this kind of prize-sales now came to an end. The material on auctions contained in the *Gazette* cannot be seen as conclusive, but rather represents a case study. It is perfectly possible that auctions were held without a prior notice in this particular publication or, indeed, in areas it did not cover, such as the western coast north of Stavanger, or in what we would now call the Oslofjord region. What this evidence *does* reveal, however, is the nature of the system adopted by the French and Dutch consuls to effectuate the sale of prizes in Norwegian ports, and that, in this, they were able to draw upon the support of Norwegian merchants and others. As Olav Arild Abrahamsen pointed out in his study of the port of Farsund in this period, holding the position of commissioner for prize sales was lucrative, resulting in competition between Norwegian merchants for appointment.[144] The case of the auctions advertised in the *Christiansand Weekly Gazette* thus suggests that sales were good, but it does not answer the question of who bought the prizes.

While no comprehensive study of the purchase of prize goods and vessels in Norwegian ports town during the 1790s has yet been carried out, the issue has been addressed in a couple of local-historical works, most notably by Olav Arild Abrahamsen. What Abrahamsen found was that both goods and vessels were typically purchased by the senior merchants in town—which in the case of Farsund meant the Lund family—often to be sold on to an overseas market, and that many prize vessels were subsequently repurchased by the original owners. This appears to have been the case for Kristiansand too.[145] As we saw in Chap. 2, the British government did not accept the sale of prize vessels to Danish subjects if these vessels had been condemned in Norwegian ports, and threatened to retake them, but what about repurchases by the original owners? Having observed such repurchases in Kristiansand himself, Mitchell questioned Evan Nepean at the Admiralty if they were legal, and if the ships in question would be 'entitled to a British Register?'[146] It is not clear what, if any, reply Mitchell received to his query. The problem went beyond the mere *re*-purchases of prize vessels and goods, however. As Mitchell complained less than a year later, British merchants were lining up to purchase *any* prize vessels and goods that were put up for sale. 'A number of British Vessels & their Cargos', brought into Bergen by French privateers, had recently been 'bought in for British & Irish Account', Mitchell reported in late May 1796, and the same scenario was now about to repeat itself in Kristiansand. '11 British Vessels & Cargos, Prizes to the Dutch are to be sold here', Mitchell wrote, and he was 'sorry to see' that 'several British & Irish Merchants' were on site 'intending to purchase both the Vessels & Cargoes'. Faced with this situation, Mitchell stated:

> I have done everything in my Power to discourage this Commercial intercourse with our Enemies, but while such Captured Vessels & Cargos are permitted to be entered in Great Britain & Ireland my Endeavours are of no Effect. This Commercial intercourse between British Merchants and the Enemy, or their Agents here is a great encouragement to Privateering.[147]

Eventually, legal advice was sought to determine the issue, and John Nicholl—who succeeded William Scott as king's advocate in November 1798—was of the clear

> Opinion that these purchases by British Subjects are illegal in themselves, and highly injurious to the Interests of this Country—Such Purchases, if immediately from the Enemy, are not only Acts of trading with the Enemy, (which is prohibited to all His Majesty's Subjects) but aggravated, by directly aiding them in giving Success to their Hostilities against the British Commerce.[148]

By the time Nicholl presented his assessment in May 1799, however, the closure of the Norwegian ports to privateers was just around the corner.

Conclusion

The experience of French (and Dutch) privateers operating out of Norwegian ports in the 1790s arguably serves to demonstrate two things. At a more general or overall level it reveals that—no matter how well established the institution of privateering had become by the later eighteenth century, governed as it was by an extensive set of commonly agreed rules (letters of marque, prize courts, etc.)—it was still difficult to ensure that these rules were adhered to in practice. This was then further complicated by the special case of privateers using neutral ports, for which there were little in terms of clear rules either in specific treatises or in the Law of Nations. Seen from the British perspective, the situation appeared rather hopeless by the time the Norwegian ports were finally closed to privateers in 1799. The British envoy to Copenhagen at the time, Robert Stephen Fitzgerald, summed up the accumulated British grievances in an unusually fiercely worded note to Bernstorff written shortly after he had been notified about the closure.

The occasion was a recent 'dispute' that had arisen 'between British and Danish commanders regarding a neutral ship apprehended and captured' in the Mediterranean, and which Fitzgerald felt he had to address. From this individual case, however, Fitzgerald proceeded to review British-Danish relations in general, focusing on the visitation issue and British captures of Danish vessels carrying contraband goods to France and on French privateers in Norwegian ports. The note, which was in French, was written in a rhetorical style, containing statements such as:

> To hear all the petty evils of which Denmark likes to complain so loudly, is it to be believed that the circumstances of a war without parallel [have] in themselves led, in this area of the Globe as in any other, in a more or less great proposition, to this country *alone* suffering all the sorrows, all the indignities, enduring all the calamities, and that Great Britain *alone* was the one who bestowed it upon them?

No, quite to the contrary, Fitzgerald held that 'the speculative charges of violence, intimidation, infractions of territory, and excesses that are attributed to the English nation' by the Danish government 'will disappear before the presentation of England's very different and more serious Table of Grievances'. The Danes 'ever meek and obliging towards France, ever rigid and terse towards England' had demonstrated their 'Partiality' for Britain's enemies beyond any doubt. Nowhere could this be more clearly seen than in relation to French privateers, both with respect to individual cases and in terms of the overall Danish approach. '*The Favourite of London*, a superb merchant vessel', Fitzgerald wrote, had been

> apprehended by the Order of the Government in Bergen since 18th May of the simple suspicion, articulated by an Agent of France, that the Captain of the Vessel had favoured the clandestine seizure of another merchant ship from his Nation that the Enemy had brought to Norway.

The case of Captain Lawson was, of course, an unusual one, but the Danish (and Norwegian) pro-French attitudes could be seen in other cases too. While the privateers *Le Petit Diable*, *Le Petit Furet* and *Vlugheid* had all been 'loyally returned' to their owners, Fitzgerald wrote, the 'English merchant ship, *The Nancy of Ayr*' had been held in a Norwegian port, and only returned to its owners after 'three years of requests, delays and enormous expenses for those concerned'. The situation was no better as far as the general picture was concerned:

> Can it be believed that, after more than six years, the Ports of Norway offer every encouragement to the Enemy Privateers to take their seizure there and offload them at a good price; provide them assistance in war munitions as well as in victuals, procure for them the means to recover and rebuild from accidents at sea as well as to escape from the Vigilance of the British War Vessels?

Clearly, this state of affairs was not in line with the agreement reached in 1793, but to make matters worse the Danish government had permitted the French consuls

> to establish their private quarters in Norway in so many independent Admiralty Courts of the sovereign Jurisdiction of the Country, where they judge, pass sentence, condemn and order the Sale of Property abducted from the Subjects of a Power friendly towards His Majesty the King of Denmark.[149]

Fitzgerald's tirade was arguably slightly odd since all the problems he complained of, as far as privateering was concerned, were meant to be resolved by the forthcoming closure of the ports and, in that sense, this was all old news, but it nevertheless spoke to the exasperation felt on the British side by 1799. It was also, of course, a very different version of events compared to that presented in the Danish declaration and, for that reason, could be seen as a British riposte to the official Danish view. The question now was whether the closure of the ports would be accepted and honoured by all sides, and we will return to this issue in Chap. 6.

Notes

1. Patrick Crowhurst, *The Defence of British Trade 1689–1815* (Wm Dawson & Sons, Folkstone, 1977), pp. 46–54.

2. Crowhurst, *Defence of Trade*, p. 55; and Richard Hill, *The Prizes of WAR: The Naval Prize System in the Napoleonic Wars, 1793–1815* (Sutton Publishing, Phoenix Mill, 1998), p. 8.
3. Hill, *Prizes of WAR*, p. 8.
4. 22 Geo. II c.33, Article XVII 'of not taking Care of Ships under Convoy', as cited in: N. A. M. Rodger, *Articles of War: The Statutes which Governed our Fighting Navies 1661, 1749 and 1886* (Kenneth Mason, Homewell, 1982), p. 25. The 'Articles of War', or 'Laws of War and Ordinances of the Sea', was the 'rulebook' of the Royal Navy, and dated from 1661, but the original Act had not included any article on convoys. Convoy duty was not very popular in the Royal Navy, and commanders would therefore often try to avoid it. See: Hill, *Prizes of WAR*, pp. 60–61; and N. A. M. Rodger, *The Command of the Ocean: A Naval History of Britain, 1649–1815*, (Penguin, London, 2006), pp. 15, 59–60.
5. See: Rodger, *Command of the Ocean*, p. 559; and Patrick Crowhurst, *The French War on Trade: Privateering 1793–1815* (Scholar Press, Aldershot, 1989), pp. 31–32.
6. 38.Geo III c. 76 §2 [1798]; and 41 Geo III c. 57 §3 [1803].
7. Crowhurst, *Defence of British Trade*, pp. 38, 72–74. Convoys bound for Archangel were also assembled at the Nore.
8. National Archives [NA], ADM 1/3841, Admiralty, Letters to British Consuls, N. Fenwick to Philip Stevens Esq., 10 September 1793. Letters to British Consuls for the period covered here are contained in boxes 3841–3845.
9. NA, ADM 1/3842, N. Fenwick to Evan Nepean Esq., Elsinore 29 August 1795; N. Fenwick to Evan Nepean Esq., Elsinore 8 August 1797; Charles Fenwick to Evan Nepean Esq., Elsinore 30 June 1798; and Charles Fenwick to Evan Nepean Esq., Elsinore 25 May 1799.
10. *Ibid.*, N. Fenwick to Evan Nepean Esq., Elsinore 12 April 1796; and N. Fenwick to Evan Nepean Esq., Elsinore 4 July 1795.
11. *Ibid.*, N. Fenwick to Evan Nepean Esq., Elsinore 10 October 1795; and N. Fenwick to Evan Nepean Esq., Elsinore 3 October 1795.
12. *Ibid.*, N. Fenwick to Evan Nepean Esq., Elsinore 24 June 1797. See also: NA, ADM 1/3841, N. Fenwick to Philip Stevens, Elsinore 16 August 1794.
13. NA, FO 22/21, Foreign Office Correspondence, Denmark, fos. 108–110, James Craufurd to Lord Grenville, Copenhagen 27 December 1794 [quote fo. 108v-109.
14. Unfortunately, the convoy had to return due to contrary winds, and the stay at Elsinore turned out to be a lengthy one after all. John Barney, 'North Sea and Baltic Convey 1793–1814: As Experienced by Merchant

Masters Employed by Michael Henley & Son', *The Mariner's Mirror*, 95/4 (2009), pp. 430–431.
15. NA, ADM 1/3842, N. Fenwick to Evan Nepean Esq., Elsinore 29 July 1797.
16. NA, ADM 1/3841, N. Fenwick to Philip Stevens Esq., Elsinore 5 November 1793.
17. *Ibid.*, N. Fenwick to Philip Stevens Esq., Elsinore 13 July 1793.
18. The squadron consisted of twelve battleships and eight frigates, all of which were placed under the command of Duncan, see: Eunice H. Turner, 'The Russian Squadron with Admiral Duncan's North Sea Fleet, 1795–1800', *Mariner's Mirror*, 49/5 (1963), pp. 213–215.
19. NA, ADM 1/3842, N. Fenwick to Evan Nepean Esq., Elsinore 5 November 1796.
20. NA, ADM 1/3841, N. Fenwick to Philip Stevens Esq., Elsinore 20 August 1793, and N. Fenwick to Philip Stevens Esq., Esingoer 19 October 1793.
21. NA, ADM 1/3842, Charles Fenwick to Evan Nepean Esq., Elsinore 24 November 1798.
22. See: James Davey, 'Supplied by the enemy: the Royal Navy and the British consular service in the Baltic, 1808–12', in *Historical Research*, 85 (2012), p. 273.
23. NA, ADM 1/3842, Charles Fenwick to Evan Nepean Esq., Elsinore 24 November 1798.
24. NA, ADM 1/3841, J. Wallace to Philip Stevens Esq., Bergen 22 June 1793.
25. *Ibid.*, N. Fenwick to Philip Stevens Esq., Elsinore 6; 13; and 16 July; and 30 November 1793. See p. 151 above.
26. *Ibid.*, N. Fenwick to Philip Stevens Esq., Elsinore 11 January 1794. See also: *ibid.*, N. Fenwick to Philip Stevens, Elsinore 25 January 1794.
27. She was, for example, reported to have captured 3 British, 1 Dutch and 1 Prussian vessel in March the same year, 2 in May, as well as another 13 ships in the summer of 1796, see: NA, FO 22/18, fos. 187–188, John Mitchell to Lord Grenville, Christiania 29 March 1794; NA, FO 22/19, fos. 56–57, John Mitchell to Lord Grenville, Christiania 3 May 1794; and NA, ADM 1/3842, J. Wallace to Evan Nepean Esq., Bergen 4 June 1796.
28. NA, ADM 1/3841, J. Wallace to Philip Stevens Esq., Bergen 20 September 1794.
29. *Ibid.*, J. Wallace to Philip Stevens Esq., Bergen 6 December 1794. Generally speaking, Baltic Sea merchant vessels which were caught by French privateers were brought into ports on the Southern coast of Norway, while ships in the Archangel trade seem to have been landed predominantly in Bergen, but there were exceptions. In late January

1794, for example, Nicholas Fenwick could report that 'two large Dutchmen, for the Baltick' had been carried into Bergen by two French privateers. NA, ADM 1/3841, N. Fenwick to Philip Stevens Esq., Elsinore 25 January 1794.

30. Crowhurst, *Defence of British Trade*, p. 70.
31. Turner, 'The Russian Squadron', p. 220.
32. NA, ADM 1/3841, N. Fenwick to Philip Stevens Esq., Elsinore 3 August 1793. The Dutch were, of course, an ally of Britain at this time in the war.
33. NA, ADM 1/3842, J. Wallace to John Mitchell Esq., Bergen 25 May and 24 September 1796; and *ibid.*, John Mitchell to Evan Nepean Esq., Christiansand 9 October 1796.
34. *Ibid.*, Alex Grieg to Evan Nepean Esq., Bergen 29 July, 19 August, 9 September and 18 November 1797.
35. NA, FO 22/22, fos. 115–116, Thos. Erskine ot J. B. Burgess Esq., Norfolk Street No 7, 31 March 1795 [quote fo. 116]; and *ibid.*, fo. 117, Thos. Erskine to Giert Torreson, London 30 March 1795.
36. NA, ADM 1/3842, John Mitchell to Evan Nepean Esq., Christiansand 1 September 1795 [information about the Admiralty decision has been added to Mitchell's letter]. Mitchell had already presented similar ideas to the Foreign Office, see: NA, FO 22/23, fos. 246–247, John Mitchell to Lord Grenville, Christiania 25 August 1795.
37. NA, ADM 1/3842, John Mitchell to 'Sir' [Evan Nepean], Christiansand 9 October 1796.
38. NA, FO 22/18, fos. 30–31, John Mitchell to Lord Grenville, Christiansand 14 February 1794 [quote fo. 30]. Daniel Hailes, the British envoy to Copenhagen, backed Mitchell's request a week later: *ibid.*, fos. 38–39, D Hailes to Lord Grenville, Copenhagen 22 February 1794. See also: FO 22/19, fos. 56–57, John Mitchell to Lord Grenville, Christiania 3 May 1794.
39. NA, ADM 1/3842, John Mitchell to 'Sir' [Evan Nepean], Christiansand 7 December 1795.
40. NA, ADM 1/3841, N. Fenwick to Philip Stevens Esq., Elsinore 7 September 1793.
41. *Ibid.*, N. Fenwick to Philip Stevens Esq., Elsinore 3; and 17 August 1793 [original emphasis].
42. NA, ADM 1/3842, N. Fenwick to Evan Nepean Esq., Elsinore 6; 9; and 13 August 1796.
43. Davey, 'Supplied by the Enemy', p. 275. The Baltic Sea Fleet was in operation from 1808 to 1812. See: Tim Voelker, *Admiral Saumarez versus Napoleon: The Baltic, 1807–1812* (The Boydell Press, Woodbridge, 2008), p. 1.
44. See Chap. 2, p. 19.

45. Robert Gardiner (ed.), *Fleet Battle and Blockade: The French Revolutionary War 1793-1797 (Chatham Publishing, London, 1996)*, p. 58.
46. See Chap. 2, pp. 19–20.
47. See Chap. 2 on the French policy. In practice, the policy does not appear to have been adhered to very consistently by French privateers, as was revealed in a report Daniel Hailes sent in November 1793: 'Some of the prizes are sent to France, and others brought into Bergen and other Ports in Norway'. NA, FO 22/17, fo. 161, D. Hailes to Lord Grenville, Copenhagen 30 November 1793.
48. NA, ADM 1/3841, J. Wallace to Philip Stevens Esq., Bergen 2 August 1794.
49. *Ibid.*, J. Wallace to Philip Stevens Esq, Bergen 4 October 1794.
50. NA, FO 22/20, fos. 261–262, John Mitchell to Lord Grenville, 'Mandall by the Naze of Norway', 1 October 1794 [quote fo. 261]. See also: NA, FO 22/20, fos. 245–246, D. Hailes to Lord Grenville, Copenhagen 20 September 1794.
51. NA, FO 22/21, fos. 21–22, James Craufurd to Lord Grenville, Copenhagen 1 November 1794 [quote fo. 21]; and *ibid.*, fos 92–95, James Craufurd to Lord Grenville, Copenhagen 29 November 1794.
52. See Mitchell's report to Fitzgerald from November 1796 discussed in Chap. 2.
53. NA, ADM 1/3842, John Mitchell to Evan Nepean Esq., Christiansand 3 June 1796.
54. *Ibid.*, John Mitchell to Evan Nepean Esq., Christiansand 7 June 1796.
55. Joseph Allen, *Battles of the British Navy, Volume 1* (2 vols., Henry G. Bohn, London, 1853), pp. 431–432.
56. NA, ADM 1/3842, Alex Grieg to Evan Nepean, Bergen 21 October 1797 [a list of the captured vessels was included]; and NA, FO 22/29, fo. 170, Robt Steph Fitzgerald to Lord Grenville, Copenhagen 4 November 1797.
57. Allen, *Battles*, p. 517.
58. NA, FO 22/16, fos. 183–186. John Mitchell to Lord Grenville, Christiania 24 June 1793 [quote fo. 183].
59. Informed by Mitchell, Daniel Hailes jumped to the conclusion that 'the Danish Flag and Passports are granted without difficulty, to every Smuggling Adventurer that chuses to apply for them'. NA, FO 22/17, fo. 41, Copenhagen 22 July 1793.
60. NA, FO 22/17, fos. 99–100, John Mitchell to Lord Grenville, Christiania 24 August 1793 [quote fo. 99]; and *ibid.*, fos. 101–105, John Mitchell to Count Bernstorff, Christiania 24 August 1793 [quotes fos. 101-103].
61. *Ibid.*, fos. 162–163, John Mitchell to Lord Grenville, Christiansand 3 December 1793 [quote fos. 162v–163].
62. NA, ADM 1/3841, N. Fenwick to Ph. Stevens Esq., Elsinore 13 July 1793.

63. NA, FO 22/18, fos. 15–16, John Mitchell to Lord Grenville, Christiansand 31 January 1794 [quote fos. 15v–16].
64. See: NA, FO 22/23, fos. 182–183, John Mitchell to Lord Grenville, Christiansand 28 July 1795; and FO 22/24, fos. 185–186, John Mitchell to Lord Grenville, Christiania 23 November 1795.
65. NA, FO 22/29, fos. 233–234, J. Wood to Lord FitzGerald, His Majesty's Sloop Hound, Christiansand, 7 December 1797 [quote fo. 233v].
66. Archives du Ministère des affaires étrangeres, Paris [AMAE], Correspondance politique, Danemark, vol. 169 [CP, Danemark, vol. 169], fos. 138–139, Framery to Citizen Minister, Copenhagen 29 June 1793 [translated from French]; *ibid.*, fos. 155–164, Framery to Le Citoyen Le Brun Ministere des affaires étrangeres, Copenhagen 9 July 1793; fos. 226–227, to Framery, Paris 26 August 1793; fos. 240–241, 'Report on the Measures that have been Taken by the Minister of Foreign Affairs on the Purchase of Saltpetre in Denmark', Paris 4 September 1793 [title translated from French].
67. Daniel Hailes was given clear instructions in March 1793 that 'By Contraband Goods, the British Government mean to understand all the Articles specified in the Convention signed on the 4th July 1780 between Great Britain and Denmark': NA, FO 22/16, fos. 76–82. 'Draft to Mr Hailes', Whitehall 29 March 1793 [quote fo. 79].
68. NA, FO 22/21, fos. 16–18, James Craufurd to Lord Grenville, Copenhagen 25 October 1794 [quote fo. 16v]. See also: FO 211/5, Foreign Office and predecessor, Embassy, Consulate and Legation, Denmark: General Correspondence—Secret Communications, No. 3 to 'My Lord', Copenhagen 25 October 1794.
69. NA, FO 22/27, fos. 96–100, John Mitchell to Lord Robert Fitzgerald, Christiansand 18 November 1796 [quote fo. 96v; this letter has been misplaced in volume 27 of the FO 22 series]; and *ibid.*, fos. 131–132, to Lord Robert Fitzgerald, Downing Street 2 March 1797.
70. *Ibid.*, fos. 175–176, Robt Steph Fitzgerald to le Comte de Bernstorff, Copenhagen 23 March 1797.
71. NA, FO 22/34, fos. 452–456, Rob Steph Fitzgerald to Lord Grenville, Copenhagen 35 May 1799 [quote fo. 453v].
72. NA, FO 22/45, fos. 167–168, Chas Adam to Rear Admiral Vashon, Leith Roads 6 September 1804.
73. NA, FO 22/18, fo. 36, John Mitchell to Lord Grenville, Christiansand 16 February 1794.
74. NA, FO 22/21, fos. 104–105, James Craufurd to Lord Grenville, Copenhagen 16 December 1794; and FO 211/5, No. 13 to 'My Lord', Copenhagen 16 December 1794 [quote fos. 104–104v].
75. NA, FO 22/21, fos. 108–110, James Craufurd to Lord Grenville, Copenhagen 27 December 1794 [quotes 108 and 109]; and FO 20/25,

fos. 63-69, James Craufurd to Lord Grenville, Copenhagen 20 February 1796 [quote fo. 69]. The complete 'regulations' can be found in a proclamation issued on 24 March 1794: NA, FO 22/18, fos. 193–195 [untitled].

76. NA, FO 22/17, fos. 51–52, D. Hailes to Lord Grenville, Copenhagen, 27 July 1793 [quote fo. 52].
77. NA, FO 22/24, fo. 130, 'To the Right Honbl Lord Grenville Principal Secretary of State for Foreign Affairs &c &c. The Humble Petition of Menzies Goalen Ship Carpenters in Leith, Proprietors of the Cargo of the Vessel after mentioned: and of Robert Young, Alexander Allan, Robert Sands, Walter Wood, Alexander Wood, George Sinclair, Jas Borrowman, James Mackell, William Sibbald, David Low, Francis Sharp, John Spence, and John Thomson Junior, Underwriters upon the Vessel & part of the Cargo', Edinburgh 9 October 1793.
78. NA, FO 211/4, Foreign Office and predecessor, Embassy, Consulate and Legation, Denmark: General Correspondence, Grenville, to Daniel Hailes Esq., Whitehall 26 July 1793; and *ibid.*, Sam Thornton to Lord Grenville, London 22 July 1793.
79. NA, FO 22/21, fos. 5–6, John Mitchell to J. B. Burgess Esq., Christiania 12 October 1794.
80. See, for example, a series of letters from the dual-monarchy's Norwegian ambassador to London, Count Wedel Jarlsberg, to Grenville from 1794: NA, FO 22/18, fos. 81, 83, 92, 94–96, 157, 206, 267 and 269.
81. At least one attempt was made to recover a vessel on the grounds that it had been condemned and sold in a port in Norway, rather than taken to France in line with the established rules for privateering. This concerned the vessel the *Star* of Leith, which had been captured in 1795. Five years later, the ship was discovered in the port of Banff in Scotland, arrested there and an 'Action of Restitution' raised before the Court of Admiralty of Scotland. It is not clear what the outcome was. NA, FO 22/38, fos. 165–166, Geo Buchan Hepburn to Lord Advocate for Scotland, Edinburgh 21 November 1800.
82. Wyndham L. Walker, 'Territorial Waters: The Cannon Short Rule', in *British Yearbook of International Law*, vol. 22 (1945), p. 212.
83. The established rule was that a blockade had to be effectively maintained by warships in order to be legitimate. It was not sufficient for a belligerent power to proclaim that the port(s) of the enemy was under blockade. See: Hill, *Prizes of WAR*, pp. 10, 34–42.
84. Walker, 'Territorial Waters'; H. S. K. Kent, 'The Historical Origins of the Three-Mile Limit', in *American Journal of International Law*, vol. 48, no. 4 (1954), p. 542; and Stephen C. Neff, *Justice among Nations: A History of International Law* (Harvard University Press, Cambridge, Massachusetts, 2014), pp. 203–205.

85. A continuous belt could, of course, be utilised by merchant vessels seeking protection from privateers too, since they would be legally immune from attack as long as they stayed within the belt.
86. Kent, 'Historical Origins'; and Walker, 'Territorial Waters'.
87. In late May 1799, for example, Fitzgerald admitted that the capture of the French privateer *Vengeur* by the British ship *Martin* was illegal as it had taken place 'two English Miles from the shore whereas the territorial Sovereignty is considered as extending a Danish Sea League or four English Miles from the Land into the Sea'. A complicating factor in this case was the fact that the *Vengeur* had been chasing a British merchantman at the time, whereby it was also violating neutral waters. NA, FO 22/34, fos. 452–456, Robt Steph Fitzgerald to Lord Grenville, Copenhagen 25 May 1799 [quote fo. 452v].
88. ADM 1/3842, John Wallace [?] to Evan Nepean Esq., Bergen 2 June 1796; and D. H. Reid, 'Danish Neutrality and the Royal Navy 1795–7', in *Mariner's Mirror*, Vol. 76, issue 2 (1990), p. 180.
89. NA, FO 22/27, fos. 96–100, John Mitchell to Lord Robert Fitzgerald, Christiania 18 November 1796 [quote fos. 97v–98].
90. NA, FO 22/17, fos. 75–76, John Mitchell to Lord Grenville, Christiania 3 August 1793 [quote fos. 75-75v].
91. NA, FO 22/31, fos. 80–82, Robt Steph Fitzgerald to Lord Grenville, Copenhagen 19 June 1798 [quote fo. 81].
92. *ibid.* See also: *ibid.*, fos. 197–198, Robt Steph Fitzgerald to Lord Grenville, Copenhagen 11 August 1798; and FO 22/30, fos. 81–83, Robt Steph Fitzgerald to Lord Grenville, Copenhagen 17 February 1798.
93. Hill, *The Prizes of WAR*, p. 123.
94. NA, FO 22/23, fo. 261, John Mitchell to Lord Grenville, Christiansand 30 August 1795; and *ibid.*, fo. 262, John Mitchell to Lord Grenville, Christiansand 31 August 1795.
95. NA, FO 211/5, No. 48 to 'My Lord', Copenhagen 19 September 1795.
96. NA, FO 22/41, fos. 514–556, 'Explanatory Notes upon the Remarks on the Northern Pretention of Free Ship making Free Cargos. By Mr. Mitchell', undated [quote, fo. 521].
97. NA, FO 22/17, fos. 111–112, D. Hailes to Lord Grenville, Copenhagen 7 September 1793 [quotes fos. 111–111v]; and Brian Lavery and Geoff Hunt, *The Frigate Surprise: The Complete Story of the Ship made famous in the Novels of Patrick O'Brian* (W. W. Norton & Company, New York, 2009), p. 36. See also: NA, FO 22/17, fos. 95–96, D. Hailes to Lord Grenville, Copenhagen 24 August 1793; and FO 22/19, fos. 226–227, John Mitchell to Lord Grenville, Christiania 8 June 1794.
98. NA, FO 22/25, fos. 188–193, James Craufurd to Lord Grenville, Copenhagen 14 May 1796 [quote fo. 189; original emphasis].

99. NA, FO 22/25, fos. 211–212, L W. Halsted to Admiral Duncan, Phænix at Sea, 27 April 1796 [quote fo. 211v].
100. NA, ADM 1/2131, Letters from Captains, Surnames M: 1796, Mirajah Malbon to Evan Nepean Esq., Kite Sloop Nore, 4 May 1796; and *ibid.*, Mirajah Malbon to Evan Nepean Esq., Little Nore, His Majesty's Sloop Kite 6 May 1796.
101. NA, FO 22/25, fos. 213–214, 'Extract of a Letter from Adm. Duncan to Evan Nepean Esq., dated Venerable at Sea, 27 April 1796' [quote fo. 213v]; and NA, ADM 1/523, Letters from Commanders-in-Chief, North Sea, 1796, fos. 222–223 [same letter].
102. NA, FO 22/25, fos. 188-193, James Craufurd to Lord Grenville, Copenhagen 14 May 1796 [quotes fo. 189v]; *ibid.*, fos. 194–195, James Craufurd to Lord Grenville, Copenhagen 21 May 1796 [quotes fos. 194-194v]. See also: NA FO 211/5, No. 20, to 'My Lord', Copenhagen 14 May 1796; and No. 26, to 'My Lord', Copenhagen 28 June 1796.
103. Scott was appointed judge at the High Court of Admiralty in 1798.
104. NA, FO 22/25, fos. 217–218, W. Scott to Lord Grenville, 30 May 1796.
105. *Ibid.*, fos. 246–250, James Craufurd to Lord Grenville, Copenhagen 28 June 1796; and ibid., 251–256, James Craufurd to Lord Grenville, Copenhagen 2 July 1796.
106. *Ibid.*, fos. 233–234, 'Memorial from Caleb Fletcher, Merchant of Liverpool, to Grenville', London 8 June 1796.
107. NA, FO 22/26, fos. 129–130, Henry Wray to Evan Nepean Esq., His Majesty's Sloop Sea Gull, 'Fahrsund Norway', 18 September 1796; *ibid.*, fos. 127–128, Evan Nepean to Geo Hammond, Admiralty Office 4 October 1796; *ibid.*, 133–134, Löwenörn, Adjutant General and Captain of the [blank] to Henry Wray Esq. Commanding His Britannic Majesty's Sloop Sea Gull, undated; and *ibid.*, 246–247, Robt Steph Fitzgerald to le Comte de Bernstorff, undated.
108. NA, FO 22/26, fos. 201–203, Downing Street to Fitzgerald, Nov 1796 [quote fos. 202v-203].
109. *Ibid.*, fos. 271–272, Evan Nepean to Geo Hammond Esq., Admiralty Office 20 November 1796; ibid., fos. 273–274, Henry Wray to Evan Nepeans Esq., Sea Gull, Yarmouth Roads 29 November 1796; *ibid.*, fos. 286–287, Evan Nepean to Geo Hammond, Admiralty Office 8 December 1796; and NA, ADM 1/3842, John Mitchell to Evan Nepean Esq., Hamburg 11 April 1797.
110. NA, FO 22/24, fos. 175–176, Mirajah Malbon to John Mitchell Esq., His Majesty's Ship Dryad, 'Christian Sands' 28 October 1795.
111. *Ibid.*, fos. 214–215, Mirajah Malbon to Evan Nepean Esq., Sheerness 21 November 1795 [quote fo. 214]. It is not fully clear if this meant that Malbon thought the cannon shot rule applied.

112. *Ibid.*, fos. 206–209, John Mitchell to Governor Levitzen [*sic*], 30 October 1795; and *ibid.*, fo. 210, John Mitchell to Governor Levitzen [*sic*], 31 October 1795 [quotes 206v, 207v, 208, 209, 210v, original emphasis].
113. *Ibid.*, fos. 171–174, James Craufurd to Lord Grenville, Copenhagen 14 November 1795 [quotes fos. 172–172v].
114. NA, FO 97/117, Foreign Office and predecessors: Political and Other Departments: Supplement to General Correspondence before 1906, fos. 332–334, 'To His Most Excellent Majesty The King of Denmark. The Humble Memorial of Ninian Douglass of the Island of Guernsey Merchant a Subject of his Majesty The King of Great Britain.' London 15 November 1795.
115. NA, FO 22/36, fos. 203–204, Chas. Bicknell to Evan Nepean Esq., Norfolk 2 April 1800. See also: NA, FO 97/117, fo. 362, 'From Mr. Doune Attorney of Mr. Douglass', undated.
116. NA, FO 22/36, fos. 231–232, 'Draft to Mr. Merry', Downing Street 15 April 1800 [quote fo. 231v]. See also: *ibid.*, fo. 201, Evan Nepean to George Hammond Esq., Admiralty Office 4 April 1800; *ibid.*, fo. 279, Ant. Merry to le Comte de Bernstorff, Copenhagen 1 May 1800; *ibid.*, fos. 276–278, Ant. Merry to Lord Grenville, Copenhagen 3 May 1800; and NA, FO 22/37, fos. 5–6, Ant. Merry to Lord Grenville, Copenhagen 6 May 1800.
117. The ship was referred to as the *Favorite* by its owners, which means that this was probably the correct spelling of the name.
118. NA, FO 22/30, fos. 55–56, Alex Grieg to Lord Grenville, Bergen 27 January 1798 [quotes, fos. 56v]. See also Fitzgerald's report: *ibid.*, fos. 81–83, Robt Steph Fitzgerald to Lord Grenville, Copenhagen 17 February 1798.
119. NA, FO 22/31, fos. 63–64, 'Memorial of John Roberts &Co Merchants No. 37 Old Broad Street London' to Grenville [quote, fo. 63v]; enclosed with: *ibid.*, f. 62, 'Memorial of John Roberts &Co Merchants Old Broad Street London' to Lord Grenville, London 7 June 1798.
120. Regional State Archives of Stavanger [RSAS], Sorenskrivaren i Ryfylke, Tingbok C 6a-b, fos. 403–404, 'Præliminair Forhör angaaende Priisslupskibet Belandile, Bell and Anna kaldet, dets Borttagelse af Höyevarde Havn den 23de Jan: 1798' [translated from Danish].
121. RSAS, Tingbok C 6a-b, fos. 418–420, 'Extra Rets Tingsvidne paa Höyevarde i Augvaldsnæs Skibrede' [translated from Danish].
122. *Ibid.*, fos. 420–424 [translated from Danish]. Contemporaries tended to refer to the Danish currency of *rigsdaler* as rixdollars.
123. In this part of the protocol, the surname 'Meeling' is added to Endresen, and this may suggest that he was another family member of the Mælands, Meeling being a misspelling.
124. *Ibid.*, fos. 427–431 [translated from Danish].

125. NA, FO, 22/30, fos. 160–161, Alex Grieg to Lord Grenville, Bergen 31 March 1798; and *ibid.*, fos. 174–175, Alex Grieg to Lord Grenville, Bergen 7 April 1798. As a compromise solution, Grieg was able to persuade the governor to let Lawson sell the cargo—which was in a 'perishing condition'—as long as the proceeds were deposited for the time being. NA, FO 22/31, fos. 16–17, Alex Grieg to Lord Grenville, Bergen 14 May 1798 [quote fo. 16].
126. *Ibid.*, fos. 87–88, from Count Wedel Jarlsberg to Milord Grenville, London 23 June 1798 [translated from French]. Fitzgerald had been informed about the Danish government's position two months earlier: FO 22/30, fo. 218, Robt Steph Fitzgerald to Lord Grenville, Copenhagen 28 April 1798.
127. NA, FO 22/31, fo. 62, 'Memorial of John Roberts &Co Merchants Old Broad Street London' to Lord Grenville, London 7 June 1798.
128. NA, FO 22/33, fos. 200–201, G. H. Schönborn to Milord Grenville, London 18 December 1798 [translated from French].
129. NA, FO 97/118, fo. 3, John Roberts &Co. Thorntons & Smalley, 'To his Danish Majesty. The Humble petition of the Undersigned British Merchants who are interested in the British Ship Favorite, and her Cargo, arrested and detained at the Port of North Bergen in Norway'; and *ibid.*, fo. 1, John Roberts &Co, Thornton & Smalley, 'To the Right Honble Lord Grenville, His Majesty's Principal Secretary of State, for Foreign Affairs. The Memorial of British Merchants and Ship Owners, concerned in the Ship Favorite, and her Cargo, detained at North Bergen', London 20 February 1799.
130. NA, FO 22/36, fo. 59, Ant. Merry to Monsieur le Comte de Bernstorff, Copenhagen 23 January 1800 [translated from French].
131. NA, FO 22/36, fos. 57–58, Ant. Merry to Lord Grenville, Copenhagen 25 January 1800 [quote fo. 57v]
132. NA, FO 22/41, fos. 400–401, Alex Grieg to Lord Hawkesbury, Bergen 15 November 1801 [quote fo. 401].
133. NA, FO 22/24, ff. 185–186, John Mitchell to Lord Grenville, Christiania, 23 November 1795. See Chap. 2, p. 39 for Mitchell's argument.
134. See Chap. 2, pp. 41-44. The *Christiansand Weekly Gazette* was Mitchell's own translation of *Kristiansand Adresse Kontors Efterretninger*. As in the other chapters, we have adopted the English name in the text and the references here.
135. National Library of Norway [NLN], *Christiansand Weekly Gazette*, No. 21, 20 May 1796.
136. *Ibid.*, No. 5, 29 January 1796 [translated from Danish].
137. *Ibid.*, No. 9, 3 March 1797 [translated from Danish].
138. *Ibid.*, No. 17, 27 April 1798 [translated from Danish].

139. *Ibid.*, No. 4, 26 January 1798 [translated from Danish].
140. *Ibid.*, No. 27, 5 July 1799 [translated from Danish; by now, Kielland had clearly secured his appointment as commissioner].
141. *Ibid.*, No. 38, 21 September 1798 [translated from Danish].
142. *Ibid.*, No. 22, 31 May 1799 [cargo]; *Ibid.*, No. 29, 19 July 1799 [ship and inventory]. Final advertisement in No. 31, 2 August 1799.
143. *Ibid.*, No. 32, 9 August 1799.
144. Olav Arild Abrahamsen, *Farsund bys historie*, i, *En by blir tid. Fra stedets oppkomst til 1850* (3 volumes, Farsund kommune, 1997), p. 61.
145. Abrahamsen, *Farsund bys historie*, i, pp. 59–65; Sverre Steen, *Kristiansands Historie 1641–1814* (Grøndahl, Oslo, 1941), p. 394; and Berit Eide Johnsen and Gustav Sætra, *Sørlandsk skipsfart 1600–1920* (Portal forlag, Kristiansand, 2016), p. 78.
146. NA, ADM 1/3842, John Mitchell to Evan Nepean Esq., Christiansand 1 September 1795.
147. *Ibid.*, John Mitchell to Evan Nepean Esq., Christiansand 31 May 1796.
148. NA, FO 22/34, fo. 473, J. Nicholl to Lord Grenville, Lincolns Inn Fields 28 May 1799.
149. NA, FO, 22/35, fos. 123–131, Robt Steph Fitzgerald to Count Bernstorff, 17 July 1799 [translated from French; original emphasis].

CHAPTER 5

The Dutch Change of Sides in the War

In January 1795, the United Provinces of the Netherlands—also known as the Dutch Republic—were overrun by the military forces of the French Republic, and the last Dutch *Stadholder* William V fled to Britain. The Netherlands was now occupied by France, who proceeded to establish the Batavian Republic, a new Dutch state under French control. Since the Dutch had been an ally of Britain in the war against France before 1795, the establishment of the Batavian Republic meant that they were forced to change sides, and this had important implications for both privateering and the war in the North Sea in a wider sense. Soon, the Dutch began to equip their own privateers to hunt for British merchant ships, and they also sent out warships on commerce raiding. Moreover, since the Dutch Navy was no insignificant force, the change of sides could be said to have had a double negative impact for Britain. Before 1795, Dutch warships had, for example, escorted convoys to and from the Baltic Sea, and they had presented an additional challenge to French privateers and warships operating in northern European waters.[1] Now, this asset was lost to Britain, but gained by France.[2] The Admiralty responded to the new challenge by appointing Admiral Adam Duncan as commander-in-chief of the North Sea, allocating more resources to the fleet under his command. Although it arguably made up a 'cinderella force', consisting of whichever units were available at a point when the better ships had already been allocated to the fleets operating in the English Channel, Mediterranean and West Indies, the presence of a reinforced North Sea Fleet after 1795 did at

A. L. Wold, *Privateering and Diplomacy, 1793–1807*,
https://doi.org/10.1007/978-3-030-45186-8_5

least have the advantage of strengthening the operational force in those waters where the privateers were operating.[3] Alongside the main task of watching the Dutch Fleet at the Texel, detachments of Duncan's squadron could be sent on patrol duty further north and, as we saw in Chap. 4, this was done with good result. Nevertheless, the involvement of the Dutch Fleet on the side of France undoubtedly worsened the situation in the North Sea as seen from a British point of view, and it remained difficult until the defeat of the Dutch Fleet at the Battle of Camperdown, in the words of one historian, 'eased the strategic problem of controlling the North Sea'. Thereafter, the Royal Navy arguably held the upper hand.[4]

The Dutch change of sides in the war also raised questions concerning their loyalty, however. Why would they be prepared to join their occupiers in a war against their former allies, the British? One reason could be their previous position in the eighteenth century as a 'profiteering neutral', pursuing policies similar those adopted by Denmark-Norway. During the American War of Independence, for example, the Dutch had been involved in an arms trade with the Americans, and this had been one central element in the build-up to the fourth Anglo-Dutch war in 1780–1784. It may be that the possibilities of reaping profits from joining the French in their privateering war were just too tempting to be ignored. Of greater importance were probably the internal affairs of the Dutch Republic itself. In the later eighteenth century, the United Provinces had been fraught by an intensifying division between so-called Patriots and Orangists where the latter supported the House of Orange as *stadholders* and the political status quo—broadly speaking—whereas the former sought reforms. Organised in 1781, the Patriots were initially a movement looking back to the 'Golden Age' of the Dutch Republic in the seventeenth century, but from 1784 onwards, it became increasingly radicalised. As the situation intensified and brought the country to the brink of civil war, thousands of Patriots fled to France. By the time of the French Revolution in 1789, therefore, there were many Dutchmen of radical political views in exile abroad, waiting for an opportunity to return, and this opportunity came with the outbreak of war on the continent in 1792. A 'Batavian Revolutionary Committee' was organised by Patriots in exile that year, intended to function as a 'provisional government'. The following year, the Patriot Herman William Daendels led a 'volunteer foreign legion' raised in France in an invasion of the homeland, supported by French troops. The initial assault was repulsed by Prussian and Austrian troops, but the Patriot-French forces returned, and were able to hold on to a part of the southern Netherlands thereafter.[5] Defending Dutch independence from France was a central British war aim, and a British expeditionary force under the command of the Duke of York was sent across to Flanders in 1793 to fight the French. The expedition was no great success, but the force remained in the field until it was pushed back and withdrew via Bremen in 1795.[6] Because of the conflict between Patriots and Orangists, and the former group's involvement in the invasion and setting up of the Batavian Republic, the loyalties of the Dutch were arguably divided thereafter. The question of loyalty was to prove crucial in relation to the Dutch involvement in privateering too.

The previous three chapters of this book have touched upon Dutch privateering in those contexts where it was of relevance to the topics raised. This shorter chapter will not return to all of these issues, but rather focus on those particular concerns the Dutch change of sides in 1795 gave rise to; first in a section addressing several themes, and then in relation to one individual case of particular interest: that of 'Captain von Dirking'.

The Impact of 1795

Although the Batavian Republic was arguably a French 'satellite' state in real terms, it was officially a 'sister republic' with its own constitution (from 1798) and Dutch government.[7] As far as privateering was concerned, this official Dutch 'independence' had some actual implications, particularly relating to the ports in Norway, and the Dutch consular representation there.

In July 1793, the British consul at Kristiansand, John Mitchell, had informed Foreign Secretary Lord Grenville that as there was 'no Person in my District' to look after the affairs of the Dutch Republic, he had ordered his agents to look out for Dutch vessels that had recently been 'brought in to the western Ports' as prizes. His intention thus seemed to be to utilise his own network of agents in Norway to assist Britain's Dutch allies, in a situation where they did not have any consular representation of their own that could support them (at Kristiansand).[8] After 1795, however, the Batavian Republic appointed the Norwegian merchant Daniel Isaachsen as their 'Commissioner and Consul' to cover the entire length of the Norwegian coastline from Bergen on the western coast to Halden on the border to Sweden. This, Isaachsen did from his base at Kristiansand. His main task as consul was no longer to assist Dutch merchantmen, however, but to take care of the prizes brought in by Dutch privateers and warships.

Both prize cargos and vessels were, as we saw in Chap. 4, sold at auctions, and it was Isaachsen's task to organise these auctions. This meant that the sale of prizes captured by Dutch privateers took place separately and independently from the sale of French prizes.[9] What did the Danish authorities make of this? In the British-Danish debate on privateering in 1793, the Danish government had pursued an impartiality-type argument of neutrality, stating that the privateers of both belligerent powers, France and Britain, were welcome to call upon the ports of Norway. Now there was a third belligerent country involved, and the Danish Minister A. P. Bernstorff addressed this new situation by simply expanding on the arrangement that had already been adopted. The occasion was the arrival at Kristiansand of four British merchant ships captured by three 'Dutch Armed Brigs' in August 1795. Informed of this by Mitchell, the British chargés d'affaires in Copenhagen, James Craufurd, raised the 'subject of these Prizes' in a meeting with Bernstorff, who informed him that 'the Danish Government would adopt the same line of conduct respecting them, as they had followed respecting those brought in by the French'. Presumably, this meant that the condition set out in the British-Danish agreement of August 1793 was to apply for Dutch privateers also. The Danish minister proceeded to reflect further upon the new situation, however, expressing his surprise 'that the Dutch should venture to commence actual hostilities, for, as he justly observes, from that moment they can have no hope that their Ships, which are detained in England, will escape confiscation'. Bernstorff had a clear opinion as to the reason for this Dutch policy, Craufurd wrote:

> he says that they have been forced into all this by the French, who, to give some appearance of foundation to their boasts of the assistance which they were to derive from the Dutch Navy, forced them to send their Fleet to Sea for the purpose of making a vain demonstration.[10]

The Dutch were under French pressure, and that was the reason for their cooperation with the French. The relative independence of the Dutch representatives is also illustrated by the occasional quarrel some of them had with their French counterparts. In the wake of the abortive raid conducted by the illustrious French Captain Jean Jacques de St Faust and his 'Batavian Auxiliary Naval Force' off Bergen in 1804,[11] 'Several of the Men belonging to the armed Vessels lately under the command of M. St Faust' were reported by the British chargés d'affaires in Copenhagen, Francis Hill, to 'have arrived here'. Hill thought that most of them were 'French gunners', but 'some altercation' nevertheless ensued between the Dutch and French representatives on the question of whose responsibility it was to provide for their 'protection and support'. The Dutchman claimed that they were 'French Soldiers' and therefore the responsibility of the French, while the French consul 'insisted that as they were in the Dutch service it was he that should provide for them'.[12]

A central issue that arose immediately in the wake of the Dutch change of sides was the question of what should be done about the Dutch merchant ships which had been brought into Norwegian ports as prizes by French privateers. Should they be restored to their original owners, who were now supposedly the allies of the French? The Danish government tried to resolve this through an order from the Chancery stating that all such prizes could be sold, but, as we saw in Chap. 2, the mistake (or omission) in the wording of the order whereby the word 'Dutch' was missing had led to misunderstandings, which it took some time to resolve. The attempt to settle the issue quickly was thus botched.[13] Moreover, the threat to Dutch shipping was not at an end with this. As Ole Feldbæk has pointed out, Dutch East India Company ships sometimes sought refuge in Bergen and Trondheim on their way to the Texel, and now this exposed them to the new threat of British warships and privateers cruising in the North Sea.[14] This was probably no improvement on the previous threat posed by French privateers and warships, and an incident from the autumn of 1798 demonstrates both the new challenge British naval power posed to Dutch shipping and the attempts the Dutch sometimes made to adjust to this new situation.

The incident concerned four small fishing vessels sailing under Danish flags, but whose names were conspicuously Dutch sounding: *De Jonge Maartje*, *De Jonge Pieter*, *De Drie Gebroeders* and *De Jonge Pieter* (thus two ships with the same name). All four had been captured by British warships while 'employed in the Fishery on the Coast of Holland', and had 'sailed under Danish Colours when taken'. Officially, these vessels belonged to 'Danish Subjects residing at Blankenese' (near Hamburg), but British investigations revealed that the 'Proofs of Danish Property are by no means clear'. Instead, the 'strongest presumptions arise that they are really owned by Dutchmen, and collusively documented as Danes to prevent Capture'. Until 1795, the very same vessels had sailed under Dutch colours, and had been owned by Dutchmen. Moreover, interviews with the masters of the four ships made it clear that they were all of Dutch origin, but that they had been admitted as burghers of Blankenese shortly after the Batavian Republic was formed. One of them, Ionnies Non Beck of the *De Jonge Pieter* (first of the two) claimed to have resided at Blankenese since then, but admitted that his family was still in Holland, while Jacob Moodyks of the second *De Jonge Pieter* stated that he had spent no more than two days there after his admission as a burgher. The crews were also predominantly Dutch.[15] This evidence was submitted to the king's advocate John Nicholl, who gave legal advice on the case. In Nicholl's opinion, 'there appears sufficient ground to maintain, that these vessels are to be considered as Dutch'. Not only did the 'entire management' consist of Dutch merchants, but the crews were 'principally' Dutch; the masters of the ships Dutch; the vessels were involved in the 'Dutch Fishery'; they were sailing to and from Dutch ports; and the 'pretended Transfer of the Property to Danes and the Danish Papers appear strongly colorable [*sic*]'. Nicholl also held that the residence of the owner did not affect the Dutch 'Character' of the ships under the Law of Nations. It was an example of the use of false flags, and the capture was therefore legitimate.[16] The British consul at Bergen, John Wallace, reported on a different kind of attempted deception in early 1797. The Dutch privateer the *Waaghals* had arrived in port with 'black sides' and 'no head', which made her 'look like a Merchant Ship', Wallace stated. Whether this was instrumental in the *Waaghals'* subsequent success as a privateer cannot be said for certain, but it could be seen as a variation on the use of false flags to disguise the real identity of the vessel, adopted by some of the French privateers. By April, Nicholas Fenwick at Elsinore felt the need to stress that, in light of news that the *Waaghals* had 'gone to sea again … a good look out on the Coast of Norway will be daily wanted'.[17]

Just as British naval power presented a challenge to the Dutch from 1795 onwards, so the Dutch warships operating in the North Sea formed a new, and possibly even more dangerous threat to British shipping than the French naval units that had been involved in commerce raiding and support for privateers up until then. As the then British envoy at Copenhagen, Robert Fitzgerald, pointed out to Grenville in October 1796:

> It were much to be wished My Lord, that a Stop were put to the Depredations made on the British Trade; by the Dutch Cruizers on the Coast of Norway. The Success of the Dutch Frigates, Venus and Scipio, which have long been stationed at Bergen, is severely felt by the homeward bound Archangel Men, and calls for Redress.[18]

The general impression was that the Dutch naval units sent out into the North Sea were particularly adept at commerce raiding, and Fitzgerald's comment on the two frigates that were 'stationed' at Bergen is also telling. Unlike the French warships, which made 'only occasional visits' to Norwegian ports, many Dutch cruisers were literally based there, forming a more permanent threat, at least until they were withdrawn in the spring of 1797.[19] The frigates *Scipio* and *Venus* which attacked the Archangel trade from their base at Bergen were examples of the kind, as was another frigate, the *Jason* of 36 guns, which operated out of Trondheim for a while in the spring of 1796.[20] Finally, the constant threat posed by the Dutch Fleet on the Texel inspired the ever-energetic Mitchell to send frequent reports from his new base at Hamburg, containing whatever intelligence he was able to obtain on fleet movements, and preparations to sail. On 19 May 1797, for example, he reported to the Admiralty that the Dutch Fleet, consisting of '14 Sail from 68 to 40 guns', as well as '6 or 8 Armed India Ships, Several Frigates, & a number of Transport with Troops onboard, were under Sailing orders at the Texel' issued five days earlier. In Mitchell's view, the 'most probably conjecture' was that they were planning to 'land their Troops in Some Part in the North of Ireland', but so far, unfavourable winds had delayed the departure of the fleet.[21] A month later, the invasion fleet was still in port, but Mitchell—who was now in Hannover—could provide further information on the invasion force, now relating to the number of transports, and the artillery some of them carried.[22] In the end, the planned invasion never materialised, and the Dutch Fleet was, of course, defeated on 11 October the same year at Camperdown, removing the particular threat of an invasion launched from the Batavian Republic for the immediate future. The Dutch had fought well in what one naval historian described as 'a most determined and sanguinary fight', leaving little doubt as to the loyalty of the crews to the new regime it would seem.[23] Before the battle, however, reports had suggested that this might not be the case. In July, Mitchell could convey news from a 'Correspondent of mine in Amsterdam', who had claimed that 'great Confusion prevails in the Dutch Fleet at the Texel', where there was 'no Confidence amongst the Officers, nor Subordination amongst the Crews'. The situation had even deteriorated to the degree that 'Sailors parading about Swear publicly that they will never fire a Short at a British Man of War'.[24] In the event, they were clearly prepared to do so, but reports from Norway pointed in the same direction as that of Mitchell's correspondent, suggesting that the crews of individual Dutch ships were prepared to surrender to the British without a fight. Thus in April the same year, it was reported that 'should any British Ships of War come into Drontheim', the sailors on board a few Dutch ships currently at anchor there would 'deliver up their Ships to the Enemy'.[25] The question of the loyalty of Dutch crews was at the centre of the individual case we will turn to next.

The von Dirking Case

Captain von Dirking—or Arnold Christiaan Leopold van Dirckinck, as was his real name—was the commander of the Dutch 36-gun frigate the *Argo*, which had narrowly escaped its British pursuers into the port of Hidra on 22 August 1795 together with an unnamed cutter of 12 guns, while its companion, another 36-gun frigate the *Alliance* had been captured.[26] From then onwards, an extraordinary story concerning defection, loyalty and remuneration unfolded.

Both the *Argo* and the cutter had sustained 'Considerable Damage in their Rigging etc.', as well as casualties, and remained at Hidra for several months thereafter.[27] There was, in other words, little doubt that these naval vessels from a belligerent nation obtained repairs in a neutral port, though no mention was made of strict contraband goods being supplied. By 18 October, the ships were still at Hidra, but on 7 December, Mitchell could report that they were preparing to sail for Kristiansand. Meanwhile, 'three Dutch Armed Briggs', the *Echo* of 18 guns, and the *de Gier* and *Mercury* of 14 guns each, had brought four British merchantmen into Kristiansand, and had subsequently positioned themselves, first at Flekkerøy and then at Mandal, before returning to Kristiansand together with the *Argo* in late December.[28] Thereafter, this group of Dutch naval vessels remained in port until May the next year, and formed the basis for a negotiated deal between Mitchell as the British representative, and Captain von Dirking.

It began while the *Argo* was still at Hidra. In a report to Grenville—where he outlined how he was trying to lure the Dutchmen into leaving port by 'industriously' circulating (false) rumours that the British naval vessels in the area had sailed for Britain—Mitchell also stated the following:

> Should these Dutchmen not think themselves safe to proceed to Holland this fall, I am clearly of opinion that I could at a moderate Expense persuade them to proceed to England. Money & not the Services is the only object of the Dutch Officers who command these Vessels, particularly the Captain of

> the Argo; and they are all in Some Measure devoted to their former government, or at any rate ill pleased with the present System.[29]

Mitchell did not state how he had come by this information, but it seems likely that his network of informants along the southern coast of Norway had played a role in it. However that may have been, London immediately warmed to his idea, and in a direct reply from Downing Street, Mitchell was informed that: 'Instructions will be given by the Lords of the Admiralty to such Officers in His Majesty's Naval Service as they shall judge to be the best qualified for the Undertaking'. These officers were then meant to cooperate with Mitchell to find 'the Measures the most likely to prevail on the Dutch Officers in question to pursue the Line of Conduct' he had outlined. Moreover, 'in order to accelerate this design', Mitchell was 'hereby authorized to advance any reasonable Sums of Money', which he and the 'Officer so acting in Conjunction' with him might think necessary to achieve the 'Object'. He was, however, warned that he should 'not on any Account' feel 'at liberty to exceed' such sums as the officer agreed to.[30] Mitchell was, in other words, entrusted with the task of negotiating with enemy naval officers but, as always, the British government was concerned to keep a tight string on any expenditure involved. For the time being, however, Mitchell was uncertain about the motives of the Dutch, stating that 'I have not yet had opportunity to learn much of Captain Dirking's Projects or Principles', though it was clear that he now had 'all the Dutch Cruisers on this Coast under his Orders'.[31] Why was he, as Mitchell had stated, prepared to 'proceed to England', and what exactly did that mean? Once von Dirking had arrived at Kristiansand this became clearer, and a plan began to take form.

According to von Dirking himself, he was no supporter of the new Dutch regime, and his reason for staying in the Dutch Navy in the wake of the 'Revolution of January 1795' was primarily 'to watch a favourable opportunity to leaving it in his power to be of use to the Prince of Orange', although he also had hopes of 'Recovering a large Arrears due to him by the Marine Department'. Von Dirking was, therefore, a true Orangist, and although he had not yet received the money due to him, he was nevertheless prepared to 'put the Squadron under his orders into His Majesty's possession'.[32] His plan was, in other words, to defect to Britain with the ships under his command, which—for the moment—consisted of the *Argo*, the cutter and the three Briggs. A main obstacle to this plan was the 'Patriotick' Captain Kile, the commander of the *Echo*, who was likely to oppose it, but an incident in late January removed this particular problem for the time being, while arguably also wedding von Dirking to his planned defection. In order to 'commemorate the Restoration of their so called Batavian Liberty', Mitchell reported to Grenville on 27 January, the Dutch consul at Kristiansand had organised 'a grand Entertainment to the Dutch officers, the Governor, the French Consul, & the Magistrates and principal Inhabitants' on the 21st of that month. At the party, a 'serious Scuffle' had ensued between Captain Kile and another Dutch officer (who was presumably an Orangist), and this had given von Dirking the 'opportunity of ordering Kile to repair onboard of his Ship & Remain there untill [*sic*] further orders'. Kile refused, but the other officers supported von Dirking, arguing that Kile should be 'put under Arrest until they arrived in Holland', and he was subsequently placed 'under Confinement in his own ship'. In Mitchell's view, this was a beneficiary turn of events, since 'von Dirking's Authority is for the present consolidated, & the greatest obstacle to the success of my Negotiations with him is Removed', but the fact that he had placed a Patriot under lock and key, also meant that von Dirking could not now 'Return to Holland with any hopes of personal safety while the present System predominates in that Country'.[33] For von Dirking, it was more important than ever to carry through the plan, but neither the other officers, nor the crews of the five ships appear to have been aware of his intentions, and it could not be known if they would support the defection. How was this to be organised in practice? The Dutchman had devised a preliminary plan, which he presented to Mitchell. First, a 'small fast sailing Cutter' would need to be placed at the disposal of Mitchell, for the purpose of efficient communication with British naval forces. Then, von Dirking would provide Mitchell with full details on 'the Circumstances under which he would sail', including 'the courses he would steer with such & such winds & weather, the sail & colors [*sic*] which he carry & the Signals which he would make upon seeing ships at Sea'. This detailed information should then be dispatched to a waiting British naval force (using the cutter) 'at a proper period prior' to the departure of the Dutch Squadron, so that this naval unit could intercept and capture the Dutch ships. It was crucial that the British forces were superior to von Dirking's own squadron, since his officers and crew would then be 'easily persuaded to Surrender without Bloodshed'. It was necessary to arrange this 'surprise' attack by British warships as von Dirking did not have 'confidence enough in his officers & men to Risk an attempt to carry his Squadron direct to England alone'.[34] There was one way in which at least the Dutch officers might be placated, however. If the planned defection could be given the approval of the 'Prince of Orange', in the shape of a 'Note or order from the Prince expressing His Serene Highness' will, wish, or Pleasure', then von Dirking was convinced that 'no opposition would be made in the Squadron to his intended proceedings'. He based this assumption on his own estimate that three quarters of the 'Officers & men in the present Dutch Navy' were of his own 'Principles'.[35] Since von Dirking was expecting orders to sail home to arrive any day, he had deployed a delaying tactic by indirectly favouring 'the Desertion of a large Proportion of the Sailors from the Briggs', and placing '30 of his own best men on the sick List'. He did assure Mitchell that he would not sail until he was sure 'there is a British Squadron waiting for him', but there was clearly a need to act quickly if the planned defection was to succeed.[36] Shortly afterwards, Mitchell received full backing of the British government in a letter which also contained outright praise: 'your Conduct in this business has been much approved by his Majesty's Ministers'.[37] The urgency to act, which von Dirking had hinted at, was confirmed by the arrival of orders from the Dutch *Comité de Marine* on 16 March.

Although this meant that his initial plan had to be revised, it made the intended defection no less interesting to the British side. Von Dirking was now instructed to be in charge of a convoy operation from Norway to the Texel. Two vessels had been dispatched by the *Comité*, one for Bergen and the other for Trondheim, with 'orders for the Dutch East India Ships' presently in those two ports to 'Repair with all possible dispatch' to Skudeneshavn on the southern tip of the island of Karmøy, north of Stavanger. There, they would meet up with von Dirking's squadron, which would escort them '& Such other Vessels belonging to the Batavian Republick as may be there or in that Neighbourhood' back to Holland. It was important that von Dirking dispatched his 'fastest sailing Brigg' to the Texel before departing with the convoy, so that the commander of the Dutch Fleet, Admiral de Winter, could send out ships to meet them, and should the vessels from Trondheim be delayed or not arrive, von Dirking was to sail with the 'Bergen Ships & the Squadron' alone. Two vessels had also been dispatched for Skudeneshavn with 'Supernumerary Seamen' to bring the complement of von Dirking's ships up to normal.[38] The addition of the East India Ships made the potential catch all the more promising, of course, and Mitchell estimated that there were eight of them in total.[39] In early January, Captain Hale—the officer sent by the Admiralty to cooperate with Mitchell—had met with von Dirking, and inspected the Dutch vessels. In his estimation, the Frigate and the three Briggs were worth upwards of £38,000, and two of the Briggs were, according to Mitchell, 'Remarkably fine Vessels'.[40] The addition of the merchant ships undoubtedly hiked up this value significantly, but what was more was that their capture would deal a 'Mortal Blow' to the 'Enemies of the Prince & of Social order', von Dirking argued. The reason was that this would 'cut off the only Resource which they have at this moment to depend upon, namely their Remaining East India Ships'.[41] It is perhaps questionable if the loss of these vessels would have been that severely felt, but the point remained that there was a potential double benefit to be had: a material gain for Britain and a loss for the Batavian Republic. And this would come in addition to the negative 'Effect which the Desertion' of von Dirking's squadron would have on the 'Naval Operations' of the Batavian Republic.[42]

Mitchell, von Dirking and Captain Hale now sat down and composed a 'Memorandum', a new and ambitious plan, the purpose of which was 'not only the Capture of the Dutch Convoy, but also the annihilation of the present Dutch Marine'.[43] The plan was set out in nine points, where the first stated that a 'British Fleet of at least 8 or 10 Sail of the Line and as many Frigates' should be sent out to intercept von Dirking's convoy. For this to work out successfully, it was stated in point two that secrecy about the British Fleet was paramount as 'the Dutch Committee have their Friends & Spies in every corner'. Point three concerned the use of false flags to create deception before the interception, while point four addressed von Dirking's emphasis on deploying superior force, particularly in the attack on the *Argo* since, 'when she strikes, the other Dutch Ships will also strike'. Point five added that 'von Dirking should be left in safe possession of his Baggage & Papers & particularly cared for', while point six said the opposite for the *Argo's* first lieutenant who should be 'carefully secured with all his Papers'. Points seven and eight concerned the Dutch Fleet which was expected to sail out from the Texel under the command of Admiral Braak to meet von Dirking's convoy. It was stated in point eight that if the Dutch Fleet was not 'along with the Convoy when the British Fleet intercepts it, the British Fleet after disposing of the Convoy should proceed direct to the Texel'. This would be a sensible move since 'von Dirking has the private Signals whereby the British Fleet may enter the Texel as friends & make themselves masters of the Whole Dutch Fleet, & of the Texel, without Opposition'. The final point simply restated the need for a fast vessel to be placed at Mitchell's disposal, and it was added in a 'PS', that the 'Captain of the Echo Mr. Kile' should be secured and 'his Papers taken from him'.[44] It was a spectacular, complicated and, as far as the planned capture of the entire Dutch Fleet was concerned, perhaps not entirely realistic plan. The Admiralty does not seem to have taken it very seriously. In any case, it depended on the successful departure of the Dutch convoy from Norway, and this proved difficult.

On 19 March, John Wallace reported to Mitchell that the 'Dutch are lying still quietly here', and that the vessels at Trondheim were 'disabled to proceed for want of hands'. A number of sailors had 'deserted' their ships (probably due to lack of pay), and Norwegian seamen had proved difficult to hire, quite simply because most of them had been ordered to Copenhagen to man Danish warships, and there were 'consequently none to spare'.[45] Having 'received no Fresh Orders or Official Information from Holland' since February, von Dirking had consequently informed Mitchell that he intended to go for plan B, and 'proceed to Schuderness for the Bergen Ships'. The delay this caused meant, however, that the Dutch squadron under the command of Admiral Braak, which had sailed to meet von Dirking, had already arrived, and an opportunity had been lost. As Mitchell wrote to Admiral Duncan:

> Von Dirking expresses much Vexation that his Arrangement with me on the 20th and 21st February was not more attended to, because had the British Fleet been upon the spot pointed out at the time requested (the 5th March) Braaks Squadron must have inevitably fallen into your Hands.[46]

Instead, Braak's ships escaped. There were problems related to von Dirking's attempt to depart for Skudeneshavn too. First, he had moved his squadron to the outport of Flekkerøy, where he was only awaiting a favourable wind, when a 'Report of His Majesty's Squadron under your Command being off the Coast reached the Dutch Consul & consequently von Dirking dared not to purpose leaving the port'. Then, when von Dirking tried to make another attempt to leave, a mutiny on board the *Argo* and desertion of a considerable number of sailors in his squadron forced him to return to Kristiansand. The mutiny concerned lack of pay and provisions, and was later resolved, but the return of the squadron to Kristiansand gave Mitchell an extraordinary idea: 'I then advised von Dirking to invite Captain Alms to take possession of the Dutch in the Port'. Captain Alms commanded the detachment of British warships, which had followed von Dirking into Kristiansand, and Mitchell's proposal, had it been carried through, would have constituted a clear breach of Danish-Norwegian neutrality, with likely repercussions. Upon 'Consideration', however, Mitchell, von Dirking and Captain Alms agreed not to go through with the idea, since they were all

> apprehensive that some of the Patriotick officers or men in the Squadron might be able to set some of the Ships on fire before they could be firmly taken possession of, in which case the British Squadron, & also the Town and Port of Christiansand, would have been in too great Danger.

Both Mitchell and von Dirking were unhappy about the British squadron sailing so close to the shore as to be detected, though, since the agreement had been that British warships 'should keep at *a distance* from the Coast until the Dutch Convoy got fairly to Sea', as Mitchell stressed in his report to Grenville.[47] By April, von Dirking was again prepared to depart for Skudeneshavn, but now there was concern if the Dutch India ships at Bergen would dare to venture out into the open sea as they had been 'Alarmed' by news of the 'British Squadron lately at Flekkeröe'.[48] In the event, von Dirking did not sail this time either, but not because the merchantmen remained at Bergen. Instead, it was a repeat of the incident in March, which prevented him from departing, or so von Dirking and Mitchell argued. The British squadron under the command of Captain Robert Watson had, according to von Dirking, come 'so near the Coast, that he could perfectly distinguish the different Ships'. Watson, however, disputed this and insisted that he had come no 'nearer the Shore than 11 or 12 Leagues'.[49] He also questioned the reliability of von Dirking, suggesting that the Dutchman was trying to 'deceive' Mitchell.[50] Mitchell, however, dismissed the claim that the sighting of Watson's ship *Isis* was a 'falsehood invented by Von Dirking to give him a pretense [*sic*] for not Sailing', and word stood against word.[51]

In the meantime, von Dirking had received new orders, which said that he was to 'take under his Orders all the Dutch Ships of War which are in Norway', and 'proceed with them direct for Holland there to be properly equipt [*sic*] for a Summer Cruize against the British Baltic Trade'.[52] The plan to convoy the India ships home was, in other words, given up, and on 7 May, Mitchell could finally dispatch a letter to Grenville stating that von Dirking had departed at '7 o'clock this afternoon'.[53] On 12 May, von Dirking's ships were intercepted by four Royal Navy vessels dispatched by Duncan, the *Phœnix* under the command of Captain Halsted, two other frigates, the *Leopard* and *Pegasus*, and the sloop *Sylph*. After a 'very smart Action of about Half an Hour, (during which she made every Effort to get off)', Duncan wrote in his official, published report, the *Argo* struck to the *Phœnix*, but the other Dutchmen did not follow her example and tried to escape. The *Mercury* was eventually captured, but the *Echo* and the *de Gier* disappeared in haze and strong winds, only to be wrecked on the shore, and lost.[54] This was hardly the glorious outcome drawn up on the Memorandum, but at least the British side was able to secure two of the Dutch vessels, and the First Lord of the Admiralty, Lord Spencer, praised Duncan and his unit: 'I am very glad your squadron stayed out long enough to catch Von Dirking, which service appears to have been performed in a very masterly manner, and I sincerely congratulate you on the success of it'.[55] After the battle, von Dirking stayed in London for some time until he travelled on to Bocholt in Germany on promises never to serve against Britain,[56] while his ship, the *Argo,* was commissioned by the Royal Navy under the new name of *Janus*.[57] This was not, however, the end of the matter. As Mitchell had indicated in his first letter to Grenville from October 1795, the whole operation would need to be financed, and the financing also caused difficulties.

Early on, an agreement had been reached that von Dirking would be paid a substantial sum to cover various expenses such as necessary provisions for his vessels, as well as some of that money he was owed by the Dutch Navy. This was necessary to enable von Dirking to sail, since the arrangements of the Dutch Navy were such that the captains were the 'Pursers or as they call themselves the Commissaries for Victualling their Ships or Squadrons', and therefore had to 'procure their Provisions & Necessaries from their private Agent to whom they are answerable for the Payment'. The total sum of this amounted to £18,000, of which £12,500 had already been paid out by Mitchell before von Dirking sailed for the Texel on 7 May. The remainder was due to be paid once the Dutch captain had arrived in London, but by early July, it became clear that the British government was reluctant to do so.[58] A clearly annoyed Mitchell made little attempt to moderate his views in a letter to Grenville, in which he also summarised the wider implications of the von Dirking-case:

> I yesterday Received a Letter from Mr. von Dirking wherein he mentions that your Lordship has declined to pay any Part of my last Assignment to him £18000 Stg owing as von Dirking supposes to its having been insinuated to your Lordship that he (Dirking) never seriously intended to perform

> what he promised but on the Contrary had endeavoured to escape with his squadron & the money which he had Received.

This insinuation was unheard of, Mitchell thought, and 'All I can say upon this matter', he continued, was that von Dirking had 'Regularly produced to me every original Information & order which he Received from Holland'. This included a plan 'whereby to put 23 Sail of Dutch Ships of War, and 7 East India & 2 West India Ships, at once into His Majesty's Possession', as well as accurate, updated and detailed information for the whole period of 7 months in which he remained in the port of Kristiansand. Moreover, during this time he had let British trade pass by without ever attempting to capture prizes, even though he could easily have caught 'Two Hundred thousand pounds Sterling's Value at the most moderate calculation; From these Circumstances alone I can as little doubt von Dirking's Sincerity as I could doubt his Existence when he was in my presence', Mitchell concluded. Little had, of course, gone according to plan, but that 'the whole of Dirking's Squadron was not at last taken, was not his fault'. As for the 'pecuniary Arrangements with the Dutch', Mitchell thought they were reasonable and necessary. Based on Captain Hale's estimate of the value of the Dutch ships, the British government stood to have gained a significant profit, and to 'have offered von Dirking merely what he was inevitably to lose by his desertion' would have been to offer him 'no Reward for his Breach of trust', for the 'injury' caused to the enemy, for the 'advantage' given to Britain, 'nor any indemnification for his future Prospects'. Surely, such an offer would have been 'rejected justly with disdain' Mitchell hypothesised. Lastly, it was not the 'material Value of the Dutch Ships' that was the central issue at stake, but the opportunity to 'disarrange the Dutch Maritime Expeditions', Mitchell held, and even if the outcome had not been as wished for, he thought that his 'Lordship will not consider the Project as having been merely Chimerical'. For that reason, he hoped that von Dirking could be paid at least part of the money that was due to him, if only to reassure 'his Friends who have a wish to follow his Example'.[59] It is not clear if any further payments were made, however.

The von Dirking-case was a unique episode in the context of the war in the North Sea during the period under discussion here. There were no other examples of Dutch naval officers offering to give themselves up to the British with the vessels under their command, von Dirking's claim that three-fourths of these officers sympathised with the House of Orange notwithstanding. Nevertheless, the case still serves to illustrate the variety of complications that followed from the Danish decision to allow privateering out of the ports in Norway. This facilitated a degree of belligerent activity along the Norwegian coast, which it is unlikely would have materialised had the ports been closed from the start of the war in 1793. In 1799, however, the ports *were* closed, and the next chapter addresses the development thereafter until Denmark-Norway entered the war in 1807.

Notes

1. On convoys escorted by Dutch warships, see: National Archives [NA], ADM 1/3841, Admiralty, Letters to British Consuls, N. Fenwick to Philip Stephens, Elsinore 20 August 1793.
2. French cavalry had been able to capture the frozen-in Dutch Fleet by 'galloping over the ice'. Robert Gardiner (ed.), *Fleet Battle and Blockade: The French Revolutionary War 1793–1797* (Chatham Publishing, London, 1996), p. 170.
3. Gardiner, *Fleet Battle*, p. 170; and Robert Adam Philip Haldane Camperdown, *Admiral Duncan* (Longmans, Green, and Co, London, 1898), pp. 35–41.
4. N. A. M. Rodger, *The Command of the Ocean: A Naval History of Britain, 1649–1815* (Penguin, London, 2006), p. 456.
5. Friso Wielenga, *A History of the Netherlands: From the Sixteenth Century to the Present Day* (Bloomsbury Academic, London, 2015), pp. 111–143 [quotes, pp. 127–128]. The account given here is obviously little more than a very brief sketch of internal Dutch, and Dutch-French relations before and during the Batavian Republic. The seminal study of this topic is Simon Schama, *Patriots & Liberators: Revolution in the Netherlands 1780–1813* (Harper Press, London, 2005 [Collins, 1977]). Schama discusses, for example, the extent to which the Patriot attempt to carry through a genuinely Dutch revolution succeeded, and how Patriot-French relations remained fraught in many respects after 1795.
6. On the British 'Flanders Campaign', and the war strategy in general during first three years of the war, see, for example: Ian R. Christie, *Wars and Revolutions: Britain 1760–1815*, (Arnold, London, 1982), pp. 229–234.
7. Wielenga, *History of the Netherlands*, p. 135.
8. NA, FO 22/17, Foreign Office Correspondence, Denmark, fos. 29–30, John Mitchell to Lord Grenville, Christiania, 13 July 1793 [quote fos. 30–30v].
9. National Library of Norway [NLN], *Christiansand Weekly Gazette*, No. 9, 13 March 1797 [translated from Danish]. The title was John Mitchell's

translation of the original Danish: *Kristiansands Adresse-Kontors Efterretninger*. We have adopted Mitchell's English version here.

10. NA, FO 22/24, fos. 22–25, James Craufurd to Lord Grenville, Copenhagen 5 September 1795 [quote fo. 23–23b]; and FO 211/5, Foreign Office and predecessor, Embassy, Consulate and Legation, Denmark: General Correspondence—Secret Communications, No. 46 to 'My Lord', Copenhagen 5 September 1795.
11. See: R. P. Fereday, *Saint-Faust in the North 1803–4: Orkney and Shetland in Danger, An Abortive Raid and its Consequences* (Tempvs Reparatvm, Oxford, 1995), p. 1.
12. NA, FO 22/45, fos. 115–118, Francis Hill to Lord Harrowby, Copenhagen, 18 August 1804 [quote fos. 117–117v]. We will return to the St Faust-case in Chap. 6.
13. See Chap. 2, p. 43.
14. Ole Feldbæk, 'Danish Shipping in War and Peace, 1750–1807', in David J. Starkey, E. S. van Eyck van Heslinga and J. A. de Moor (eds.), *Pirates and Privateers: New Perspectives on the War on Trade in the Eighteenth and Nineteenth Centuries* (University of Exeter Press, Exeter, 1997), p. 236.
15. NA, FO 22/33, fos. 98–100, Jas. Heseltine to Mr. Nepean, Doctors Commons 15 November 1798 [quotes 98v–99].
16. *Ibid.*, fos. 132–133, J. Nicholl to Lord Grenville, 23 November 1798 [quote fo. 132]. The Dutch fisheries were hard hit by the war; first pursued by the French, and then by the British after 1795. See: Schama, *Patriots & Liberators*, pp. 370–371.
17. NA, ADM 1/3842, Letters to British Consuls, J. Wallace to Evan Nepean Esq., Bergen 7 January 1797; and ibid., N. Fenwick to Evan Nepean Esq., Elsinore 1 April 1797. For subsequent reports on the *Waaghals*, see: ibid., Alex Grieg to Evan Nepean Esq., Bergen 8 April 1797; and John Mitchell to Evan Nepean Esq., Hamburg 11 April 1797.
18. NA, FO 22/26, fos. 163–165, Robt Steph Fitzgerald to Lord Grenville, Copenhagen 15 October 1796 [quote f. 164].
19. D. H. Reid, 'Danish Neutrality and the Royal Navy 1795–7', in *The Mariner's Mirror*, 76/2 (1990), p. 178.
20. NA, ADM 1/3842, Wallace [?] to Evan Nepean Esq., Bergen 2 June 1796. On the *Scipio* and *Venus*, see Chap. 4, pp. **140**.
21. NA, ADM 1/3842, John Mitchell to Evan Nepean Esq., Hamburg 19 May 1797; and Kent Library and History Centre, U1968/O426/3, John Mitchell to Lord Grenville, Hamburg 23 May 1797.
22. NA, ADM 1/3842, John Mitchell to Evan Nepean Esq., Hannover 24 June 1797.
23. William Laird Clowes, *The Royal Navy: A History from the Earliest Times to the Present* (Chatham Publishing, London, 1997 [1899]), p. 329.

24. NA, ADM 1/3842, John Mitchell to Evan Nepean Esq., Christiansand 19 July 1796.
25. *Ibid.*, John Mitchell to Evan Nepean Esq., Christiansand 3 April 1796.
26. A. J. van der Aa, *Biographische woordenboch der Nederlanden. Deel 4* (J. J. van Brederode, Harlem, 1858), cited on: *biografisch portaal van nederland:* http://www.biografischportaal.nl/persoon/00449704. For the sake of consistency, we have used 'von Dirking', as adopted by the British side here. On the battle where the *Alliance* was captured, and the *Argo* escaped, see Chap. 4, p. **158**.
27. NA, ADM 1/3842, John Mitchell to Evan Nepean Esq., Christiansand 1 September 1795.
28. See three letters from Mitchell to Evan Nepean, the secretary at the Admiralty: NA, ADM, 1/3842, John Mitchell to Evan Nepean Esq., 1 September 1795; 18 October 1795; and 8 December 1795; and one letter to Grenville: *ibid.*, John Mitchell to Lord Grenville, Christiansand 29 December 1795.
29. NA, FO 22/24, fos. 139–140, John Mitchell to Lord Grenville, Christiansand 17 October 1795 [quote fo. 139v].
30. *Ibid.*, fo. 167, to Mr. Mitchell, Downing Street 10 November 1795.
31. NA, ADM 1/3842, John Mitchell to Lord Grenville, Christiansand 29 December 1795.
32. NA, FO 22/25, fos. 12-13, John Mitchell to Lord Grenville, Christiansand 6 January 1796 [quote fos. 12–12v].
33. *Ibid.*, fos. 19–20, John Mitchell to Lord Grenville, Christiansand 27 January 1796.
34. *Ibid.*, fos. 33–34, John Mitchell to Lord Grenville, Christiansand 5 February 1796 [quotes fos. 33v–34].
35. *Ibid.*, fos. 37–38, John Mitchell to Lord Grenville, Christiansand 6 February 1796 [quote, fo. 37v].
36. *Ibid.*, fos. 44–45, John Mitchell to Lord Grenville, Christiansand 7 February 1796 [quotes fos. 44–4v].
37. *Ibid.*, fos. 53–54, to Mr. Mitchell, Downing Street 13 February 1796 [quote fo. 53].
38. *Ibid.*, fos. 72–73, 'Extract of order transmitted by the Dutch Comité de Marine to Captain von Dirking Commander of the Dutch Squadron in the Ports of Norway', John Mitchell, Christiansand 19 February 1796. Mitchell sent the order on to London, see: *ibid.*, fos. 61–62, John Mitchell to Lord Grenville, Christiansand 19 February 1796.
39. *Ibid.*, fos. 70–71, John Mitchell to Lord Grenville, Christiansand 20 February 1796.
40. NA, ADM 1/3842, John Mitchell to Lord Spencer, Christiansand 7 February 1796.

41. NA, FO 22/25, fos. 76–77, John Mitchell to Lord Grenville, Christiansand 21 February 1796 [quote fo. 77].
42. NA, ADM 1/3842, John Mitchell to Lord Spencer, Christiansand 7 February 1796.
43. NA, FO 22/25, fos. 76–77, John Mitchell to Lord Grenville, Christiansand 21 February 1796 [quote fo. 76].
44. NA, FO 22/25, fos. 78–80, 'Memorandum', Mitchell, Christiansand 24 February 1796.
45. NA, ADM 1/523, Admiralty, Letters from the Commanders-in-Chief, North Sea, 1796, fo. 192, J. Wallace to John Mitchell Esq., Bergen 19 March 1796; and ibid., fo. 194, 'Extract of a Letter received by Captain Von Dirking from the Commodore of the Dutch East India Ships in Drontheim, dated Drontheim the 4th March 1796 and addressed to Von Dirking at Schuterness—and received by Von Dirking here the 29th March', John Mitchell, Christiansand 30 March 1796.
46. NA, ADM 1/523, fos. 196–197, Secret, John Mitchell to Adam Duncan Esq., Christiansand 30 March 1796.
47. NA, FO 22/25, fos. 198–199, John Mitchell to Lord Grenville, Christiansand 22 March 1796 [quote fos. 198v–199; original emphasis]. See also: NA, ADM 1/3842, John Mitchell to Evan Nepean [?], Christiansand 19 March 1796; and *ibid.*, N. Fenwick to Evan Nepean Esq., Elsinore 19 March 1796.
48. NA, ADM 1/3842, John Mitchell to Evan Nepean Esq., Christiansand 3 April 1796.
49. NA, ADM 1/523, fos. 198–199, Adam Duncan to Evan Nepean Esq., Venerable at Sea 21 April 1796.
50. *Ibid.*, fo. 205, Robt. Watson to 'Sir', Isis at Sea 18 April 1796.
51. *Ibid.*, fos. 210–211, John Mitchell to Adam Duncan Esq., Christiansand 23 April 1796 [quote fo. 210v].
52. *Ibid.*, fos. 188–189, John Mitchell to Adam Duncan Esq., Secret, Christiansand 12 April 1796 [quote fo. 188].
53. NA, FO 22/25, fos. 182–183, John Mitchell to Lord Grenville, Christiansand 7 May [quote fo. 182].
54. *The London Gazette*, 17–21 May 1796.
55. Lord Spencer to Duncan, 18 May 1796, cited in: Camperdown, *Admiral Duncan*, p. 65.
56. A. J. van der Aa, *Biographische woordenboch der Nederlanden. Deel 4* (J. J. van Brederode, Harlem, 1858), cited on: *biografisch portaal van nederland:* http://www.biografischportaal.nl/persoon/00449704.
57. NA, ADM 2/278, Admiralty out-letters: Lord's Personal Letters, pp. 544–545, P. Stephens, J. Gambier, W. Young to Navy Board, 28 June 1796. Since the name *Argo* was already in use for a Royal Navy warship at

the time, the Navy deviated from its normal practice of retaining the names of captured vessels in this particular case.

58. NA, FO 22/25, fos. 133–134, John Mitchell to Lord Grenville, Christiansand 6 April 1796 [quote fo. 133v]. See also: ibid., fos. 81–82, John Mitchell to Lord Grenville, Christiansand 26 February 1796; and *ibid.*, fos. 161–162, John Mitchell to Lord Grenville, Christiansand 22 April 1796.
59. *Ibid.*, fos. 261–264, John Mitchell to Lord Grenville, Christiansand 5 July 1796.

CHAPTER 6

After the Closure of the Ports in 1799

The official closure of the Norwegian ports to privateers in July 1799 also meant that the diplomatic debate on privateering and neutrality came to an end but, as we discussed in Chap. 2, it remained to be seen how the closure would work out in practice. During the remainder of the period when Denmark-Norway pursued a policy of neutrality, however, the situation changed on two occasions. First, the diplomatic relations between Britain and Denmark-Norway were suspended due to the conflict over the League of Armed Neutrality, officially entered into by Denmark-Norway on 26 September 1800 until the British attack on Copenhagen on 2 April 1801. At that point, the two countries were on the brink of a state of war. Diplomatic relations were, however, gradually resumed thereafter, and relations returned to their previous positions of Britain as a belligerent in the war, and Denmark-Norway as a neutral country.[1] From March 1802 to May 1803, however, the Peace Treaty of Amiens ended hostilities between Britain and France, and during these 14 months, French privateers could no longer attack British shipping. Doing so would have been an act of piracy, but the short-lived nature of the peace treaty meant that privateers could again be deployed from May 1803 onwards. In the following years, the war intensified, and in 1807, Denmark-Norway's near century-long policy of neutrality was at an end. The developments of the post-1799 years have been addressed in two main sections here, before and after the Peace of Amiens.

A. L. Wold, *Privateering and Diplomacy, 1793–1807*,
https://doi.org/10.1007/978-3-030-45186-8_6

Privateer Activity from 1799 to 1802

At the time of the official closure of the ports in Norway in 1799, the British government had expressed concerns about the possibility that French privateers might try to continue as before. There was also the question of whether the Danish government, as well as the local officials in the Norwegian port towns, would make serious attempts to uphold the closure. The new British representative at Copenhagen, Anthony Merry, was therefore asked to instruct the consuls in Norway to keep their eyes open, and so they did.[2]

Although there was some privateering activity in the later summer and autumn of 1799—the *Tay Greenlandman* was, for example, captured in July, just after the Danish declaration had been issued (but probably before a copy had reached Bergen)—there were no further reports on privateering sent by the British representatives in Denmark-Norway until well into the next year.[3] The privateers had not disappeared, however. 'The Vice Consul at Christiansand has reported to me the Arrival of a French Lugger Privateer, of 14 Guns and 70 Men', Anthony Merry wrote to Foreign Secretary Lord Grenville in late April 1800. Christian Höyer, the vice consul, had written to the 'Governor of the Castle for the Privateer to be immediately ordered out of Port, and to quit the Coast', and the governor could confirm that such orders had already been issued. The French consul, however, insisted that a little delay was necessary before the French ship could sail, simply because 'she had been chased in by a British Cruizer, and, to avoid being captured, had been obliged to throw overboard Nine of her Guns, and her only Boat, together with almost all her Water and Provision'. The French consul promised to send the vessel 'instantly' out to sea again, as soon as a 'Supply of the Two latter Articles' had been taken on board.[4] Since the Danish proclamation on the closure of the ports from July 1799 permitted privateers to go into Norwegian ports when pursued by the enemy, the French privateer had done nothing wrong on this occasion. There were, however, cases of privateers attempting to bring prizes into port, more or less as before.

On 3 January 1801, the British consul at Elsinore in Denmark, Charles Fenwick, submitted a report to the Admiralty on recent privateering activity along the Norwegian coast, which revealed that the French privateers were trying to circumvent the closure as best they could. 'Letters from Stavanger' had informed him of several captures of prizes by French privateers, and a tendency on the part of the privateers to come up with a variety of excuses for going into port in Norway with their prizes. The *Snow Henry* of Newcastle, for example, was sent into a port in the vicinity of Stavanger after being captured by a French privateer, and two days later, the privateer followed 'under pretence that he was chased in by an English Frigate'. The prize master on board the *Henry* had then stated that the ship was 'leaky' and could not 'go to Sea without the Cargo being delivered and Ship repaired'. Whether 'delivered' meant an intension of *selling* the cargo was not made clear, but the approach chosen by the French privateer captain was no doubt pushing the limits of the rule set up in 1799.[5] Christian Höyer presented a similar report a few weeks later, stating that 'A Number of French privateers have lately been in Norway', but in some cases it was the privateer only that came into port for repairs, while captured ships were sent for France. Such was the case for the *Le Voyageur* of 14 guns and 54 men, which had arrived at Flekkefjord with a 'broken Mast', while her two prizes, the *John & Mary* of Hull and the *Diligence* of Liverpool, had been sent to France with prize crews. Höyer also felt the need to stress that 'all this [*sic*] privateers are not coming on purpose on this Coast, but mostly driven over from the English coast, where they have made their precis'.[6] About the same time, Fenwick had received information from 'His Majesty's Hired armed Cutter the Fox', which had recently been at Christiansand and, while there, had observed two French privateers, both of which were in port to receive repairs.[7] There was, in other words, some privateering activity in Norwegian ports, but no confirmed—or even suspected—cases of prizes being condemned and sold. Nevertheless, the British chargés d'affaires in Copenhagen, William Drummond, was not content with this state of affairs.

On 9 January 1801, he wrote to Lord Grenville concerning information he had obtained from Fenwick, stating that 'two French Privateers', the *Marengo* and *Chasseur*, had brought two British ships into the port of Tananger (near Stavanger) as prizes. Similarly, 'another privateer, the Voltigeur, had arrived at Christiansand', landing the crew from a British ship she had captured. 'As these proceedings, my Lord, are direct infringements of a treaty, lately established with Denmark', Drummond wrote, he intended to 'make a strong remonstrance upon the subject to Count Bernstorff' at the first opportunity.[8] At the subsequent meeting Drummond stressed—referring to the treaties of 1670, 1701 and 1780—that 'if the French privateers were suffered, not only to enter the ports of Norway, but to refit, and revictual there, I could consider it, only, as an avowed breach of treaty, and open indication of hostility'. These were strong words, but Drummond was pleased to say that 'the answer of Count Bernstorff was perfectly clear, explicit, & decided'. He had assured Drummond that the 'most positive orders' would be dispatched to Norway, stating that privateers would not be allowed to enter 'the Ports of his Danish Majesty upon any pretext whatever'. Bernstorff even suggested that if Drummond would like to 'address a note to him, proposing a better method for preventing the evil complained of', he would be happy to 'carry it into effect'. Drummond was content with the response, but Bernstorff's reply seemed to suggest that privateers could now no longer enter Norwegian ports under *any* circumstances, and that was neither in line with the declaration of 1799 nor would it be adhered to in practice thereafter.[9]

There was also at least one example of the commander of a British warship overstepping his mark before 1802. On 7 March 1801, Charles Fenwick reported that the 'last Norway Mail' had 'brought the intelligence of His Majesty's Ship the Shannon Captain Pater, having taken several British Vessels out of the neighbourhood of Stavanger which had been carried in there as prizes by French Privateers'.[10] The port in question was Egersund, and the British vice consul in Stavanger, Gabriel Schancke Kielland, hoped that the action of Captain Peter, the commander of the *Shannon*, 'will save our Harbour from being troubled more with French prizes this War'. For a British warship to go into a Norwegian port to recapture prize vessels in this way was arguably in breach of Danish-Norwegian neutrality, even if French privateers were no longer permitted to bring prizes into these ports in the first place, and Kielland was clearly aware of the problem. As he stated to Mitchell: 'I hope, Sir, that you will give me a hint, if anything can yet be feared, but according to the report from Copenhagen, this Post, they hope it will be Settled amicably'.[11] Nothing further was heard of the matter, suggesting a settlement was reached.

Privateer Activity from 1803 to 1807

During the four years which passed from the end of the Peace of Amiens in May 1803, and Denmark-Norway's entry into the war in August 1807, the question of privateering in the North Sea was arguably dominated by one particular case—that of the French captain Jean Jacques de St Faust. This case has been studied in detail by R. P. Fereday, and the account here is based partly on his work.

St Faust was a naval captain who was tasked with a somewhat unusual mission in August 1803. At a time when Napoleon was planning his invasion of Britain, it was thought useful to deploy a force in the North Sea as a diversionary tactic to draw British naval forces away from the English Channel. St Faust was hired by the so-called Batavian Privateer Company of Amsterdam, and commissioned with three vessels, the schooners *L' Union* and *La Vengeance*, and the cutter *La Terreur*.[12] The purpose was now to carry out a 'raid' on either the Shetland, the Orkneys or the North of Scotland and, for that reason, St Faust's two supporting ships would also carry a contingent of French troops to be landed on shore. The squadron would fly the Batavian flag, which—in addition to St Faust's employment by a Dutch privateering enterprise—was meant to serve a propaganda purpose. It would demonstrate 'Dutch enthusiasm for the war against Great Britain, and contradict the general impression that most Dutchmen were apathetic allies of Bonaparte'.[13] St Faust's was, in other words, no ordinary privateer undertaking, but capturing merchant vessels was still within his brief. In September, he sortied from the Texel on a trial mission where he first encountered and damaged, but failed to capture the Royal Navy cutter the *Princess Augusta*, before sailing further into the North Sea, capturing four British merchant vessels and burning another five. One of these vessels, the *Good Intent* of Newcastle, was caught off Mandal, and subsequently sent into Kristiansand. Christian Höyer did not let this pass without due attention and, 'having learnt from some Norway Pilots that the vessel had been seized within too small a distance from the Shore', he 'requested of the Governor of the Province that the matter should be enquired into, and that in the meantime the prize should be taken possession of by the Danish Government'. This was 'complied with' by the governor, who transmitted the case to Copenhagen, confirming in his report that the capture had taken place within territorial waters. In the view of Robert Liston, the British envoy at Copenhagen, this was reassuring. It demonstrated that:

> While the Administration of this Country are anxious to preserve a rigid neutrality in the present contest between Great Britain & France, there is some satisfaction in observing that they seem disposed to repress a practice which has in former wars given just cause of umbrage to His Majesty's Government,—the reception of Enemies' privateers & their prizes into the Harbours of Norway.[14]

Once the case had moved on to Copenhagen, the 'Batavian Minister' there had 'done every thing in his power to make it be considered a lawful prize', the British chargés d'affaires, Francis Hill, reported, but the Danish government ordered the vessels to be released, and the Dutch consul at Kristiansand acquiesced.[15]

In the meantime, St Faust had returned to the Texel, and preparations began for his real mission. He received a larger brig, also called *L'Union*, in replacement for the schooner of the same name, and on 20 December 1803, he finally sailed. The aim now was to attack Fort Charlotte in Lerwick, but this was thwarted by the appearance of a British frigate on patrol in the North Sea, the *Amethyst*. St Faust was able to escape into Bergen harbour with *L'Union*, but the two other vessels under his command—the *La Vengeance* and *La Terreur*, which were carrying the troops—were both wrecked and sank. In Bergen, however, were three other Dutch naval vessels, the schooners *De Wolff* and *De Snuffelaar*, and the corvette *De Spion*, which were now placed under St Faust's command, refitted and renamed as *La Vertu*, *L'Honneur* and *La Foi Batave*. St Faust's stay in the port of Bergen—which proved lengthy—created a situation, which in some ways was analogous to that of the *Shannon* three years earlier. When the French were arguably violating the proclamation of 1799 by equipping and preparing a privateer force for action while in a Norwegian port, were the British simply to sit idly by and wait, or could they act? The Admiralty approached Foreign Secretary Lord Hawkesbury, wondering what action could legally be taken in a situation where an enemy force 'appears to have taken a Station on the coast of a Neutral Nation for the purpose of effecting depredations from thence on the Northern limits of Great Britain'. Would it not

> be advisable to order a Frigate to Bergen to watch the motions of the Enemy and, in the event of their quitting that port, to follow them immediately, and having gained sufficient distance from the Danish Territory to preclude a possibility of any complaint being made of a violation of it, to capture or destroy them?[16]

An alternative approach was to try to make the Danish government act on the matter, and the British government opted for this, instructing the envoy at Copenhagen, Robert Liston, to raise the issue with Bernstorff. The force 'in the Port of North Bergen, should be obliged to depart from thence without delay', London demanded, because it 'obviously' formed a 'part of the General Plan which is projected against these Kingdoms'.[17] In Copenhagen, Liston had already observed that the 'Danish & German Newspapers have lately contained various accounts of the arrival of Dutch Vessels of War, and of Dutch Troops, in the Port of Bergen'. One such account stated that there were six Dutch warships in total, but as he had 'received no information' to confirm this 'from any Consul or Vice-Consul in that part of the Country' Liston was unsure. He did as London requested, however, and emphasised to Bernstorff the

> propriety of sending orders to the Governor & other publick [*sic*] officers in Norway to enquire into the fact & to take measures to prevent irregularities which might give a Danish harbour the appearance of *a place d'armes* calculated perhaps to facilitate some desultory attack upon the Coast of Scotland.

Bernstorff agreed, and a 'promise was very readily made that this suggestion should be complied with'. Since then, however, it had emerged that the account of six ships had been 'extremely exaggerated', that there were only three ships 'of a Small size', and that 'instead of receiving reinforcements, their commanders have formed the project of sending their crews to Holland & of disarming & laying up the vessels'. This latter point was hardly true, but for now, it meant that the Danish government decided to take no further action.[18] On 1 March, St Faust sailed from Bergen to make another attempt at carrying out his planned raid. His squadron consisted of the four ships he had available: the *La Foi Batave* of 18 guns, the *L'Union* of 18 (lighter) guns and the two schooners, the *L'Honneur* of 8 guns and the *La Vertu* of 6 guns. Two days later, they were sighted by the *Amethyst*, which immediately laid chase to them. Commanding a 36-gun frigate, which also mounted 8 carronades, the commander of the *Amethyst*, Captain Campbell, was well placed to defeat his four opponents, but in the ensuing battle, St Faust was able to beat off his superior adversary, causing significant damage to Campbell's ship. Although this was a surprise victory to the Frenchman, and a major embarrassment to the British captain, St Faust's own ships had been sufficiently damaged to force him to abort his mission and return to Bergen. Campbell tried to sail for Britain, but contrary winds and poor weather forced him to seek refuge in Bergen on 19 March, and thereafter the two enemies were in the same port. On 5 April, St Faust sent the *L'Union* out, and in line with common practice, the governor of Bergen withheld the *Amethyst* in port for 24 hours before she was permitted to sail in pursuit. For two weeks, Campbell sailed between Bergen and the Naze, hunting for the brig and hoping for St Faust to emerge out of port, but with his own ship in increasingly poor repair, he eventually returned to Britain.[19] The *L'Union*, however, was able to capture three British vessels, the *Nancy & Margrete* of Peterhead, and the *Michael* and the *Meanwell*, both of Newcastle. The first and last sailed in ballast and were burnt, while the *Michael* 'was sent into Holland'.[20] A fourth vessel captured by the privateer caused greater controversy however.

In July 1804, the commander of the British revenue vessel the Royal George, Captain Carmichael, reported that, 'an English Brig had been captured by the Union Dutch Privateer and carried into Bergin [*sic*] where she remained near two months, but was at length ordered away by the Danish Government'. The privateer had then 'quitted Bergen', but the prize master on the captured vessel proceeded to paint a new name on its stern, the *Mercurius von Embden*, and sailed to Egersund under Prussian colours, claiming that the ship was Prussian and in need of repairs as she had supposedly 'sprung a Leak'. Carmichael had received his information from a Norwegian pilot, and decided to investigate the matter further, sailing to Egersund himself. Once on port, he 'found the vessel laying there', which a few of his own crew could identify as 'either the Lark or Minerva of Aberdeen', and consequently that 'every thing the Pilot had told me was perfectly true' (Carmichael could also confirm this himself by examining the sails of the ship). The official in charge in Egersund, Mads Nissen, had, however, 'taken charge' of the vessel, and 'landed the Cargo, consisting of grain in his own Warehouse', but 'Judging that the faith of Nations had been violated by her being permitted to remain so long in a Neutral port', Carmichael wrote, 'I claimed her as British Property'. Nissen refused to release the vessel, and Carmichael responded by sending an official protest to Copenhagen.[21] A few weeks later, Francis Hill raised the issue with Bernstorff, who promised to look into it, assuring Hill that 'it was far from the intention of this Government to countenance any unfair transactions', but it is not clear if the ship and cargo were ever restored.[22]

Following its solitary operations, the *L'Union* was able to return safely to Bergen, but there, St Faust and his men were 'beginning to outstay their welcome', Fereday writes.[23] A fight at a tavern between some of St Faust's men and local inhabitants on 3 April led to growing tensions and, eventually, St Faust decided that it was time to depart. He ordered the *L'Union* to leave first, on 8 May, but as the British had intensified their patrols, she was captured by the frigate *Ethalion* once out in the open sea. Unable to leave port without risk of being captured himself, St Faust eventually abandoned the *La Foi Batave*, and purchased a small sloop in which he was able to escape, returning to the Netherlands via Denmark. His ship remained in Bergen, however, and was sold some time later by the Dutch consul there, Hendrich Fasmer. In December 1804, Francis Hill could reassure London that, as St Faust had returned home, 'there are no remains of that Armament which had been for a while very troublesome to the British Trade'.[24] As far as Captain Campbell and St Faust were concerned, however, there was arguably no winner. Campbell was court-martialled and dismissed from duty for his failure to defeat an inferior enemy, while St Faust was hired for another mission in 1805, which ended with his capture by British forces and nine years in British prison hulks. Was it all a failure for St Faust? While his foray into the North Sea could hardly be seen as great a success as far as the original objective or carrying out a raid was concerned, in terms of attracting attention, generating concern in Britain and tying up British naval resources, the mission was arguably successful from the start. In addition to the threat St Faust was seen to pose to Shetland and the Orkneys, the Admiralty even suspected that he might be headed for Hudson Bay in Canada, and exaggerated figures were also published in the press on the number of troops held on board his ships.[25]

While St Faust remained in Bergen, the British chargés d'affaires at Copenhagen, Francis Hill, was ordered by Hawkesbury to raise the issue of privateers in Norwegian ports with the Danish government. Stressing the 'impropriety of admitting Privateers of the Nations at War with Great Britain into the Ports of Norway', Hill conveyed the expectation of the British government that immediate measures be taken to bring this kind of activity to an end and, to this, the Danish minister was most accommodating. In fact, he held that the

> inconvenience of admitting Privateers into the Danish Ports had already been very severely felt during the last War, and that consequently the strictest Orders had been given and every measure taken to prevent such Vessels from entering into the Ports of His Danish Majesty's Dominions, except in those cases of distress in which humanity directed assistance to be granted to the Ships that stood in need of it.

Moreover, Bernstorff 'assured' Hill 'most positively that all Privateers would be excluded from the Danish Harbours and more particularly those of His Majesty's Enemies'.[26] It sounded much like a repeat of the many assurances given before the closure in 1799, but the problem was again, of course, that the Danish government could not fully control or monitor attempts made by privateers to circumvent the rules, be that by the adoption of false flags, fictitious claims to 'distress' or other. Arguably, the permission given to privateers to enter neutral ports *both* in cases of distress *and* when pursued by enemy warships in the declaration of July 1799 was an invitation to such abuses, but it would, in any case, have been difficult to deny them access on the grounds of distress. After all, the general rule was that a ship should be allowed to go into port in an emergency caused, for example, by adverse weather. Although the St Faust-case dominated, there were also other cases of note from May 1803 onwards, most notably one which concerned an alleged British violation of neutral waters.

In late August 1803, two British warships, the cutter *Fox* and frigate *Carysfort*, had laid chase to a French vessel they had discovered out at sea, west of Bergen. The French ship, called the *Dunkerque*, had tried to escape by heading east for the Norwegian mainland, and after sailing for several hours with the British ships in pursuit, the master, Pierre Charles Cailliez, had 'hoisted a signal which brought a Pilot on board'. The pilot had guided the ship close to a small island or rock, and 'brought her safe to anchor' there, presumably thinking that they were now safely within neutral waters.[27] While the *Dunkerque* laid at anchor, however, a boat had been sent over from the *Carysfort*, and the crewmembers on board had seized control of the French ship. Thereafter, the *Dunkerque* had been taken to Britain, and condemned as a good prize by the High Court of Admiralty. The capture and subsequent court case gave rise to a controversy, which arguably concerned the nature of the neutral 'belt' along the coast of Norway. As we saw in Chap. 4, there were two alternative ways of 'measuring' the width of this belt. Either it could be seen as going from the mainland itself, or it should be measured from the outermost island, and it was not until 1812 that the Danish government decided in favour of the latter. Several months after the incident off Bergen, the French representative at Copenhagen protested against the capture, claiming that it was a 'violation of the neutrality of the Danish Territory' since the ship had been captured 'within so small a distance of the Land of Norway that she was secured by cables fastened to the shore'. Fearing that Napoleon 'would perhaps be happy to find, in a denial of justice on the part of

England, and a supposed collusive submission in the part of the Court of Copenhagen' a 'pretext' for an invasion of Denmark, the leading Danish minister Count Bernstorff responded to the French protest by instructing his ambassador at London, Count Wedel Jarlsberg, to raise the issue with the British government.[28] Since this was an Admiralty case, it fell upon the Secretary to the Admiralty, William Marsden, to investigate the matter further, and he did this by requesting the commander of the *Carysfort*, Captain Robert Fanshawe, to submit a report, explaining his actions. In the report, Fanshawe argued against the view that the French vessel had been secured to the 'shore'. Although he admitted that the *Dunkerque* had been secured with cables fastened on land, the 'Rock' in question 'could not be considered as belonging in Sovereignty to the Crown of Denmark' as it was 'so inconsiderable that it is not to be found in any Chart of the Coast of Denmark that I have seen altho' I have consulted the best that could be produced'. The fact that there were some metal 'rings' on this rock to which the cables had been attached—as Wedel Jarlsberg had stressed—did not change this, Fanshawe insisted. The problem was, of course, that Fanshawe did not know the exact location of this rock or tiny island; the best he could come up with was that it was the 'most Western from the Island of Sartoroe' (possibly Sotra).[29] Alexander Grieg, the 'acting' British consul at Bergen, had, however, submitted a report to Hawkesbury as early as 3 September 1803, in which he held that the capture had taken place in 'a Harbour on the Coast called Backesund'. Bakkasund is an island just south of Sotra, the main larger island outside Bergen, and it can hardly be described as simply a 'rock', nor is it very far out at sea. If Grieg was correct, Fanshawe's line of argument rested on flimsy grounds, but none of this seems to have had any implications for the case. By the time Fanshawe submitted his report, both ship and cargo had already been sold, and a later report on the case indicated that an 'amicable' settlement was in the process of being reached.[30] The whole affair was, arguably, quite odd, but it serves to demonstrate that the problem of deciding when belligerent action had taken place in neutral waters and not, persisted after 1799. Furthermore, Grieg had warned of possible negative consequences for the British. Since the 'Transaction so contrary to the rights of Neutrality has created great Sensation here', he wrote, Grieg predicted (correctly) that there would be protests, and that 'if such infringements are tolerated [*sic*] by the British Government, all the Pilots on the Coast will be forbid from giving any assistance to any Ship of War that may come upon the Coast'. The consequences of that could potentially be 'fatal'.[31] Grieg's dire predictions did not materialise, and after 1804, there were only a handful confirmed cases of privateers operating in Norwegian waters, or coming into ports in Norway.[32]

In March 1805, Francis Hill found reason to convey 'some Information' to Foreign Secretary Lord Mulgrave, 'which though not of much importance, still deserves some degree of Attention'. A French privateer had recently come into a port nearby Kristiansand, 'being forced to do so by a strong western Gale'. Since French privateers 'think it profitable to cruise off the coast of Norway, as they have often an opportunity of falling in with the English Vessels that sail towards the Cattegate [*sic*] in their way to the Baltic', Hill reasoned, he thought it would be 'advantageous to the safety of the British Navigation in those Seas', if 'one of His Majesty's Frigates should be stationed in them, that the enemy's Privateers may by that means lose all hopes of remaining in a situation which is so greatly conducive to their Purposes'.[33] This was hardly a very original or new idea by 1805, but then Hill was also new at the job, and may not have been familiar with the British strategies adopted to defend the Baltic Sea trade against privateers in the 1790s.[34] A year later, in March 1806, a 'French Cutter Privateer' was reported to have captured two British vessels, the *Hull Packet* of Newcastle and *Venus* of Hull, and to have 'landed' the captains of both ships as well as five sailors in Stavanger, where they were 'delivered' to vice consul Gabriel Kielland upon his 'request'. The captain of the Venus, John Smith, had told Kielland that he thought the privateer was heading for Kristiansand, and Kielland subsequently sent an 'Express' to Christian Höyer to 'acquaint' him of this, and to 'ask if You have the means in Your corner for here are none, of conveying the English Captains and Seamen to their Mother Country'. Kielland was thus trying to fulfil his duties as vice consul, but faced the now familiar problem of having no financial means to do so.[35] Höyer passed the letter on to Benjamin Garlike, the British envoy at Copenhagen, who does not seem to have addressed the issue of finance, but responded to the threat posed by the privateer. 'Mr. Hoyer is of opinion that the French Privateer has been driven on the Norway coast by stress of weather', he wrote to Foreign Secretary Charles James Fox, and while it is 'not likely that she can remain there … she will nevertheless hope to catch some of the Merchant Ships which may happen at this season of the year to separate from their convoy on their passage to or from the Baltic'. For that reason, Garlike had 'transmitted the same intelligence to Mr. Fenwick at Elsinore, and to the Commander of His Majesty's Ships on the Yarmouth Station' (meaning Admiral Duncan).[36]

Thus even as late as in 1806, nearly seven years after the closure of the ports, there was still a need to patrol the seas off Norway.

The experience of the period from 1799 to 1807 points in the direction of three to four main findings. The first is that the closure of the ports seems to have worked, broadly speaking. Although there were attempts made by privateers to utilise Norwegian ports more or less as before, indications are that these attempts were not very numerous, nor did they really succeed to any extent. The second is that there is little in terms of direct evidence that prizes were sold in Norwegian ports. Admittedly, this is a statement based primarily on negative evidence, that the topic was not raised by the British diplomatic correspondence for the period, but it can also be deduced from the experience of the 1790s. Given the readiness with which the British side reacted to sales that were not in line with the agreement of August 1793 before 1799, it seems unlikely that they should have let sales pass without protest after the closure, had they taken place. A third finding is that the Danish authorities seemed prepared to police the closure as effectively as they could, and a fourth that the more central cases, such as that involving St Faust or Captain Fanshawe, were out of the ordinary, and perhaps not very representative of the 'mainstream' privateering that took place before 1799.

In what was possibly the last report on privateer activity on the Norwegian coast, Benjamin Garlike stated that: 'I learn from Mr. Hoyer at Christiansand that a French Privateer Lugger rigged, the Ratafia of six Guns and forty Men commanded by M. Forest, which had been chased from the English Coast has taken refuge at Christiansand in Norway'.[37] This was in April 1807, and thereafter, it turned quiet. When Denmark-Norway entered the war on the side of Napoleon in the wake of the Danish defeat in the Second Battle of Copenhagen a few months later, the situation changed markedly. Any French (or Dutch) privateer that sailed along the coast of Norway would now be operating in the waters of an allied country, and all the questions and problems related to privateering out of neutral ports were a thing of the past and of no relevance anymore. More importantly, though, the dual-monarchy's emergence as a belligerent in the war provided new opportunities to the inhabitants in the many port towns along the southern coast of Norway. On the same day as the British attack commenced, on 16 August, the Danish government issued a royal proclamation stating that the country was in a state of war. The next day, Crown Prince Fredrik, the Prince Regent, sent out a circular order to all the governors in the dual-monarchy, authorising them to issue letters of marque 'to any of His Majesty's subjects' who might wish to hunt for British ships. Thus rather than simply 'receiving' prizes brought in by French and Dutch privateers, the Norwegians now could, and did, equip their own vessels to hunt for British merchantmen. The 'privateering war' which ensued has, however, been studied in considerable detail already, and it is, in any case, a different story from the one told here.[38]

Notes

1. On the League of Armed Neutrality, see: Ole Feldbæk, *Denmark and the Armed Neutrality 1800–1801: Small Power Policy in a World War* (Akademisk Forlag, Copenhagen, 1980), p. 79. While the British envoy Baron Whitworth left Copenhagen on 26 September 1800, William Drummond arrived to act as chargé d'affaires on the same day, remaining until 21 March 1801. Nicholas Vansittart arrived as 'Plenipotentiary on a Special Mission' on 9 March 1801, remaining until he left together with Drummond. Alleyne Fitzherbert, Baron St Helens, then acted as Britain's chief negotiator until Denmark's accession to the Convention of St. Petersburg on 23 October 1801. On 24 March 1802, Francis Hill took up the post of chargés d'affaires, and diplomatic relations could be said to have been resumed, though there was no British envoy at Copenhagen until the arrival of Robert Liston in June 1803. See: S. T. Bindoff, *British Diplomatic Representatives (1789–1852)* (The Royal Historical Society, London, 1934; reprint by: Facsimile Publisher, Delhi, 2017), pp. 41–43.
2. See: National Archives [NA], FO 22/35, Foreign Office Correspondence, Denmark, fos. 91–100, To 'Mr. Merry', Downing Street, 9 July 1799, cited in Chap. 2, pp. **54–55**.
3. For the case of the British merchant vessel, the *Tay Greenlandman*, see Chap. 1, p. 1.
4. NA, FO 22/36, fos. 269–279, Ant. Merry to Lord Grenville, Copenhagen 29 April 1800 [quotes fos. 269v–270].
5. NA, ADM 1/3842, Admiralty, Letters from British Consuls, Charles Fenwick to Evan Nepean Esq., Elsinore 3 January 1801.
6. *Ibid.*, Chr. Höyer to Evan Nepean Esq., Christiansand 22 January 1801. See also: *ibid.*, John Mitchell to Lord Grenville, Hamburg 13 January 1801.
7. *Ibid.*, Charles Fenwick to Evan Nepean Esq., Elsinore 24 January 1801.
8. NA, FO 22/40, fos. 28–32, W. Drummond to Lord Grenville, Copenhagen 9 January 1801 [quote fo. 32].
9. *Ibid.*, fos. 38–42, W. Drummond to Lord Grenville, Copenhagen 13 January 1801 [quote fos. 40–40v]. See also: *ibid.*, fos. 51–53, W. Drummond to Lord Grenville, Copenhagen 20 January 1801.

10. NA, ADM 1/3842, Charles Fenwick to Evan Nepean Esq., Elsinore 7 March 1801.
11. *Ibid.*, G Schancke Kielland to John Mitchell Esq., Stavanger 20 February 1801.
12. R P Fereday, *Saint-Faust in the North 1803–1804: Orkney and Shetland in Danger, An Abortive Raid and its Consequences* (Tempvs Reparatvm, Oxford, 1995), p. 5.
13. Fereday, *Saint-Faust*, p. 17.
14. National Library of Scotland [NLS], MSS 5602, Official correspondence between Robert Liston and Lord Hawkesbury, 1803–1804, No. 1, fos. 79–80, Robert Liston to Lord Hawkesbury, Copenhagen 7 January 1804.
15. FO 22/44, fos. 321–323, Francis Hill to Lord Hawkesbury, Copenhagen 5 May 1804 [quote fo. 321]; and Fereday, *Saint-Faust*, p. 71.
16. NA, FO 22/44, fo. 62, T. Troubridge and J. Markham to Lord Hawkesbury, Admiralty 7 February 1804. Also cited in: Fereday, *Saint-Faust*, p. 45.
17. NA, FO 22/44, fos. 70–72, 'Draft to Mr Liston', Downing Street 8 February 1804. Cited in: Fereday, *Saint-Faust*, p. 46.
18. NLS, MSS 5602, fos. 95–96, Robert Liston to Lord Hawkesbury, Copenhagen 3 March 1804 [quote fo. 95v; original emphasis]. Same letter: FO 22/44, fos. 174–175. See also: *ibid.*, fos. 198–199, Francis Hill to Lord Hawkesbury, 14 March 1804.
19. For a detailed account of the battle and the subsequent developments described here, see: Fereday, *Saint-Faust*, pp. 57–75. Carronades were a type of heavy short-range guns of a unique Scottish design, normally mounted on the upper deck. The majority of the Amethyst's regular 'long' guns were significantly heavier than those carried by St Faust's ships. On carronades, see: B. Lavery, 'Carronades and Blomefield Guns: Developments in Naval Ordnance, 1778–1805' in Robert D. Smith (ed.), *British Naval Armaments* (Royal Armouries, London, 1989), pp. 15–28.
20. NA, FO 22/44, fo. 344, 'Repport' [*sic*], signed Kielland, British Consulate Office Christiansand, Bergen 3 May 1804.
21. NA, ADM, 1/689, Letters from Commander-in-Chief, Leith, 1803–1805, Rt Carmichael to Rear Adml Vashon, Royal George Leith 22 July 1804; or NA, FO 22/45, fos. 74–75.
22. NA, FO 22/45, fos. 115–118, Francis Hill to Lord Harrowby, Copenhagen 18 August 1804 [quote fo. 117].
23. Fereday, *Saint-Faust*, p. 71.
24. NA, FO 22/45, fos. 272–273, Francis Hill to Lord Harrowby, Copenhagen 18 December 1804 [quote fo. 272v].
25. Fereday, *Saint-Faust*, pp. 39–40.

26. NA, FO 22/44, fos. 288–291, Francis Hill to Lord Hawkesbury, Copenhagen 10 April 1804 [quote fo. 288–288v].
27. NA, FO 97/118, Supplementary, Denmark, fos. 160–163, 'Extract from the Depositions, Pierre Charles Cailleiz the Master', Admiralty Court of Prize 12 March 1804 [quote fo. 161].
28. NLS, MSS 5602, No. 28, ff. 77–78. RL [Robert Liston] to Lord Hawkesbury, Copenhagen 31 December 1803.
29. NA, FO 97/118, fos. 150–154, Robert Fanshawe to 'Sir', No 10 John Street Adelphi 3 March 1804 [quotes fos. 150b and 151b]. See also: *ibid.*, fo. 148, W. Marsden to C. Arbuthnot, Admiralty Office 12 March 1804.
30. NA, FO 22/46, fos. 244–246, B. Garlike to Lord Mulgrave, Copenhagen 14 May 1805 [quote fo. 244]. Garlike did not state what the settlement involved.
31. NA, FO 22/43, fos. 260–261, Alex Grieg to Lord Hawkesbury, Bergen 5 September 1803 [quote, fo. 260].
32. The possibility to trade with the USA from 1804 onwards arguably made privateering less appealing. See Chap. 2, p. 17.
33. NA, FO 22/46, fos. 126–127, Francis Hill to Lord Musgrave, Copenhagen 16 March 1805 [quotes fos. 126v].
34. See Chap. 4 on the British defence of trade.
35. NA, FO 22/48, fos. 94–95, 'Extract of a Letter from Mr. Kielland Vice Consul at Stavanger to Mr. Hoyer His Majesty's Consul at Christiansand dated 30th March 1806'; 'In Mr. Garlike's N. 99 of 12th April 1806' [quote fos. 94v–95].
36. NA, FO 22/48, 92–93, B. Garlike to Charles James Fox, Copenhagen 12 April 1806 [quotes fos. 92v–93].
37. NA, FO 22/51, fos. 212–214, B. Garlike to Lord Howick, Copenhagen 2 April 1807 [quote fo. 213].
38. The seminal work on this is: Joh. N. Tønnessen, *Kaperfart og Skipsfart 1807–1814* (J. W. Cappelens forlag, Oslo, 1955). The quote is from p. 21 [translated from Norwegian].

CHAPTER 7

Conclusion

During one of the periods of the most intense French privateering activity in the 1790s, in May 1797, the British consul at Elsinore in Denmark, Nicholas Fenwick, expressed his exasperation with the situation he had to handle. The problem concerned British merchantmen travelling through the Kattegat, and their protection against privateers. Through a recent report, Fenwick had been informed that the 'French Lugger Courageux' of 16 guns and 40 men had just caught the British vessel *Pallas* near the Scaw (Skagen) on the northernmost tip of Jutland, and sent her into Marstrand in Sweden. This had prompted him to contact the British envoy at Copenhagen, Robert Stephen Fitzgerald, in hopes that he might 'apply to the Danish Court, for Protection of the Cattegat, from these kind of Vermin', lest there should be 'no where safe' left.[1] Fenwick's view of French privateers as a pest could be said to chime with the more general view predominant among the British government's men in Denmark-Norway at the time, and probably with the government in London too. These privateers were clearly a danger to British seaborne trade, but also a time- and resource-consuming nuisance. Privateering was, of course, a legitimate and broadly speaking acknowledged form of warfare in the eighteenth century, and one to which Britain also subscribed, but the permission French privateers had been given by the Danish authorities to operate out of neutral Norwegian ports was arguably never really fully accepted by the British side, the agreement from August 1793 notwithstanding. The problem was made worse by what appeared to be a lax

A. L. Wold, *Privateering and Diplomacy, 1793–1807*,
https://doi.org/10.1007/978-3-030-45186-8_7

attitude adopted by the Danish government, which did not seem to be very concerned to uphold the agreement, and suspicions of underhand collaboration between the local officials in the Norwegian coastal towns, and the French and Dutch privateers who brought prizes into these ports. The attempts made by the British government and its diplomatic and consular representatives in Denmark-Norway to address this problem formed the main point of departure in this book.

At the start of the war in 1793, the British government's men had good reason to be suspicious, they thought. Previous experience from the eighteenth century seemed to prove beyond doubt that the Danish policy of neutrality was really one of 'profiteering neutrality'. The Danish government would insist officially that it was upholding a strict neutrality in all affairs but, in reality, it would do whatever it could to exploit the wartime situation to achieve as much financial benefit as possible. The main thrust of this policy came in the shape of neutral trade with the belligerent nations, and reached its peak in the 1790s with the Danish attempt to introduce convoys for its trade in 1798, whereby the Danish government sought to resist the 'visitation' right of the belligerents. All this is, however, well known from the existing literature on Danish foreign policy in the period. Less well known is the impact of privateering out of neutral ports. Yet, this phenomenon deserves attention too, as it was both of considerable interest to Denmark-Norway and perceived as a serious problem by Britain. The sale of prizes brought into port by privateers from the belligerents generated economic activity in the Norwegian port towns, and provided the dual-monarchy with much needed shipping for, precisely, the neutral trade it was trying to expand upon. As the British consul to the town of Kristiansand in Norway stated in letter to Foreign Secretary Lord Grenville in 1794:

> A maritime war wherein Great Britain is concerned is ever the Harvest of the Northern States; A naval Equipment, or a Sea Fight, is as glad Tidings to these so called neutral Speculators as the loss of a Revenue Cutter is pleasing to a Smuggler; when extraordinary gain is in view neither political Treaties nor Domestick Ordinances can bind Adventurers to Respect the one or obey the other.[2]

This was a British view of the situation, of course, presented early in the war, and one which did not take into account the increasingly difficult situation the Danish government found itself in, pressed as it was from both sides by two of the great powers at war, France and Britain. Nevertheless, it was knowledge of how Denmark-Norway had operated as a neutral country during the previous wars of the eighteenth century which informed the British approach adopted in the wake of the first observations of privateers on the coast of Norway. The expectation was that the Danish government would permit French privateers to operate from the ports of the dual-monarchy unless Britain acted to put a stop to it. The means of trying to achieve this was diplomacy and an appeal to bilateral treaties and international law, or the 'Law of Nations' in the contemporary parlance. Posed differently, the British government sought to get its will by means of persuasion. This proved partially successful only, as the Danish government insisted on keeping the ports in Norway open to privateers, but the British side was able to secure a few concessions nonetheless, primarily related to the sale of prizes in Norwegian ports. According to the agreement reached in August 1793, such sales were only meant to take place when the vessels in question carried the so-called *perishable goods*. The diplomatic-legalistic approach adopted by the British government formed the central focus of Chap. 2, and a striking feature of the development in the 1790s is the consistency with which the British side stuck to this approach. Some more or less open threats were admittedly put forward but, by and large, emphasis was placed on arguing Britain's case, and on protesting against breaches of the agreement of 1793. When the ports were finally officially closed to privateers in July 1799, it was *not* done primarily because of British pressure, suggesting that the British approach, in the end, was not very effective in terms of achieving the stated objective, the closure of the ports. Part of the problem was that there existed very little in terms of legal material on the specific question of privateers operating out of neutral ports, be that either in terms of actual rules stated in treatises, prize court rulings or deliberations by legal scholars. Although attempts were certainly made by the British government's men to find such a rule in existing treatises with Denmark-Norway, or in existing practice on privateering, none was discovered. To this problem was then added the question of what constituted 'proper' neutral behaviour, often seen in light of the so-called rights and duties of neutral nations. Should privateers be excluded from neutral ports on the basis of the principle of *abstention*, or was it acceptable for a neutral country to allow privateers from belligerent countries to enter its ports, as long as the 'invitation' applied equally for all—in other words, based on the less strict principle of *impartiality*? There was no ready answer to this, and it cannot really be said that the British-Danish discussion resolved the issue either. It provided little in terms of clear precedence that could be applied if the problem should re-emerge in the future. Where Chap. 2 focused on this principled discussion, Chap. 3 looked at the job performed by the British representatives in Denmark-Norway.

The focus on resolving the matter by means of discussions through diplomacy meant that the British government's men in the dual-monarchy played a central role in the ongoing debate between the British and Danish authorities. Yet, while the British envoy at Copenhagen took care of the actual debate with the Danish government, the British consuls played an equally if not more important role as the eyes and ears of the diplomatic service. At the start of the period, Britain had relatively more consuls in Denmark-Norway than on most other stations, and the service was particularly well-staffed in Norway, with three consuls and possibly as many as six vice consuls. Together with the one consul in Denmark, positioned at the strategically important point of Elsinore, the British government enjoyed the services of an arguably well-functioning network of representatives. This meant that London could stay well-informed about the development of privateering in the seas off Denmark-Norway throughout the whole period 1799–1807, and that it was at times even better informed than the government in Copenhagen. Although the consuls proved very valuable to the Foreign Office, tasked as they could be with a wide range of work, the service suffered from poor financial arrangements, which caused major difficulties from time to time. This was particularly the case with respect to the return to Britain of British seamen, the crews of captured British merchant vessels landed in Norwegian ports, which was, of course, a task specifically linked to the phenomenon of privateers operating out of neutral ports. Above all, however, it was the great energy and many initiatives of the consul at Kristiansand in Norway, John Mitchell, that stood out and made the consular service so useful. Mitchell's system of informants along the southern coast of Norway arguably represented an extraordinary feat of organisation, and proved very helpful in the war against privateers. That said, Nicholas Fenwick's efforts to keep the Admiralty informed of the movements of merchant vessels in and out of the Sound was no doubt of great use too.

The British-Danish debate covered in Chap. 2 gave clear indications that the agreement of 1793 was not being adhered to in Norway, and the aim of Chap. 4 was to look at the actual experience of privateering on the coast of Norway. This was partly a matter of determining whether it was true as John Mitchell stated in 1795—that the Governor of Kristiansand was selling prizes on a 'daily' basis—that is, that the agreement of 1793 was not respected, and partly to look into the day-to-day practice of privateering.[3] What kind of issues emerged in individual cases, and were there any general concerns that kept recurring? Who was in the right and who was in the wrong in an individual case of conflict? One main finding was that the question of neutral waters—the part of the sea immediately adjacent to the shore of a neutral country—and belligerent action within these waters, was probably the most frequent cause of controversy. Such violations of neutral waters were perpetrated as much by British warships as they were by French privateers, it turned out, and were at the centre of the extraordinary *Bell & Ann*-case, which was addressed in detail. This chapter also provided an, at least partial, answer to the question raised in Chap. 2: why did the British government not place greater pressure on its Danish counterpart to close the ports? The deployment of British naval forces in the North Sea, benefitting from a steady supply of intelligence from the consuls in Denmark and Norway, meant that Britain had a means of countering the privateers, and this seems to have made it less pressing to force through a closure of the ports. The British government was, in any case, aware that too much pressure on the Danes might push them into the arms of the French. Lastly, the case of the auctions advertised in the *Christiansand Weekly Gazette* suggests that Mitchell was right.

The main focus of the British government and its representatives in Denmark-Norway throughout the period examined in this book was on *French* privateers. Yet, the French occupation of the Dutch Republic in 1795 and subsequent establishment of the Batavian Republic meant that the Dutch changed sides in the war and equipped their own privateers. These Dutch privateers were no less dangerous than were the French, and their entry into the war probably led to an increase in the total number of privateers operating in the North Sea. In addition came the changeover of the Dutch Fleet from an ally to an enemy of the Royal Navy. Uncertainty remained, however, with respect to the loyalty of the Dutch, not the least because of the long-standing conflict between the so-called Patriots and Orangists in the Dutch Republic before the 1790s. This question of loyalty was a central theme in Chap. 5, and particularly in the 'von Dirking'-case to which the bulk of the chapter was devoted. Captain von Dirking's defection to Britain was masterminded by John Mitchell, and the initial plans arguably looked too good to be true, or at least to be realistic. Although a reasonably successful operation was in the end carried through, it was far from what had been envisaged at the outset. Finally, Chap. 6 addressed the question raised at the end of Chap. 2: would the closure of the ports in 1799 be effective? The answer is a qualified yes. Indications are that the Danish government did try to police the closure, and that there were far fewer privateers operating in the North Sea compared to before 1799 (although it fluctuated significantly during those years), but that there were some privateers who tried to utilise Norwegian ports now also. The Peace of Amiens from 1802 to 1803 meant that there were no privateers in the North Sea for the duration of this accord, and thereafter the case which attracted the most attention was that of the French Captain St Faust's attempted raid on Shetland. This, and other cases, arguably demonstrated the possibilities the Danish declaration of 1799 gave to privateers in terms of using Norwegian ports as 'safe havens', places to which they could escape from British warships. In a way, this could be seen as an invitation to operate in the neutral waters of the dual-monarchy. In terms of the main problem in the 1790s, however, the bringing into port in Norway of prize vessels, and subsequent sales of both ships and cargoes there, indications are that this activity came to an end. By way of conclusion, therefore, the historical phenomenon of privateers operating out of neutral Norwegian ports in the period 1793–1807 could be said to hold a position of being both relevant and not so relevant. For privateering in general, it was arguably not too relevant since the general rule was that privateers should operate out of ports in the home country. As long as they did so, the question of whether a neutral country could permit privateers in its ports was not an issue (although the problem of *captures* in neutral water could still be an issue, of course). For the relationship between neutrals and belligerents, however, it was arguably both relevant and interesting because of the way in which it shed light on the relative rights and duties of the two. Moreover, for the British merchants doing their trade on the Baltic Sea or Archangel, it *was*, no doubt, of relevance whether the enemy privateers were waiting for them along the coast of Norway, or whether these privateers had to travel all the way back and forth from their home ports in France or the Batavian Republic.

Notes

1. National Archives [NA], ADM 1/3842, Admiralty, Letters to British Consuls, N. Fenwick to Evan Nepean Esq., Elsinore 13 May 1797.

2. NA, FO 22/20, Foreign Office Correspondence, Denmark, fos. 40–42, John Mitchell to Lord Grenville, Christiania 28 June 1794 [quote, fo. 40].
3. See: NA, FO 22/24, fos. 185–186, John Mitchell to Lord Grenville, Christiania, 23 November 1795.

Index

A. L. Wold, *Privateering and Diplomacy, 1793–1807*,
https://doi.org/10.1007/978-3-030-45186-8

D

Neutrality
  Danish policies on, 30–31, 34–45, 50–61, 154, 193–195, 213, 229–232
  French policies on, 55–58
  legal aspects, 3, 9–11, 20–28, 32–35, 48–50, 177

The manufacturer's authorised representative in the EU is Springer Nature Customer Service Centre GmbH, Europaplatz 3, 69115 Heidelberg, Germany. If you have any concerns regarding our products, please contact ProductSafety@springernature.com

Printed and bound by CPI Group (UK) Ltd, Croydon, CR0 4YY
30/09/2026
02225460-0004